The
New Public
Service

The
New Public
Service

Serving, not Steering

Janet V. Denhardt and
Robert B. Denhardt

M.E. Sharpe
Armonk, New York
London, England

Library of Congress Cataloging-in-Publication Data

Denhardt, Janet Vinzant.
  The new public service : serving, not steering / by Janet V. Denhardt and Robert B. Denhardt.
  p. cm.
Includes bibliographical references and index.
ISBN 0-7656-0845-6 (cloth : alk. paper) ISBN 0-7656-0846-4 (pbk : alk. paper)
  1. Public administration. 2. Public administration—United States. 3. Civil service. 4
Civil service—United States. I. Denhardt, Robert B. II. Title.

JF1351 .D4495 2002
351—dc21

2002066974

Printed in the United States of America

The paper used in this publication meets the minimum requirements of
American National Standard for Information Sciences
Permanence of Paper for Printed Library Materials,
ANSI Z 39.48-1984.

BM (c) 10   9   8   7   6   5   4   3   2   1
BM (p) 10   9   8   7   6   5   4

To the women and men of the public service

Contents

Preface

This book has two primary aims. The first is to synthesize some of the many ideas and voices calling for the reaffirmation of democratic values, citizenship, and service in the public interest as the normative foundations for the field of public administration. The second is to provide a framework to organize those ideas around principles, giving them a name, a mantle, and a voice that we believe has been lacking. This book is a call to think about and act on our values. It is intended as a challenge for us to think carefully and critically about what public service is, why it is important, and what values ought to guide what we do and how we do it. We want to celebrate what is distinctive, important, and meaningful about public service and to consider how we might better live up to those ideals and values.

There are two themes that form both the theoretical core and the heart of this book: (1) to advance the dignity and worth of public service, and (2) to reassert the values of democracy, citizenship, and the public interest as the preeminent values of public administration. It is our hope that the ideas presented here may help us not only to initiate more conversations, but also to look within ourselves for the soul of what we do. We want words like "democracy" and "citizen" and "pride" to be more prevalent in both our speech and our behavior than words like "market" and "competition" and "customers." *Public servants do not deliver customer service; they deliver democracy.*

These themes—the dignity and worth of public service and the values of democracy, citizenship, and the public interest—were the subject of two on-line articles we wrote for the American Society for Public Administration Web site following the September 11 attacks on the United States. In the first article, we expressed our grief and disbelief, along with our admiration for the brave public servants who went to the aid of those in need. The story of the police and firefighters running up the stairs of the World Trade Center as others struggled down was particularly compelling to us:

> These people showed America, once again, that they stand apart. What makes them different is their quiet, often anonymous heroism. They are public servants. They serve their fellow citizens in a way that many people would find very difficult if not impossible to understand. . . . In a peculiar way, this ghastly act of terrorism reminds us of why we are in the public service. We care about our country, our community, and our neighbors. Each of us, whether we wear a uniform, a suit, a jacket, coveralls, or a hard hat, plays a role in improving the lives of others. Service to the public—helping people in trouble, making the world safer and cleaner, helping children learn and prosper, literally going where others would not go—is our job and our calling. (Denhardt and Denhardt 2001a)

In the second article, we wrote about our continuing admiration for the many public servants who work tirelessly on our behalf and also about the importance of citizenship and our responsibility to promote citizens' active involvement in their government:

> The spirit of public service extends beyond those formally working for government, those we think of as public servants. Ordinary citizens have also wished to contribute. However, the avenues through which they might bring their many talents to bear have been somewhat limited, in part, we think, because over the past several decades we have severely constrained the citizenship role, preferring to think of people as customers or consumers rather than citizens. (Denhardt and Denhardt 2001b)

We were gratified and a little surprised at the response. Many people wrote to us and talked with us about what the articles meant to them, and most importantly, how much they wanted to hear and talk about the values, the soul, and the nobility of public service. In this book, we are trying to extend that discussion by grounding it in history and in the development of thought and practice in public administration. The ideas are not new, but they are beginning to have a clearer voice and spark a renewed interest. What happened to the ideals of public service and when did we stop hearing about them? How have changes in management philosophy and theories about the proper role and identity of government altered how public servants act, think, and behave? What values of public service, especially those that give the field dignity, courage, and commitment, have been lost in the process? How can we rediscover and affirm them?

We do not pretend to provide all the answers or to stake a claim to articulating the "correct" values of the field; rather, we want people to start talking about them again, a little louder and a little more forcefully. We want to initiate conversations about the nobility and calling of public service and to help public servants rediscover the soul and meaning of what they do and why they do it.

Janet and Robert Denhardt
March 2002

Acknowledgments

We are indebted to many people for their guidance and help during our work on this project. We especially want to acknowledge the important models of public service and civic engagement provided by forward-looking public servants and active and engaged citizens across the country and around the world. These are the people who have already established "the New Public Service." We have simply given their work a name. We also want to thank friends and colleagues in the academic community for their assistance and support during our work on this project. Among the many practitioners and academics we might mention, we especially want to recall the intellectual contributions, support, and friendship of such people as Marvin Andrews, Maria Aristigueta, Lynn Bailey, Joel Benton, Eric Bergrud, Dick Bowers, Harry Briggs, Patra Carroll, Joe Cayer, Linda Chapin, Jeff Chapman, Tom Eichler, Eileen Eisen, Frank Fairbanks, Mark Glaser, Joe Gray, Joe Grubbs, Jay Hakes, John Hall, Mary Hamilton, Mark Holzer, Ed Jennings, Cheryl King, Christiaan Lako, Roz Lasker, Brian Marson, Barbara McCabe, Cynthia McSwain, John Nalbandian, Nico Nelissen, Robert O'Neill, Phil Penland, Jan Perkins, Mark Platts, Jeff Raffel, Dan Rich, Faye Schmidt, Camilla Stivers, Larry Terry, John Thomas, and Orion White. We also owe a very special thanks to Kelly Campbell, our wonderful research assistant, whom we know will make great contributions to the field of public administration. A sincere thanks to all! And as always, we want to express our love and admiration for our children: Michael, Ben, Cari, and Mary.

The
New Public
Service

Chapter 1

Public Administration and the New Public Management

Government shouldn't be run like a business; it should be run like a democracy. Across this country and around the world, both elected and appointed public servants are acting on this principle and expressing renewed commitment to such ideals as the public interest, the governance process, and expanding democratic citizenship. As a result, they are learning new skills in policy development and implementation, recognizing and accepting the complexity of the challenges they face, and treating their fellow public servants and citizens with renewed dignity and respect. Public employees are feeling more valued and energized as this sense of service and community expands. In the process, public servants are also reconnecting with citizens. Administrators are realizing that they have much to gain by "listening" to the public rather than "telling," and by "serving" rather than "steering." At the invitation of public servants, even their urging, ordinary citizens are once again becoming engaged in the governance process. Citizens and public officials are working together to define and to address common problems in a cooperative and mutually beneficial way.

We suggest that this new attitude and new involvement are evidence of an emerging movement in public administration, which we will call "the New Public Service." The New Public Service seeks to pose and inform a number of central normative questions about the field. How can we define the essential character of what we do in the public service? What is the motivating force that propels our actions? What gives us strength and capacity when the trials and turmoil of our work get us down? How can we keep going even as we face problems that are complex and intractable with extremely limited resources and a public that often resents and criticizes what we do? We think the answer lies in our commitment to public service.

We find no other reasonable explanation for the extraordinary dedication and commitment of the people who work to make the world safer and cleaner, to improve our health, to teach our children, and to unravel the host of societal maladies that confront us. Where else can we find the foundations for our efforts to facilitate citizenship and public engagement as a central part of our work? What else can keep the firefighters, the police officers, the social workers, the planners and the inspectors, the receptionists and the clerks, the managers and the analysts serving their communities and their country with energy, resolve, and determination?

Research tells us that the ideals of public service are critically important in understanding how public servants can be successful in the work they do. But what seems missing today is a unifying set of themes and principles that both express and reaffirm the importance of these public service values. Questions about these values have, of course, been debated throughout the history of public administration in this country and elsewhere, but there seems to be more concern for these issues today than before. Certainly there are some important "driving forces" that have been widely discussed in the field of public administration recently: the New Public Management, the National Performance Review, the Managing for Results movement, and total quality management (TQM)—to name just a few. While all these influences have been important, none has satisfied our more basic yearning to answer some core questions: Who are we? Why are we here? What does all this mean? People in public administration throughout the history of our field have been encouraged to make things work, but that's only a partial answer. We also want to do something of societal value.

Therein lies the soul of public administration. What is most significant, and most valuable, about public administration is that we serve citizens to advance the common good. Public administrators are responsible for improving the public health, for maintaining public safety, for enhancing the quality of our environment, and myriad other tasks. Ultimately, for them, for us, what really matters is not how efficiently we have done our jobs, but how we have contributed to a better life for all. In this book, we call for an affirmation of the soul of the profession through the New Public Service, a movement grounded in the public interest, in the ideals of democratic governance, and in a renewed civic engagement. This movement, we will argue, is now being manifest in the way we interact with political leaders, in the way we engage with citizens, and in the way we bring about positive changes in our organizations and our communities.

We will approach the task of describing the various elements of the New Public Service by contrasting it with both traditional and more contemporary approaches to public policy and public administration. In this chapter, we will very briefly review the history and development of traditional public administration, what we must now call the Old Public Administration. Then we will outline what we see as the dominant or mainstream approach to contemporary public administration today, the New Public Management. In Chapter 2, we will note some of the most important alternative views of public administration, views that have been less than "mainstream" throughout the history of the field, but are now being voiced with increasing urgency. Having examined the context and historical grounding for understanding the New Public Service, in Chapters 3 through 9, we will explore seven aspects of the New Public Service that we find most compelling. At the outset, we should note that we have not attempted to catalog the many examples of the New Public Service that have emerged in the last couple of decades. Nor have we sought to develop a complete theoretical argument in behalf of the New Public Service. Rather our purpose here is simply to lay out, in a very basic way, the normative issues and the alternative ways of thinking about public administration that academics and practitioners are likely to confront as they work to build the New Public Service.

The Old Public Administration

While governments have used complex structures of management and organization throughout human history, public administration as a self-conscious field of study and practice is generally thought to have begun around the turn of the century. Its American version, for example, is typically dated to a well-known essay by Woodrow Wilson, then college professor, later president of the United States. Wilson acknowledged the growing and increasingly complex administrative tasks of government by commenting that "it is getting harder to run a constitution than to frame one" (Wilson 1987/1887, 200). In order to more effectively run government, Wilson advised that we look to the field of business, since "the field of administration is a field of business" (209). In order to follow the model of business, Wilson advised, government should establish executive authorities, controlling essentially hierarchical organizations and having as their goal achieving the most reliable and efficient operations possible.

Those residing at these centers of power, however, were not to be actively or extensively involved in the development of policy. Their tasks were instead the implementation of policy and the provision of services, and in those tasks they were expected to act with neutrality and professionalism to execute faithfully the directives that came their way. They were to be watched carefully and held accountable to elected political leaders, so as not to deviate from established policy. Wilson recognized a potential danger in the other direction as well, the possibility that politics, or more specifically, corrupt politicians might negatively influence administrators in their pursuit of organizational efficiency. This concern led to Wilson's well-known dictum, "Administration lies outside the proper sphere of politics. Administrative questions are not political questions. Although politics sets the tasks for administration, it should not be suffered to manipulate its offices" (Wilson 1987/1887, 210). Thus, Wilson established what was known for many years as the politics-administration (or policy-administration) dichotomy.

Two Key Themes

In Wilson's essay, we find two key themes that served as a focus for the study of public administration for the next half century or more. First, there was the distinction between politics (or policy) and administration, with its associated ideas of accountability to elected leaders and neutral competence on the part of administrators. Second, there was concern for creating structures and strategies of administrative management that would permit public organizations and their managers to act in the most efficient way possible. Each of these ideas deserves further comment.

First, the idea of separating politics and administration received much early commentary and came to guide practice in a number of important ways. For example, the dichotomy is clearly the basis for the council-manager form of local government, which involves the council being given the responsibility of establishing policy and the city manager being charged with implementing it. Of course, in the council-manager example, as in other areas, a strict separation of politics and administration proved difficult. Members of governing bodies, whether members of city councils or state or federal legislators, always maintained an active interest in the operations of administrative agencies. Especially through the oversight function, they exercised considerable influence in the operations of agencies. Conversely, administrators came to play a more active role in the policy process, especially as they brought expert advice to bear on the legislative process. Over time, many commentators such as Luther Gulick, first city administrator of New York and a founder of the American Society for Public Administration, argued that policy and administration could not be separated, that every act of a public manager involves a "seamless web of discretion and action" (1933, 561). Others, such as Paul Appleby, dean of the Maxwell School at Syracuse University, were even more to the point, "public administration is policymaking" (Appleby 1949, 170).

The distinction Wilson drew between politics and administration has certainly blurred over time. Yet, in many ways, the relationship between politics and administration remains important to the field of public administration. While a "dichotomy" between politics and administration is overdrawn, the interaction of political and administrative concerns is certainly key to understanding how government operates even today. Perhaps more important, however, the separation of politics and administration lies at the heart of the Old Public Administration's version of accountability, one in which appointed administrators were held to be accountable to their political "masters"—and only through them to the citizenry. In this view, the requirements of democratic governance are satisfied where a neutral and competent civil service is controlled by and accountable to elected political leaders. Frederick Cleveland, an early writer, commented that democratic accountability is maintained where there is a "representative body (such as a legislature) outside of the administration with power to determine the will of the membership (the citizens) and to enforce (that) will on the administration" (Cleveland 1920, 15, parentheses added). In this view, the legislature operates somewhat like a board of directors overseeing a business operation.

Second, Wilson held, and others agreed, that public organizations should seek the greatest possible efficiency in their operations and that such efficiency was best achieved through unified and largely hierarchical structures of administrative management. Certainly that view was consistent with thinking among business managers of the period. Many, such as the efficiency expert Frederick W. Taylor (1923) employed a "scientific management" approach to try to learn, through detailed "time and motion" studies, exactly how the productive process could be improved. Taylor, for example, sought to determine the "one best way" to shovel dirt by designing an experiment that would calculate the ideal weight of a single shovel full of dirt, ideal in the sense of producing the most shoveled dirt per day!

Other early theorists, such as Leonard White (1926) and W.F. Willoughby (1927), focused on building organizational structures that would operate with high efficiency. Again, most found attractive the idea of a strong chief executive vested with the power and authority to carry out the work assigned to the agency. Moreover, that chief executive would be most successful if he or she operated through an organizational structure characterized by unity of command, hierarchical authority, and a strict division of labor. The job of the executive, therefore, was to determine the best division of labor, then to develop the appropriate means of coordination and control. Or, following

Gulick's classic acronym POSDCORB, the work of the executive was planning, organizing, staffing, directing, coordinating, reporting, and budgeting (1937, 13). But again, efficiency was the key value accepted by most early writers and practitioners.

Dissenting Views

That is not to say, however, that *all* accepted efficiency as the ultimate criterion by which to judge administrators. Marshall Dimock, an academic and practitioner, challenged that idea, writing that mechanical efficiency is "Coldly calculating and inhuman," whereas, "successful administration is warm and vibrant. It is human" (Dimock 1936, 120). Successful administration, he continued, "is more than a lifeless pawn. It plans, it contrives, it philosophizes, it educates, it builds for the community as a whole" (133). Others suggested that administrators as well as political leaders were ultimately concerned with issues such as justice, liberty, freedom, and equality—issues far more formidable and difficult than efficiency alone.

Finally, many writers noted that the search for organizational efficiency might easily occur at the expense of involving citizens in the work of government. Writing somewhat later, Dwight Waldo, perhaps the best known public administration theorist of his generation, summarized the emerging orthodoxy in the field of public administration by writing that "The means and measurements of efficiency, it was felt and strongly stated, were the same for all administration. Democracy, if it were to survive, could not afford to ignore the lessons of centralization, hierarchy, and discipline" (Waldo 1948, 200). Moreover, he commented, "Both private and public administration were in an important . . . sense false to the ideal of democracy . . . by reason of their insistence that democracy, however good and desirable, is nevertheless something peripheral to administration" (Waldo 1952, 7).

So, in contrast to using efficiency as the sole criterion for assessing administrative performance, one might employ other criteria, such as responsiveness to the concerns of citizens. An appealing view, one might say. Yet these alternative voices were counterpoint at best, as the emerging field of public administration moved firmly through the ideas of "politics and administration," "scientific management," "administrative management," and "bureaucratic management." In each case, theory and practice confirmed the importance of tightly integrated hierarchical structures controlled from the top by managers interested in achieving the organization's goals and objectives in the most efficient manner possible. Interestingly, even as the field moved through the next several decades and into its behavioral or "scientific" phase, these same issues continued to be highlighted. Though the justification was somewhat different, the resulting recommendations were much the same.

The Rational Model

The classic *Administrative Behavior* (1957), written by Herbert Simon, a political scientist who later won a Nobel Prize in economics, laid out the argument best. According to the positive science viewpoint Simon represented, statements may be classified according to whether they are true or false. Scientists, of course, are concerned with establishing the truth of certain propositions. In order to do so they must strip away those pesky "values" that tend to interfere in human affairs. So those terms that speak to individual or group preferences are not to be admitted into scientific study, in this case the study of administrative behavior. Rather Simon argued that a single standard, the standard of efficiency, may be used to help remove values from the discussion of organized action.

The key to this argument is the concept of rationality. According to Simon, human beings are limited in the degree of rationality they can obtain in reference to the problems they face; but they can join together in groups and organizations to deal effectively with the world around them, and they can do so in a rational manner. After all, in the abstract, it's not hard to develop a rational course of action to achieve most objectives. The problem comes when we insert real live people, with all their human concerns and idiosyncrasies, into the picture. The issue then becomes one of how to match these people with the rational plan and how to assure that human behavior follows the most efficient path possible.

In contrast to a long philosophical tradition that holds human reason to be concerned with such issues as justice, equality, and freedom, Simon's more restricted view is that rationality is concerned with coordinating the proper means to accomplish the desired ends. In this view, rationality is equated with efficiency. For what Simon called "administrative man," the most rational behavior is that which moves an organization efficiently toward its objectives. "Administrative man accepts the organizational goals as the value premises of his decisions, is particularly sensitive and reactive to the influence upon him on the other members of the organization, forms stable expectations regarding his own role . . . and has high morale in regard to the organization's goals" (Simon, Smithburg, and Thompson 1950, 82). Then, through what is called the inducements—contributions model, by controlling the inducements offered to members of the organization, its leaders could secure their contribution and compliance with the rational design of the organization, the result being a far more efficient and productive organization.

Public Choice

Some years after Simon's work an interesting interpretation of administrative behavior, and one more closely allied with the classic "economic man" position, emerged. This new approach, called "public choice theory," actually provides an interesting bridge between the Old Public Administration and the New Public Management, for while public choice theory was developed during the time period we generally associate with the Old Public Administration, as we will see later, public choice became much more significant later as the key theoretical basis for the New Public Management. For this reason, we will only briefly outline public choice theory here, but return to it frequently throughout the material that follows.

Public choice theory is based on several key assumptions. First, and most important, public choice theory focuses on the individual, assuming that the individual decision maker, like the traditional "economic man," is rational, self-interested, and seeks to maximize his or her own "utilities." According to this view, individuals seek the greatest benefit (at the least cost) in any decision situation, acting to "always seek the biggest possible benefits and the least costs in the decisions. People are basically egoistic, self-regarding and instrumental in their behavior" (Dunleavy 1991, 3). Even if people are not that way, economists and public choice theorists argue that it enables us to better explain human behavior if we *assume* that they are. Second, public choice theory focuses on the idea of "public goods" as the output of public agencies. These can be distinguished from private goods in that a public good, like national defense, when provided to one person will be provided to all.

A third idea associated with public choice is that different kinds of decision rules or decision situations will result in different approaches to choice making. For this reason, structuring decision rules to influence human choice, and in turn human behavior, is a key to the operations of public agencies and the governance system more generally. In this view, "public agencies are viewed as a means for allocating decision-making capabilities in order to provide public goods and services responsive to the preferences of individuals in different social contexts" (Ostrom and Ostrom 1971, 207). In other words, the public choice approach involves the application of economic models and approaches to nonmarket circumstances, especially government and political science, so as to provide structures and incentives to guide human behavior.

There are a number of questions that have been raised about public choice theory. The first and most obvious is the empirical one. Do individuals really consistently act in a self-interested way so as to maximize their utilities? Obviously, there are many situations in which they do, but also many in which they do not. This means that the public choice model must sacrifice behavioral accuracy in order to put forward a key construct upon which the rest of its theorizing is based. The result is a set of logical propositions based on assumptions that may only remotely correspond to actual human behavior. To an even greater extent than Simon's model of "administrative man," the more purely "economic man" of the public choice model is based on an assumption of complete rationality. One might ask, "Why not focus on other aspects of the human experience, such as feelings or intuition?" For the public choice theorist, the answer is that, in order to provide better explanations for human behavior, we should concentrate on the way individuals and groups attempt to maximize their own interests and on the way that market mechanisms both influence and respond to individual choices.

As Yale political scientist Robert Dahl (1947) pointed out in a critique of Simon's view, a critique also applicable to the more recent public choice model, to say that an action is rational is not to say that it serves moral or politically responsible purposes, but merely to say that it moves the organization forward more efficiently. Dahl suggested that, in contrast, efficiency is itself a value and should compete with other values, such as individual responsibility or democratic morality. In many cases, argued Dahl, efficiency would not be the primary value chosen. For example, how would we evaluate the operation of the German prison camps in World War II, camps that by all accounts were run quite efficiently? Or, more to the current point, how would be balance a concern for administrative efficiency in a public agency with the need for that agency to involve citizens in its decision processes? We think that is a important question. But Dahl's point, like similar arguments made by Waldo and others, was relegated to a position somewhat outside the mainstream in the emerging dialogue about the structure and conduct of public organizations.

Core Ideas

Obviously many other scholars and practitioners contributed to the early development of the field of public administration. And, as we have seen, there is not a single set of ideas agreed to by all those who contributed over the decades to the Old Public Administration. However, we think that it is fair to say that the following elements generally represent the mainstream view of the Old Public Administration:

- The focus of government is on the direct delivery of services through existing or through newly authorized agencies of government.
- Public policy and administration is concerned with designing and

implementing policies focused on a single, politically defined objective.
- Public administrators play a limited role in policy making and governance; rather they are charged with the implementation of public policies.
- The delivery of services should be carried out by administrators accountable to elected officials and given limited discretion in their work.
- Administrators are responsible to democratically elected political leaders.
- Public programs are best administered through hierarchical organizations, with managers largely exercising control from the top of the organization.
- The primary values of public organizations are efficiency and rationality.
- Public organizations operate most efficiently as closed systems; thus citizen involvement is limited.
- The role of the public administrator is largely defined as planning, organizing, staffing, directing, coordinating, reporting, and budgeting.

There's no question that the Old Public Administration should be given a considerable amount of credit. Administrators operating largely within the confines of this view made (and continue to make) dramatic and important contributions to society, in areas ranging from national defense, to social security, to transportation, to public health, and to the protection of the environment. The Old Public Administration has allowed us to deal effectively with extremely complex and difficult problems and to maintain a balance between political and administrative concerns. Given the circumstances of its time, the Old Public Administration served well, even if imperfectly. It continues to do so. Most government agencies still follow this basic model of organization and management—or at least this model seems to be the "default" position for agencies at all levels of government. But the old model has come under increasing attack, especially by proponents of what we will call the New Public Management.

The New Public Management

As it is used here, the New Public Management refers to a cluster of contemporary ideas and practices that seek, at their core, to use private sector and business approaches in the public sector. While, as we have seen, there have long been calls to "run government like a business," the current version of this debate involves more than just the use of business techniques. Rather, the New Public Management has become a normative model, one signaling a profound shift in how we think about the role of public administrators, the nature of the profession, and how and why we do what we do.

Over the past couple of decades, the New Public Management has literally swept the nation and the world. As a result, a number of highly positive changes have been implemented in the public sector (Osborne and Gaebler 1992; Osborne and Plastrik 1997; Kettl 2000a; Kettl and Milward 1996; Lynn 1996; Pollitt and Bouckaert 2000). The common theme in the myriad of applications of these ideas has been the use of market mechanisms and terminology, in which the relationships between public agencies and their customers is understood as involving transactions similar to those that occur in the marketplace. "Painted with the broadest brush, these reforms sought to replace the traditional rule-based, authority-driven processes with market-based, competition-driven tactics" (Kettl 2000a, 3).

In the New Public Management, public managers are challenged either to find new and innovative ways to achieve results or to privatize functions previously provided by government. They are urged to "steer, not row," meaning they should not assume the burden of service delivery themselves, but, wherever possible, should define programs that others would then carry out, through contracting or other such arrangements. The key is that the New Public Management relies heavily on market mechanisms to guide public programs. Harvard's Linda Kaboolian explains that these arrangements might include "competition within units of government and across government boundaries to the non-profit and for profit sectors, performance bonuses, and penalties" (Kaboolian 1998, 190). The aim is to loosen what advocates of the New Public Management see as an inefficient monopoly franchise of public agencies and public employees. Elaborating on this point, Christopher Hood of the London School of Economics writes that the New Public Management moves away from traditional modes of legitimizing the public bureaucracy, such as procedural safeguards on administrative discretion, in favor of "trust in the market and private business methods . . . ideas . . . couched in the language of economic rationalism" (1995, 94).

Following these ideas, many public managers have initiated efforts to increase productivity and to find alternative service-delivery mechanisms based on economic assumptions and perspectives. They have concentrated on accountability to customers and high performance, restructuring bureaucratic agencies, redefining organizational missions, streamlining agency processes, and decentralizing decision making. In many cases, governments and government agencies have succeeded in privatizing previously public functions, holding top executives accountable for measurable performance goals, establishing new processes for measuring productivity and effectiveness, and reengineering departmental systems to reflect a strengthened commitment to accountability (Barzelay 2001; Boston et al. 1996; Pollitt and Bouckaert 2000).

Donald Kettl of the Brookings Institution sees what he calls the "global public management reform" focusing on six core issues:

1. How can governments find ways to squeeze more services from the same or a smaller revenue base?
2. How can government use market-style incentives to root out the pathologies of bureaucracy; how can traditional bureaucratic command-and-control mechanisms be replaced with market strategies that will change the behavior of program managers?
3. How can government use market mechanisms to give citizens (now often called "customers") greater choices among services—or at least encourage greater attention to serving customers better?
4. How can government make programs more responsive? How can government decentralize responsibility to give front-line managers greater incentives to serve?
5. How can government improve its capacity to devise and track policy? How can government separate its role as a purchaser of services (a contractor) from its role in actually delivering services?
6. How can governments focus on outputs and outcomes instead of processes or structures? How can they replace top-down, rule-driven systems with bottom-up, results-driven systems? (Adapted from Kettl 2000a, 1–2)

Similarly, New Zealand's Jonathon Boston had earlier characterized the central features or doctrines of the New Public Management, as follows:

> [An] emphasis on management rather than policy; a shift from the use of input controls . . . to a reliance on quantifiable output measures and performance targets; the devolution of management control coupled with the development of new reporting, monitoring, and accountability mechanisms; the disaggregation of large bureaucratic structures into quasi-autonomous agencies, in particular the separation of commercial from non-commercial functions . . . ; a preference for private ownership, contracting out, and contestability in public service provision; the imitation of certain private sector management practices, such as . . . the development of corporate plans (and) performance agreements, the introduction of performance-linked remuneration systems, . . . and a greater concern for

corporate image; a general preference for monetary incentives rather than non-monetary incentives, such as ethics, ethos, and status; and a stress on cost-cutting, efficiency, and cutback management. (Boston 1991, 9–10)

Around the World

The effectiveness of this practical reform agenda in the such countries as New Zealand, Australia, Great Britain, and later the United States put governments around the world on notice that new standards were being sought and new roles established. That is not to say that each of these countries followed exactly the same pattern in seeking management reform in the public sector. As leading European scholars Christopher Pollitt and Geert Bouckaert are careful to point out, efforts to reform are constrained by the philosophy and culture of governance within a particular country, by the nature and structure of that country's government, and by luck and coincidence. However, "Certain regimes look as though they are much more open to the 'performance-driven,' market-favouring ideas of the New Public Management that others, particularly the 'Anglo-Saxon' countries, Australia, Canada, New Zealand, the UK, and the USA" (2000, 60–61).

New Zealand's reform efforts were noteworthy, beginning in the mid-1980s as the Labor Party came to power after nine years out of office. At the time, New Zealand's economy had stagnated and the country found it hard to sustain its traditionally generous social programs and economic support. "The New Zealand reforms began with a top down approach that sought to privatize programs wherever possible, to substitute market incentives for command-and-control bureaucracies; and to focus single-mindedly on outputs and results instead of inputs." (Kettl 2000a, 8). The key principles underlying the model seemed to be that the government should only be involved in activities that could not be more efficiently and effectively handled elsewhere and that government should, wherever possible, be organized along the lines of private enterprise. Additionally, there was a strong dependence on incentive systems and the use of explicit contracts between ministers and managers or between purchasers (agencies) and providers (contractors) (Boston et al. 1996, 4–6). In terms of management systems, New Zealand essentially did away with its civil service system, allowing managers to negotiate their own contracts with employees and to introduce budget systems more focused on performance and results. The result was a massive transformation of public management in New Zealand.

Similar changes in the Australian approach to public administration and management in the 1980s and beyond were also triggered by difficult economic times but went far beyond simply enabling the government to make deep cuts in public programs. As early as 1983, the government under Prime Minister Robert Hawke had endorsed the notion of "managing for results" and had initiated a series of financial management and other reforms to achieve this objective. Again, a variety of efforts at privatization, governmental restructuring, and efforts to evaluate programs in terms of specific desired results were implemented. Managers were encouraged to use corporate-style planning processes to identify priorities, goals, and objectives, to reconstitute financial management processes so as to better track expenditures in light of desired results, and to emphasize efficiency, productivity, and accountability for results.

The British reforms largely were triggered by Margaret Thatcher's neoconservative efforts to reduce the size of the state. A key early effort was to reduce costs and spin off those activities that might be better accomplished in the private sector, while subjecting those that remained to market competition wherever possible. Additionally, the Financial Management Initiative centered on identifying specific centers of responsibility, associating costs with outcomes, and holding managers contractually responsible for achieving those outcomes. A later "citizens charter" exercise sought to hold agencies responsible for meeting specific service standards. "The (British version of) the new public management stemmed from the basic economic argument that government suffered from the defects of monopoly, high transaction costs, and information problems that bred great inefficiencies. By substituting market competition- and marketlike incentives—the reformers believed they could shrink government's size, reduce its costs, and improve its performance" (Kettl 2000a, 14).

The American Experience

These ideas were first crystallized and popularized in the United States by David Osborne and Ted Gaebler's best-selling book, *Reinventing Government* (1992; see also Osborne and Plastrik 1997). Drawing on the experiences of other countries, especially New Zealand, as well as experiences at the state and local level in America, Osborne and Gaebler, a journalist and a former city manager, provided a number of now-familiar "principles" through which "public entrepreneurs" might bring about massive governmental reform, ideas that remain at the core of the New Public Management:

1. *Catalytic Government, Steering Rather than Rowing*: Public entrepreneurs move beyond existing policy options, serving instead as catalysts within their communities to generate alternate courses of action. They choose to *steer*, recognizing a wide range of possibilities and striking a

balance between resources and needs, rather than rowing, concentrating on a single objective. Those who steer define their future, rather than simply relying on traditional assumptions (Osborne and Gaebler 1992, 35).

2. *Community-Owned Government, Empowering Rather than Serving*: Public entrepreneurs have learned that past efforts to serve clients produced dependence, as opposed to economic and social independence. Rather than maintain this approach, these entrepreneurs shift ownership of public initiatives into the community. They empower citizens, neighborhood groups, and community organizations to be the sources of their own solutions (Osborne and Gaebler 1992, 52).

3. *Competitive Government, Injecting Competition into Service Delivery*: Public entrepreneurs have recognized that attempting to provide every service not only places a drain on public resources but also causes public organizations to overextend their capabilities, thus reducing service quality and effectiveness. These entrepreneurs counter this trend by fostering competition among public, private and nongovernmental service providers. The results are greater efficiency, enhanced responsiveness, and an environment that rewards innovation" (Osborne and Gaebler 1992, 80–83).

4. *Mission-Driven Government, Transforming Rule-Driven Organizations*: Public entrepreneurs have seen how excessive rule-making in bureaucratic organizations stifles innovation and limits government performance. Such rule-making is further supported by rigid systems of budgeting and human resources. In contrast, public entrepreneurs focus first on the mission of the group—what the organization strives for internally and externally. Then, the budget, human resources and other systems are designed to reflect the overall mission (Osborne and Gaebler 1992, 110).

5. *Results-Oriented Government, Funding Outcomes, Not Inputs*: Public entrepreneurs believe that government should be dedicated to achieving substantive public goals, or outcomes, as opposed to concentrating strictly on controlling the public resources expended in doing the job. Current evaluation and reward systems focus mainly on fiscal efficiency and control, rarely asking what impacts were gained from each public initiative. Public entrepreneurs transform these systems to be more results oriented—that is, accountability based on government performance (Osborne and Gaebler 1992, 140–141).

6. *Customer-Driven Government, Meeting the Needs of the Customer, Not the Bureaucracy*: Public entrepreneurs have learned from their private-sector counterparts that unless one focuses on the customer, the citizen

will never be happy. Since legislative bodies provide most public resources to government agencies, these agencies operate completely blind
of their customer base. They function according to their own priorities, and those demanded of them by the funding source, instead of
what they customers actually need. Public entrepreneurs stand this system on its head, serving the customer first (Osborne and Gaebler 1992,
166–167).

7. *Enterprising Government, Earning Rather than Spending*: Public entrepreneurs face the same fiscal constraints as their traditional counterparts, but the difference is in the way they respond. Rather than raise
taxes or slash public programs, public entrepreneurs find innovative
ways to do more with less. By instituting the concept of profit motive
into the public realm—for example, relying on charges and fees for
public services and investments to fund future initiatives—public entrepreneurs are able to add value and ensure results, even in tight financial times (Osborne and Gaebler 1992, 203–206).

8. *Anticipatory Government, Prevention Rather than Cure*: Public entrepreneurs have grown tired of funneling resources into programs to
resolve public problems. Instead, they believe the primary concern should
be prevention, stopping the problem before it ever occurs. Government in the past prided itself on service delivery—on being able to put
forth initiatives aimed at curing public ills. However, as the problems
in postindustrial society became more complex, government lost its
capacity to respond. By returning to prevention, public organizations
will be more efficient and effective for the future (Osborne and Gaebler
1992, 219–221).

9. *Decentralized Government, from Hierarchy to Participation and Teamwork*: Public entrepreneurs appreciate the role centralized organizations served in the industrial age. These institutions represented the
first steps toward professionalization in the field of public administration. Yet, the age of the hierarchical institution has passed. Advances in
information technology, improved communications systems and increases in workforce quality have brought in a new age of more flexible, team-based organizations. Decision-making has been extended
throughout the organization—placed in the hands of those who can
innovate and determine the high-performance course (Osborne and
Gaebler 1992, 250–252).

10. *Market-Oriented Government, Leveraging Change Through the Market*: Public entrepreneurs respond to changing conditions not with
traditional approaches, such as attempting to control the entire situation, but rather with innovative strategies aimed at shaping the envi-

ronment to allow market forces to act. Each jurisdiction—whether a nation, a state, or a local community—represents a market, a collection of people, interests, and social and economic forces. Public entrepreneurs realize that these markets remain beyond the control of any single political body. So, their strategy centers on structuring the environment so that the market can operate most effectively, thus ensuring quality of life and economic opportunity (Osborne and Gaebler 1992, 280–282).

Osborne and Gaebler intended these ten principles to serve as a new conceptual framework for public administration—an analytical checklist to transform the actions of government. "What we are describing is nothing less than a shift in the basic model of governance used in America. This shift is under way all around us, but because we are not looking for it—because we assume that all governments have to be big, centralized, and bureaucratic—we seldom see it. We are blind to the new realities, because they do not fit our preconceptions" (Osborne and Gaebler 1992, 321).

In the United States, the effort to "reinvent government" came later than those in other Anglo-Saxon countries, was more highly politicized, and, in part for that reason, had its effect less on the overall structure of governance in the country and more on managerial practices. Two efforts were particularly important, the National Performance Review (NPR) and the Government Performance and Results Act. The National Performance Review was President Bill Clinton's effort, spearheaded by Vice President Al Gore, to create a government that "works better and costs less." To do so, scores of government employees were sent throughout government agencies seeking out ways in which operations could be streamlined and made less costly. Specific recommendations numbered in the hundreds and including procurement reforms, changes in personnel policy, and developments in information technology. Moreover, there was a strong emphasis on serving the "customers" of government. The National Performance Review, however, took place against a political backdrop necessitating serious cutbacks in federal employment, because this was the one activity that could produce rapid savings. Meanwhile, the congressionally driven Government Performance and Results Act required managers to establish specific performance standards and to "manage for results." Summarizing the first five years of the National Performance Review, Kettl writes that, despite its shortcomings, the NPR "saved a significant amount of money, brought substantial managerial reforms (especially in customer service and procurement processes), and promoted a more performance-based discussion about the functions of government" (Kettl 2000a, 29).

Intellectual Support

To this point, we have discussed the New Public Management in terms of the practical efforts undertaken in governments around the world to reform government operations. But we should also note the various intellectual justifications for the New Public Management. These justifications, as Lynn (1996) notes, largely came from the "public policy" schools that developed in the 1970s and from the "managerialist" movement around the world (Pollitt 1993).

The policy perspective that emerged in schools of public affairs and especially schools of public policy in the last couple of decades had its roots more clearly in economics as opposed to the more political science oriented programs in public administration. Many, though certainly not all, policy analysts and those engaged in policy evaluation were trained in or at least familiar with economics, and quite at home with terms such as "market economics," "costs and benefits," and "rational models of choice." In turn, these schools began to turn their attention to policy implementation, which they called "public management" to distinguish it from the earlier "public administration," notwithstanding the fact that both public management and public administration are both concerned with implementing public policy through the conduct and operation of the various agencies of government. (The two terms can be used synonymously and often are, but if there is a difference, it is that discussions of public management tend to show a bias toward economic interpretations of managerial behavior as opposed to discussions of public administration, more likely based in political science, sociology, or organizational analysis.)

As the ultimate extension of the economic view, the New Public Management is clearly linked to the rationalist perspective and, as we noted earlier, especially public choice theory. One important variation on public choice theory that has also influenced the development of the New Public Management is what is called "agency theory" or "principal agent theory." Simply put, agency theory is concerned with the relation between principals and agents. "Agency" refers to a situation in which one individual (the agent) acts on behalf of another (the principal). For example, if I hire a lawyer, I am the principal and the lawyer is my agent, but the lawyer has multiple incentives—win the case (my goal) and maximize billable hours (his goal). Because our objectives aren't consistent, all sorts of problems arise. In the New Public Management, agency theory can be employed either to analyze issues arising within a particular bureaucracy (e.g., what incentives might a principal provide to assume compliance on the part of an agent?) or to assess the effects of different institutional structures (e.g., how might the multiple interests influencing police officers' behavior affect a decision to privatize a police force?).

Public choice (and its companion agency theory) not only afford an elegant and, to some, compelling model of government, they have also served as a kind of intellectual road map for practical efforts to reduce government and make it less costly. For example, Boston and colleagues argue that "one of the most distinctive and striking features of New Zealand's public management reforms was the way they were shaped by . . . public choice theory and organizational economics, especially agency theory" (1996, 16). As we have seen, in its simplest form, public choice views the government from the standpoint of markets and customers. In turn, the commitment of public choice theory to rational choice implies a selection of values, most often a commitment to efficiency and productivity. It is not surprising then, as Hood suggests, that the New Public Management has clearly placed its emphasis on values such as efficiency, eliminating waste, or matching resources to clear goals (what he calls "sigma values"). However, he also points out that achieving those values may come at the expense of honesty and fair dealing, the avoidance of bias, or the pursuit of accountability ("theta values") or security, resilience, and the capacity to adapt ("lambda values") (Hood 1991; see also Hood and Jackson 1991, 14).

The second intellectual justification suggests that the New Public Management is deeply rooted in what has been termed "managerialism" or "neomanagerialism." In the managerialist view, business and public sector success depends on the quality and professionalism of managers. Christopher Pollitt has described "managerialism" as the belief that the road to social progress is through greater productivity, that such productivity will be enhanced by the discipline imposed by managers oriented toward greater efficiency and productivity, and that to perform this important (even apocalyptic) role, managers must be given what is variously termed the "freedom to manage" or even the "right to manage" (Pollitt 1993,1–3).

Some have argued, in addition, that the rise of the New Public Management is attributable not only to managerialism, but to the increasing influence of "managerialists." Interestingly, in both New Zealand and Australia, a part of transformation that occurred was very clearly linked to the emergence of a managerial class dominated by economists and those trained in economics. The Australian scholar Anna Yeatman, for example, argues that the turn toward managerialism in the Australian public service occurred when a large number of university-educated candidates, highly committed to a rationalized and task-oriented concept of public administration, were hired into high-level positions. Michael Pusey of the University of New South Wales supports that view, arguing that, in Australia's central agencies, staff drawn from economics or business-related professions—a group he terms "economic rationalists," were able to capture the line bureaucracies and, especially by threatening to withhold resources, draw them into the rationalist perspective (Pusey 1991).

We have seen that the New Public Management, as the Old Public Administration before it, is not just about the implementation of new *techniques*, but that it carries with it a new set of *values*, a set of values in this case largely drawn from market economics and business management. As already noted, there is a longstanding tradition in public administration supporting the idea that "government should be run like a business." For the most part, this recommendation has meant that government agencies should adopt those practices, ranging from "scientific management" to "total quality management," that have been found useful in the private sector. The New Public Management takes this idea one step further, arguing that government should adopt not only the *techniques* of business administration but certain business *values* as well. Today, the New Public Management is presented as a normative model for public administration and public management.

Engaging the Debate

Certainly the New Public Management has not been without its critics. Many scholars and practitioners have expressed concerns about the implications of the New Public Management and the role for public managers this model suggests. For example, in a recent *Public Administration Review* symposium on leadership, democracy, and public management, a number of authors thoughtfully considered the opportunities and challenges presented by the New Public Management. Those challenging the New Public Management in the symposium and elsewhere ask questions about the inherent contradictions in the movement (Fox 1996), the values it promotes (Frederickson 1996; deLeon and Denhardt 2000; Schachter 1997), the tensions between the emphasis on decentralization promoted in the market model and the need for coordination in the public sector (Peters and Savoie 1996), and the implied roles and relationships of the executive and legislative branches (Carroll and Lynn 1996). Others have questioned the implications of the privatization movement for democratic values and the public interest (McCabe and Vinzant 1999) and how entrepreneurship and what Terry (1993, 1998) has called "neomanagerialism" threaten to undermine democratic and constitutional values such as fairness, justice, representation, and participation.

Osborne and Gaebler (1992) told us to steer, not row, the boat. Our question is this: As the field of public administration has increasingly abandoned the idea of rowing and accepted responsibility for steering, has it simply traded one "adminicentric" view for another? In other words, have we traded one model in which public managers seek to achieve greater efficiency and productivity by controlling their agencies and their clients for another model in which the same thing occurs? Osborne and Gaebler write, "those who steer the boat have far more power over its destination than those who row it" (1992, 32). If that is the case, the shift from rowing to steering may have not only left administrators in charge of the boat—choosing its goals and directions and charting a path to achieve them—but also given them more power to do so.

In our rush to steer, perhaps we are forgetting who owns the boat. In their recent book, *Government Is Us* (1998), King and Stivers remind us that the government belongs to its citizens (see also Box 1998; Cooper 1991; King, Feltey, and O'Neill 1998; Stivers 1994a, 1994b; Thomas 1995). Accordingly, public administrators should focus on their responsibility to *serve and empower citizens* as they manage public organizations and implement public policy. In other words, with citizens at the forefront, the emphasis should not be placed on either steering or rowing the governmental boat, but rather on building public institutions marked by integrity and responsiveness.

Importantly, in making their case, proponents of New Public Management have often used the Old Public Administration as the foil against which principles of entrepreneurship can be seen as clearly superior. Note, for example, how Osborne and Gaebler contrast their principles to an alternative of rigid bureaucracies plagued with excessive rules, restricted by rule-bound budgeting and personnel systems, and preoccupied with control. These traditional bureaucracies are described as ignoring citizens, shunning innovation, and serving their own needs. According to Osborne and Gaebler, "The kind of governments that developed during the industrial era, with their sluggish, centralized bureaucracies, their preoccupation with rules and regulations, and their hierarchical chains of command, no longer work very well" (1992, 11–12). In fact, while they served their earlier purposes, "bureaucratic institutions . . . increasingly fail us" (15).

If the principles of New Public Management are compared with the Old Public Administration, the New Public Management clearly looks like a preferred alternative. But even a cursory examination of the recent literature in public administration clearly demonstrates that these two approaches do not fully embrace contemporary government theory or practice (Box 1998; Bryson and Crosby 1992; Carnavale 1995; Cook 1996; Cooper 1991; deLeon 1997; Denhardt 1993; Farmer 1995; Fox and Miller 1995; Frederickson 1997; Gawthrop 1998; Goodsell 1994; Harmon 1995; Hummel 1994; Ingraham et al. 1994; Light 1997; Luke 1998; McSwite 1997; Miller and Fox 1997; Perry 1996; Rabin, Hildreth, and Miller 1998; Rohr 1998; Stivers

1993; Terry 1995, 1998; Thomas 1995; Vinzant and Crothers 1998; Wamsley et al. 1990; Wamsley and Wolf 1996). The field of public administration, of course, has not been stuck in progressive reform rhetoric for the last hundred years. Instead, there has been a rich and vibrant intellectual and practical evolution in thought and practice, with important and substantial developments that cannot be subsumed under the title "the New Public Management." Thus there are more than two choices.

We reject the notion that the reinvented, market-oriented New Public Management should be compared only to the Old Public Administration, which, despite its many important contributions, has come to be seen as synonymous with bureaucracy, hierarchy, and control. As we said, if that is the comparison, the New Public Management will always win. In contrast, we will suggest that what is missing in the debate is a set of organizing principles for a more contemporary alternative to the New Public Management. We would like to suggest that the New Public Management should be contrasted with what we will term the New Public Service, a set of ideas about the role of public administration in the governance system that places public service, democratic governance, and civic engagement at the center.

Portions of this and subsequent chapters were extracted and adapted from a previously published article: Robert Denhardt and Janet Denhardt, 2000, "The New Public Service: Serving Rather than Steering," *Public Administration Review* 60(6): 549–59.

Chapter 2

The Roots of the New Public Service

In the first chapter, we traced the development of the Old Public Administration and the New Public Management. Before moving on, it will be helpful to review some of the themes that emerged in that analysis. First, for at least the first three quarters of the twentieth century, the mainstream model of public administration was that articulated by writers such as Woodrow Wilson, Frederick Taylor, Luther Gulick, and Herbert Simon. Even though many of its advocates portrayed orthodox public administration as neutral with respect to values, it wasn't. It was a normative model for the conduct of public agencies. Among the value choices made in the construction of this model were a particular description of the public administrator's role, especially in relation to the political (or policy) process, the choice of efficiency (as opposed to responsiveness, etc.) as the primary criterion for assessing the work of administrative agencies, and an emphasis on designing public agencies as largely closed systems, featuring a single "controlling" executive having substantial authority and operating in a top-down fashion. Perhaps the most striking feature of this model, evident in its early versions but especially clear in its later versions, was the use of "rational choice" as the primary theoretical foundation of public administration.

Second, despite the dominance of this model, the prevailing assumptions of the mainstream version of the Old Public Administration were countered, frequently and eloquently, by a series of writers and practitioners who argued for greater discretion, greater responsiveness, and greater openness in the administrative process. These alternative views—which we would associate with figures such as Marshall Dimock, Robert Dahl, and, most of all, Dwight Waldo—provided a counterpoint to the overall model, important to

remember and often accepted in particular situations, but rarely if ever dominant. Indeed, it might be proper to say that these ideas were "embedded"
within the prevailing model, to which they were largely subservient.

Third, the New Public Management has recently presented itself as an
alternative to the traditional "bureaucratic" way of conducting the public's
"business." The New Public Management holds that government should engage in only those activities that cannot be privatized or contracted out and
that, more generally, market mechanisms should be employed wherever possible so that citizens will be presented with choices among service delivery
options. In addition, the New Public Management suggests a special role for
managers, especially entrepreneurial managers, who are given greater latitude in improving efficiency and productivity, primarily through "managing
for results." Finally, the New Public Management suggests that public managers "steer rather than row," that is, that they move toward becoming moni-
tors of policy implementation or purchasers of services rather than being
directly involved in service delivery itself. At the base of these recommendations, there are theoretical commitments to such ideas as public choice theory;
agency theory; and, in general, the use of economic models in the design and
implementation of public policy

What is interesting is that while the New Public Management has been
touted as an alternative to the Old Public Administration, it actually has
much in common with the mainstream model of public administration, specifically a dependence on and commitment to models of rational choice. For
example, as we discussed earlier, principal agent theory can be applied to the
relationship between public executives and those who report to them. When
used in this way, a central question would be: What incentive structure is
appropriate to secure the cooperation or even compliance of lower employees? Such an approach bears striking similarity to Herbert Simon's inducements—contributions model of a half-century ago. In that view, a chief
question facing the organization's "controlling group" is how to provide
sufficient and appropriate inducements so that lower participants would contribute to the work of the organization. In either case, what makes the model
work is a commitment to rational choice. So while there are clearly differences
between the Old Public Administration and the New Public Management, the
basic theoretical foundations of these two "mainstream" versions of public administration and public policy are in fact very much alike.

In contrast to these mainstream models of public administration or public
management that are rooted in the idea of rational choice, we suggest an alternative, the New Public Service (see Table 1). Like the New Public Management and the Old Public Administration, the New Public Service consists of
many diverse elements, and many different scholars and practitioners have

contributed, often in disagreement with one another. Yet there are certain general ideas that seem to characterize this approach as a normative model and to distinguish it from others. While the New Public Service has emerged both in theory and in the innovative and advanced practices of many exemplary public managers, we will examine the conceptual foundations of the New Public Service. Certainly the New Public Service can lay claim to an impressive intellectual heritage, including the work of those we mentioned earlier who provided constructive dissent to the rationalist prescriptions of the mainstream model (e.g., Dimock, Dahl, and Waldo). However, here we will focus on more contemporary precursors of the New Public Service, including (1) theories of democratic citizenship, (2) models of community and civil society, (3) organizational humanism and the new public administration, and (4) postmodern public administration. We will then outline what we see as the main tenets of the New Public Service.

Democratic Citizenship

Concerns about citizenship and democracy are particularly important and visible in recent political and social theory, both of which call for a reinvigorated and more active and involved citizenship (Barber 1984, 1998; Mansbridge 1990, 1994; Pateman 1970; Sandel 1996). But citizenship can be viewed in different ways. A first and obvious definition focuses on the rights and obligations of citizens as defined by the legal system; that is, citizenship is seen as a legal status. An alternative, broader view considers citizenship as concerned with more general issues related to the nature of one's membership in a political community, including such issues as the rights and responsibilities of citizens, regardless of their legal status (Turner 1993, 3). In this view, citizenship is concerned with the individual's capacity to influence the political system; it implies active involvement in political life. It is this latter view we will focus on here and throughout this book.

Beyond these definitional concerns, there are different ways to understand what is involved in democratic citizenship. For example, one might argue that government exists primarily in order to advance the economic interests of the community and individuals within the community. In this case, the state and the relationship of citizens to the state should be based simply on the idea of self-interest. According to Sandel (1996), the prevailing model of the relationship between state and citizens is in fact based on the idea that government exists to ensure that citizens can make choices consistent with their self-interest by guaranteeing certain procedures (such as voting) and individual rights. The role of government is to make sure that the interplay of individual self-interests operates freely and fairly. Obvi-

Table 1

Comparing Perspectives: Old Public Administration, New Public Management, and New Public Service

	Old Public Administration	New Public Management	New Public Service
Primary theoretical and epistemological foundations	Political theory, social and political commentary augmented by naive social science	Economic theory, more sophisticated dialogue based on positivist social science	Democratic theory, varied approaches to knowledge including positive, interpretive, and critical
Prevailing rationality and associated models of human behavior	Synoptic rationality, "administrative man"	Technical and economic rationality, "economic man," or the self-interested decision maker	Strategic or formal rationality, multiple tests of rationality (political, economic, and organizational)
Conception of the public interest	Public interest is politically defined and expressed in law	Public interest represents the aggregation of individual interests	Public interest is the result of a dialogue about shared values
To whom are public servants responsive	Clients and constituents	Customers	Citizens
Role of government	Rowing (designing and implementing policies focusing on a single, politically defined	Steering (acting as a catalyst to unleash market forces)	Serving (negotiating and brokering interests among citizens and community groups,

Mechanisms for achieving policy objectives	objective) Administering programs through existing government agencies	Creating mechanisms and incentive structures to achieve policy objectives through private and nonprofit agencies	creating shared values) Building coalitions of public, nonprofit, and private agencies to meet mutually agreed upon needs
Approach to accountability	Hierarchical— Administrators are responsible to democratically elected political leaders	Market-driven—The accumulation of self-interests will result in outcomes desired by broad groups of citizens (or customers)	Multifaceted—Public servants must attend to law, community values, political norms, professional standards, and citizen interests
Administrative discretion	Limited discretion allowed administrative officials	Wide latitude to meet entrepreneurial goals	Discretion needed but constrained and accountable
Assumed organizational structure	Bureaucratic organizations marked by top-down authority within agencies and control or regulation of clients	Decentralized public organizations with primary control remaining within the agency	Collaborative structures with leadership shared internally and externally
Assumed motivational basis of public servants and administrators	Pay and benefits, civil-service protections	Entrepreneurial spirit, ideological desire to reduce size of government	Public service, desire to contribute to society

ously, this perspective is consistent with public choice economics and the New Public Management (see Kamensky 1996), and public choice theorists have largely endorsed this view. For example, James Buchanan, a leading public choice theorist, has argued that while altruism often enters into public deliberations, political institutions should be designed so as to minimize the extent to which institutions rely on altruistic behavior (quoted in Mansbridge 1994, 153).

Others have argued that political altruism, or what Mansbridge calls "public spirit," plays an important, even an essential role in the process of democratic governance. Sandel, for example, offers an alternative view of democratic citizenship in which individuals are much more actively engaged in governance. Citizens look beyond their self-interest to the larger public interest, adopting a broader and more long-term perspective that requires a knowledge of public affairs and also a sense of belonging, a concern for the whole, and a moral bond with the community whose fate is at stake (Sandel 1996, 5–6). Mansbridge argues that this view of citizenship provides a certain "glue" that holds the political system together. In her view, public spirit (or political altruism) involves both love and duty, each playing an important role:

> If I make your good my own through empathy (love), I will be less likely to act in ways that hurt you. If I make the collective good my own (love of nation), I will forgo my individual benefit for that good. If I am committed to a principle that for one reason or another prescribes cooperation, I will forgo self-interest for reasons of duty. (Mansbridge 1994, 147)

Mansbridge is quick to point out, however, that unrestrained altruism is not necessarily good. There is the possibility that political elites might manipulate public spirit through indoctrination or charisma, through limiting the possibilities of its expression, or through structuring public debate so that challenges to their power are prohibited.

Public spirit needs to be nourished and maintained, and that can be aided by constant attention to principles of justice, public participation and deliberation. A sense of *justice* evokes strong emotions in those who feel mistreated or exploited, and their resistance can often become quite forceful. On the other hand, a political system that seems intent on promoting justice is likely to engender affection and involvement. *Participation* is a second device for promoting public spirit. Those who are involved in decisions feel better about those decisions and are more likely to aid in their implementation; but participation can be structured so as to give people a false sense of involvement, so must be balanced with conditions of open deliberation and discourse. *Deliberation* can clarify and sometimes ameliorate perceived differences; it can provide a common ground of information so that people are at least starting "on the same page"; and it can build a sense of solidarity and commitment to solutions that may be proposed. "And good deliberation will often lead all but the most contrary-minded to change at least some of their preferences, sometimes producing agreement, sometimes clarifying conflict in ways that reveal what steps to take next" (Mansbridge 1994, 156).

Note that this alternative view of citizenship does not suggest the elimination of self-interest as an individual or social motive or its naive replacement by the notion of public spirit. To do so would neglect important and appropriate concerns—as well as longstanding debates in America and elsewhere. But this view does suggest a balancing of these "motives" and ultimately a recognition of the primary importance of civic virtue and the public interest, such as we might expect in a democratic society. The idea of deliberation, for example, suggests an initial interchange between ideas borne out of self-interest, but it also suggests that such interchange may open one to new ideas and even to new practices, including some that may eventually be pursued even though they may work against narrow self interest.

In any case, recently there have been increasing calls for a restoration of a citizenship based on civic interests rather than self-interest. In this view, citizens would be concerned with the broad public interest, they would be active and involved, and they would assume responsibility for others. As Evans and Boyte put it so eloquently, a reinvigorated notion of citizenship would include:

> a concern for the common good, the welfare of the community as a whole, willingness to honor the rights for others that one possesses, tolerance of diverse religious, political, and social beliefs, acceptance of the primacy of the community's decisions over one's own private inclinations, and a recognition of one's obligations to defend and serve the public. (Evans and Boyte 1986, 5)

In other words, citizens would do what citizens are supposed to do in a democracy—*they would run the government.* As they did so, they would contribute not only to the society's betterment, but also to their own growth as active and responsible human beings.

Though we will elaborate this point later (indeed, throughout this book), these lessons concerning a more active and vital citizenship have clearly found their way into the literature and practice of public administration. An early symposium on "citizenship and public administration," published in the *Public Administration Review,* considered a variety of theoretical and practical issues connecting emerging ideas of civics and citizenship to the profession of public administration (Frederickson and Chandler 1984). More recently, two books, *Government Is Us* (King and Stivers 1998) and *Citizen Governance* (Box 1998), have focused on how public administrators might contribute to the creation of a more citizen-centered government. Consistently with this perspective, King and Stivers (1998) assert that administrators should see citizens as citizens (rather than merely voters, clients, or "customers"), should share authority and reduce control, and should trust in the efficacy of collaboration. Moreover, in contrast to managerialist calls for greater efficiency, King and Stivers suggest that public managers should seek greater responsiveness and a corresponding increase in citizen trust. Box moves the argument specifically to the local government level, suggesting ways in which local governments might be restructured to allow for great citizen involvement in the governance process. As we will see, these and other adaptations of recent work in democratic theory, and especially theories of citizenship and civic engagement, have contributed to what we will term the New Public Service.

Models of Community and Civil Society

We can also locate important roots of the New Public Service in recent discussions about community and civil society. The widespread current interest in community is an interesting phenomenon, arising as it does in so many different arenas (Bellah et al. 1985, 1991; Etzioni 1988, 1995; Gardner 1991; Selznick 1992; Wolfe 1989) and being articulated by commentators of both the left and the right. On the one hand, those toward the left see community as an antidote to the excessive and unrestrained greed and self-interest that marks modern society, a cure for individualism run rampant. Meanwhile, those toward the right see community as an avenue to restore basic American values that were once held, but are now being challenged by forces that seem to be beyond our making or our control.

Why so many should be interested in community is an interesting question. Some suggest that Americans have become alienated by the overwhelming force of a technological society, epitomized by the assembly line or the computer, and seek a return to more "human" associations. Others blame the social and political dislocations connected with the Vietnam War and the Civil Rights movement, and hope for a time and circumstance of greater gentility and perhaps remorse. Still others cite the excesses of capitalism and the moral ineptitude of those involved in questionable market practices and "insider trading" schemes as requiring a renewed sense of social responsibility. Still others become wary at the prospect of a global economy not necessarily dominated by the United States and hope for economic certainty. Finally, some point to the degradation of the environment and the possible end of human existence implied by the existence of weapons of mass destruction; they want ecological balance and security. All seem to somehow recognize that life has gotten "out of control" and that people need a way to take back their lives.

In any case, community has become a dominant theme in American life. While different writers focus on different aspects of community, the work of John Gardner is exemplary in its clarity and persuasiveness. Gardner (1991) holds that a sense of community, which might be derived from many different levels of human association from the neighborhood to the work group, might provide a helpful mediating structure between the individual and society. Gardner writes, "In our system, the 'common good' is first of all preservation of a system in which all kinds of people can—within the law—pursue their various visions of the common good, *and* at the same time accomplish the kinds of mutual accommodation that make a social system livable and workable. The play of conflicting interests in a framework of shared purposes is the drama of a free society" (1991, 15). The shared values of a community, according to Gardner, are important but he urges that we also recognize that wholeness must also incorporate diversity. Gardner writes,

> To prevent wholeness from smothering diversity, there must be a philosophy of pluralism, an open climate for dissent, and an opportunity for sub-communities to retain their identity and share in the setting of larger group goals. To prevent diversity from destroying wholeness, there must be institutional arrangements for diminishing polarization, for teaching diverse groups to know one another, for coalition-building, dispute resolution, negotiation and mediation. Of course the existence of a healthy community is in itself an instrument of conflict resolution. (Gardner 1991, 16)

Beyond these features, according to Gardner and others, community is based on caring, trust, and teamwork, bound together by a strong and effective system for communications and conflict resolution. The interactive nature of community mediates between and reconciles the individual and the collectivity. Rosabeth Moss Kantor, the well-known management theorist, comments on this idea in some of her early work on community. She writes, "the search for community is also a quest for direction and purpose in the collective anchoring of the individual life. Investment of self in a community, acceptance of its authority and willingness to support its life can offer identity, personal meaning, and the opportunity to grow in terms of standards and guiding principles that the member feels are expressive of his own inner being" (Kantor 1972, 73).

In part, this effort depends on building a healthy and active set of "mediating institutions" that simultaneously serve to give focus to the desires and interests of citizens and to provide experiences that will better prepare those citizens for action in the larger political system. As Robert Putnam (2000) argues, America's democratic tradition is dependent on the existence of civically engaged citizens, active in all sorts of groups, associations, and governmental units. Families, work groups, churches, civic associations, neighborhood groups, voluntary organization clubs, and social groups—even athletic teams—help establish connections between the individual and the larger society. Collectively, these small groups constitute a "civil society" in which people need to work out their personal interests in the context of community concerns. Civil society is one place where citizens can engage one another in the kind of personal dialogue and deliberation that is the essence not only of community building, but of democracy itself.

A great deal of recent commentary on the notion of citizenship and civil society has focused on the apparently decreasing involvement of American citizens in politics and government. People seem disillusioned with government, they are withdrawing from the political process, and they are becoming more and more isolated in their private spaces. Public opinion polls, for example, have shown a sharp decrease in people's trust in government, especially at the federal level. For several decades, the University of Michigan's Survey Research Center has been gathering Americans' responses to the question, "How much of the time do you trust the government in Washington to do the right thing?" Forty years ago, more than three out of every four Americans said that they trusted the government "just about always" or "most of the time. Today fewer than one out of four give this response. Trust in government seems to be at an all-time low.

Some, however, have argued for a more balanced view. David Mathews of the Kettering Foundation, for example, has suggested that, while the interest of citizens in the political process may have been sublimated in recent years, it is not dead. Mathews (1994) cites a Kettering-sponsored study that discovered strong feelings of powerlessness and exclusion among citizens, but also deep concerns and an untapped sense of civic duty. Citizens felt great frustration and anger that "they had been pushed out of the political system by a professional political class of powerful lobbyists, incumbent politicians, campaign managers and a media elite. They saw the system as one in which votes no longer made any difference because money ruled. They saw a system with its doors closed to the average citizen" (Mathews 1994, 12–15). As a consequence, citizens felt alienated and detached.

On the other hand, citizens still want to act. They are proud of their communities and their country and they want to help bring about positive change. In fact, many citizens are becoming engaged in political activities of a new sort, not spending their time in electoral or party politics, which they see as closed and impenetrable, but in grass-roots citizen-based movements within neighborhoods, work groups, and associations. These activities constitute laboratories of citizenship, arenas in which people are seeking to work out new relationships with one another and the larger political order, relationships cognizant of the dilemmas of participation imposed by the modern world, but also informed by the new possibilities for activism and involvement that modern conditions offer (Boyte and Kari 1996; Lappé and DuBois 1994).

There also seems to be an important role for government in encouraging community building and civil society. Interestingly, many progressive and forward-looking civic and political leaders are coming to recognize the importance and the viability of such efforts—and are becoming involved themselves. Political leaders are reaching out to citizens in substantial ways, both through modern information technology and more conventional means. Similarly, public managers are redefining their role with respect to the involvement of citizens in the governmental process (Thomas 1995). Again, as King and Stivers (1998) point out, government can play an important and critical role in creating, facilitating, and supporting connections between citizens and their communities.

How are public administrators affected by and how do they affect community and civil society? While this question will occupy us throughout the remainder of this book, there are several general comments we can make at the outset. First, where strong networks of citizen interaction and high levels of social trust and cohesion among citizens exist, public administrators can count on these existing stock of social capital to build even stronger networks, to open new avenues for dialogue and debate, and to further educate citizens with respect to matters of democratic governance (Woolum 2000). Second, public administrators can contribute to building community and social capital. Some are arguing today that the primary role of the public administrator is that of building community (Nalbandian 1999). Others certainly argue that public administrators can play an active role in promoting social capital by encouraging citizen involvement in public decision making. Based on their experience in conducting broad-scale efforts in civic engagement, Joseph Gray and Linda Chapin comment, "citizens don't always get what they want, but including them personalizes the work we do—connects public administration to the public. And this connection leads to understanding for both citizens and administrators" (1998, 192). Such an understanding enriches both government and the community.

Organizational Humanism and the New
Public Administration

A third important theoretical root of the New Public Service is organizational humanism. Over the past twenty-five years, public administration theorists have joined colleagues in other disciplines in suggesting that traditional hierarchical approaches to social organization are restrictive in their view of human behavior, and they have joined in a critique of bureaucracy and a search for alternative approaches to management and organization. Collectively, these approaches have sought to fashion public organizations less dominated by issues of authority and control and more attentive to the needs and concerns of internal and external constituents.

Just as writers such as Dimock, Dahl, and Waldo provided a contrast to the prevailing view of public administration theory, writers such as Chris Argyris and Robert Golembiewski provided counterpoint to the prevailing view of organizational management through the last part of the twentieth century. In an early book, *Personality and Organization,* Argyris explored the impact of traditional management practices on the psychological development of individuals within complex organizations. Argyris noted that studies of the human personality indicated that people growing from infancy to adulthood move from passivity to activity, from dependence to independence, from a limited range of behaviors to a greater range, from shallow to deeper interests, from shorter to longer time perspectives, from a subordinate position to a position of equality or superordination, and from a lack of awareness to greater awareness (1957, 50). In contrast, what Argyris saw as the standard management practices of that time (and one could argue that they have not changed all that much even today) seemed to inhibit the development of employees rather than enhancing it. For example, in most organizations, people have relatively little control over their work. In many cases, they are expected to be submissive, dependent, and limited in what they can do. Such an arrangement ultimately backfires, Argyris argued, as it limits the contributions employees can make to the organization. In order to promote individual growth as well as improved organizational performance, Argyris sought an approach to management in which managers would develop and employ "skill in self-awareness, in effective diagnosing, in helping individuals grow and become more creative, [and] in coping with dependent-oriented . . . employees" (Argyris 1962, 213). As Argyris's work matured, he increasingly focused on ways that organizations could move in this direction through programs of planned change known as "organization development."

We should note that Argyris's ideas stood in direct contrast to the prevailing rational model of administration, articulated most clearly, as we saw, by Herbert Simon. Indeed, in 1973, Argyris used the pages of *Public Administration Review* to explore some limitations of the rational model (Argyris 1973). Argyris began by pointing out that Simon's rational model is quite similar to traditional administrative theory, in which management defines the objectives of the organization and the tasks to be performed, as well as training, rewarding, and penalizing employees—all within the framework of formal pyramidal structures in which authority flows from the top down. What Simon adds to this model is a focus on rational behavior, that is, behavior that can be defined in terms of means and ends. (Again, in this view "rational" is not concerned with broad philosophical concepts such as freedom or justice, but rather with how people can efficiently accomplish the work of the organization.) Given this emphasis, the rational model focuses on "the consistent, programmable, organized, thinking activities of man," it gives "primacy to behavior that is related to goals," and assumes "purpose without asking how it has developed" (Argyris 1973, 261).

Such a view fails to acknowledge the full range of human experience, the fact that people act spontaneously, that they experience chaos and unpredictability in their lives, and that they act on feelings and emotions that are far from rational. Moreover, because human growth is not a fully rational process, organizations built on this model would not support the growth, development, and "self-actualization" of the individual. Rather the rational model would give preference to those changes that would improve the rationality (the efficiency) of the organization. Those changes would likely be highly conservative, reinforcing the status quo by focusing "more on what is than is than what might be" (Argyris 1973, 261). In contrast to this view, Argyris urges greater attention to "individual morality, authenticity, (and) human self-actualization," attributes associated with the "human side of enterprise" (253).

In the field of public administration, the organization development (OD) perspective has been explored most thoroughly by Robert Golembiewski. In an early work, *Men, Management, and Morality* (1967), Golembiewski developed a critique of traditional theories of organization, with their emphasis on top down authority, hierarchical control, and standard operating procedures, arguing that such approaches reflect an insensitivity to the *moral* posture of the individual, specifically the question of individual freedom. In contrast, Golembiewski sought a way to "enlarge the area of discretion open to us in organizing and to increase individual freedom" (1967, 305). Following an OD perspective, Golembiewski urged managers to create an open problem-solving climate through the organization so that members can confront problems rather than fight about or flee from them. He encouraged them to build trust among individuals and groups throughout the organization, to supplement or even replace the authority of role or status with the authority of knowledge and competence. He suggested that decision-making and problem-solving responsibilities be located as close as possible to information sources and to make competition, where it exists, contribute to meeting work goals as opposed to win-lose competition. He said the idea was to maximize collaboration between individual and units whose work in interdependent and to develop reward systems that recognize both the achievement of the organization's mission and the growth and development of the organization's members. Managers should work, he said, to increase self-control and self-direction for people within the organization, to create conditions under which conflict is surfaced and managed appropriately and positively, and to increase awareness of group process and its consequences for performance (Denhardt 1999, 405).

Interestingly, Golembiewski, like Argyris, contrasted his more humanistic view of organization with the rational choice model, in this case through a critique of the public choice model. Golembiewski first argued that the assumption of classical rationality is a methodological construct that simply doesn't reflect reality (a point that even public choice theorists acknowledge). People don't always act rationally or even approximate rational behavior. To base a theory of choice on the assumption that they do, means that one is limited to logical propositions about how people would behave if they did act rationally. Such a view, Golembiewski argues, neglects important political or emotional considerations, which should be taken into account in developing any comprehensive theory of human behavior. Otherwise, one might conclude, with Norton Long, that public choice theorists "argue with elegant and impeccable logic about unicorns" (quoted in Golembiewski 1977, 1492).

Other important contributions to constructing more humanistic organizations in the public sector were made by a group of scholars collectively known as the New Public Administration, essentially the public administration counterpart to the late sixties/early seventies radical movements in society generally and in other social science disciplines. While the New Public Administration was never a very coherent movement, with its contributors often differing substantially with one another, some of the ideas associated with the New Public Administration are important to recall. Certainly with respect to the issue of organizational humanism, several of the scholars during that period emphasized the need to explore alternatives to the traditional top-down, hierarchical model of bureaucratic organization. Indicting the old model for its objectification and depersonalization of organizational members and calling for models built around openness, trust, and honest communications, these scholars discussed alternatives with such names as the "dialectical organization" and the "consociated model." Denhardt put it this way in his book *In the Shadow of Organization:* "The creation of settings in which creativity and dialogue can occur, in which mutuality and respect contribute both to individual growth and development as well as to enabling groups and organizations to deal more effectively and responsibly with environmental complexity, is an effort that begins with the acts of individuals" (1981, xii).

We should note that the New Public Administration contributed other dissenting viewpoints to the mainstream discussion of public administration. Specifically, there was an argument for having administrators play an even more active role in the development of public policy than had previously been the case, in part because the complexity of contemporary problems required the expertise of professionally trained administrators and their associated technical specialists, and in part simply because "somebody has to take on the challenges." There was an even more explicit recognition and discussion of the role of values in public administration. For example, George Frederickson, in his *New Public Administration*, argued in behalf of social equity as a guiding concept in administrative and political decision making, "It is incumbent on the public servant to be able to develop and defend criteria and measures of equity and to understand the impact of public services on the dignity and well-being of citizens" (1980, 46). Essentially, providing equitable solutions to public problems involves not just offering the same services to all but greater levels of service to those in greater need. Frederickson argues that public administration is not neutral and certainly should not be judged by the criterion of efficiency alone. Rather, concepts such as equality, equity, and responsiveness should also come into play.

Postmodern Public Administration

A fourth important theoretical root of New Public Management is postmodernism. In the late sixties and early seventies, scholars in public administration began to explore more critically the approach to knowledge acquisition that underlay the mainstream rational model of administration. The basis for this exploration was the idea that mainstream public administration, like other social sciences, had become dependent on a particular approach to knowledge acquisition—positivism—and that this approach subtly but dramatically limited the range of thinking possible in the field. To put it simply, the positivist approach argues that social sciences can be understood using the same approaches employed in the natural sciences. In this view, the facts of social or organizational life can be separated from values; the role of science is to focus on fact rather than value. Facts can be observed and measured, just as the behavior of physical or chemical elements can be measured. In turn, concepts and theories can be built based on these observations of "manifest behavior." The positivist approach was acknowledged as the foundation of Simon's rational model of administration and clearly came to dominate other aspects of the study of public administration, especially the policy sciences.

Critics of this view pointed out that observing human behavior "from the outside" tells us far less than understanding the *meaning* of human action. For example, you might see a man running through the woods, but you would know more about what was happening if you knew he was a criminal fleeing the sheriff. Similarly, in social life, facts and values are extremely difficult to separate and, indeed, in many cases, *values* are more important than facts in understanding human action. In any case, since human behavior differs from time to time and from culture to culture, it's impossible to formulate the same kind of enduring lawlike statements that the hard sciences seek. Moreover, describing human action in terms of "objective" observations and "law-like relationships" fails to recognize the nonrational components of human experience—intuitions, emotions, and feelings. Finally, scholars pointed out that social science is not neutral (as it claims); the measurement of human behavior can affect the behavior, as in the Hawthorne experiments when workers reacted more to the fact they were being observed than to changes the researchers made in their work environment.

On the one hand, critics pointed out that reliance on the positivist model reinforced tendencies toward objectification and depersonalization that were already part of the mainstream model of public administration. On the other hand, they also argue that relying on positivism alone simply didn't permit the fullest and most complete understanding of the meanings and values that are so much a part of human life. In a search for alternatives, scholars turned to *interpretive* approaches to knowledge acquisition, approaches that focused on understanding the meanings that people bring to their experiences, especially those experiences that they share with others. Others turned to a *value-critical* examination of the forces that underlie human experiences, especially those forces of power and domination that distort communications among human beings. Through approaches such as these, scholars hoped to build alternatives approaches to the study and practice of public administration, alternatives more sensitive to values (not just facts), to subjective human meaning (not just objective behavior), and the full range of emotions and feelings involved in relationships between and among real people.

These ideas have been even further extended in recent efforts to employ the perspectives of postmodern thinking, especially discourse theory, in understanding public organizations. While there are significant differences among the various postmodern theorists, they seem to arrive at a similar conclusion—because we are dependent on one another in the postmodern world, governance must increasingly be based on sincere and open discourse among all parties, including citizens and administrators. And while postmodern public administration theorists are skeptical of traditional approaches to public participation, there seems to be considerable agreement that enhanced public dialogue is required in order to reinvigorate the public bureaucracy and restore a sense of legitimacy to the field of public administration.

While postmodernism is extremely complex and diverse, most postmodernists would argue that a problem we face today is that we have lost the capacity to tell what is *real*. All those previously held "world-views," as well as "scientific explanations" that seemed to work in the past, have been revealed to have fatal flaws, most of these related to the fact that these explanations were the products of particular places and particular times and could only address the world from that largely unique standpoint. If we create the world through our language and our interactions, then there will inevitably be limitations on what we can claim to be "real."

The situation is even more complicated because a vast and confusing world of symbolism has come to dominate our thinking and our feeling. For example, in television commercials, sex is used to sell cars and frogs are used to sell beer. The communication is all one way. We, the passive viewers, don't have a chance to talk back. Ultimately these symbols, and others like them in the worlds of art, music, architecture, and politics (to name only a few), come to replace the "reality" from which they grew and to constitute the only culture we share in common. At the cultural level we can communicate with each other only in terms of abstractions devoid of "reality." More and more, we are forced to recognize that the only authentic communication in which we can fully engage is face-to-face interaction based on our recognition of the other as a self we share.

Public administration theorists employing the postmodern perspective are particularly critical of the field's apparent preoccupation with rationalism (especially market-based rational choice theory) and technocratic expertise. "In bureaucracy, the world of robust social action is displaced by the world of rationally organized action. Obedience of hierarchically commanded routines supersedes empathetic relationships with others. . . . In monologic communication there is no back-and-forth, no opportunity to engage in a verbal struggle to define a problem and decide what should be done about it" (Fox and Miller 1997, 70–71). In contrast, postmodern public administration theorists have a central commitment to the idea of "discourse," the notion that public problems are more likely resolved through discourse than through "objective" measurements or rational analysis (McSwite 1997, 377). The ideal of authentic discourse sees administrators and citizens as engaging fully with one another, not merely as rationally self-interested individuals being brought together to talk, but as participants in a relationship in which they engage with one another as human beings. The resulting process of negotiation and consensus building is one in which individuals engage with one another as they engage with themselves, fully embracing all aspects of the human personality, not merely rational, but experiential, intuitive, and emotional. But that change is an immensely difficult one, requiring that we come to understand (1) how it is possible to act without relying on reason and (2) how to come to terms with the idea of otherness. O.C. McSwite offers a practical first step—to open ourselves to one another. "The alternative is to *listen,* to become hollowed out, and to receive the other as oneself. This . . . is not so much the end of reason as its transformation. . . . By making people and their lives an object in its contemplations, reason separates us from one another when the reality of the human condition is, I am you" (1997, 276–277).

The New Public Service

Theorists of citizenship, community and civil society, organizational humanism and the new public administration, and postmodernism have helped to establish a climate in which it makes sense today to talk about a New Public Service. Though we acknowledge that differences, even substantial differences, exist in these various viewpoints, we would suggest there are also similarities that distinguish the cluster of ideas we call the New Public Service from those associated with the New Public Management and the Old Public Administration. Moreover, there are a number of practical lessons that the New Public Service suggests for those in public administration. These lessons are not mutually exclusive, rather they are mutually reinforcing. We will outline these ideas here, then discuss each one in more detail in the seven chapters that follow. Among these ideas, we find the following the most compelling:

1. *Serve Citizens, Not Customers:* The public interest is the result of a dialogue about shared values rather than the aggregation of individual self-interests. Therefore, public servants do not merely respond to the demands of "customers," but rather focus on building relationships of trust and collaboration with and among citizens (Chapter 3).
2. *Seek the Public Interest:* Public administrators must contribute to building a collective, shared notion of the public interest. The goal is not to find quick solutions driven by individual choices. Rather, it is the creation of shared interests and shared responsibility (Chapter 4).

3. *Value Citizenship over Entrepreneurship:* The public interest is better advanced by public servants and citizens committed to making meaningful contributions to society than by entrepreneurial managers acting as if public money were their own (Chapter 5).
4. *Think Strategically, Act Democratically:* Policies and programs meeting public needs can be most effectively and responsibly achieved through collective efforts and collaborative processes (Chapter 6).
5. *Recognize that Accountability Is Not Simple:* Public servants should be attentive to more than the market; they should also attend to statutory and constitutional law, community values, political norms, professional standards, and citizen interests (Chapter 7).
6. *Serve Rather than Steer:* It is increasingly important for public servants to use shared, value-based leadership in helping citizens articulate and meet their shared interests rather than attempting to control or steer society in new directions (Chapter 8).
7. *Value People, Not Just Productivity:* Public organizations and the networks in which they participate are more likely to be successful in the long run if they are operated through processes of collaboration and shared leadership based on respect for all people (Chapter 9).

Chapter 3

Serve Citizens, Not Customers

Serve citizens, not customers. The public interest is the result of a dialogue about shared values rather than the aggregation of individual self-interests. Therefore, public servants do not merely respond to the demands of "customers," but rather focus on building relationships of trust and collaboration with and among citizens.

The New Public Service begins, of course, with the concept of public service. But the idea of public service is intertwined with the responsibilities of democratic citizenship. In the words of Benjamin Barber, "Service to the nation is . . . the duty of free men and women whose freedom is wholly dependent on and can survive only through the assumption of political responsibilities. In this tradition service is something we owe ourselves or that part of ourselves that is embedded in the civic community" (Barber 1998, 195). Public service derives, therefore, from the civic virtues of duty and responsibility.

Respect for the idea of public service has varied over time. In some periods, the commitment of citizens to public service has been far stronger than in others. Similarly, the relationship between the public servant and the public has been characterized in different ways over time. In this chapter, we will first review several important aspects of democratic citizenship, then consider these varying views of public service in relation to citizenship. We will then examine the particular interpretation of public service in the Old Public Administration, the New Public Management, and the New Public Service.

Civic Virtue and Democratic Citizenship

We noted earlier a distinction between a legal definition of citizenship and what we might call an ethical definition of citizenship—citizenship as concerned with the nature of one's membership in a political community, including such issues as the rights and responsibilities of citizens. We will focus here on ethical interpretations of citizenship, however, even here there are questions about (1) how a "theory" of citizenship might be formulated, (2) how modern society has shaped and—we would say—restricted the role of the citizen, and (3) whether there is a rationale and hope for building more active citizen involvement in the governance process. In this section, we will briefly examine each of these topics.

Theories of Citizenship

Efforts to understand the proper roles and responsibilities of the citizen trace back to ancient Greek philosophy. Political theorist J.G.A. Pocock, in fact, suggests that the history of the concept of citizenship in Western political thought can be seen as an "unfinished dialogue" between the ideal and the real, between persons and things (Pocock 1995, 42). According to Pocock, the classical account of citizenship, that which best expresses the "ideal," was first developed in Aristotle's *Politics*. In this view, the citizen engages in the work of the *polis* because it is in that work that the individual attains his or her (for Aristotle, it was only "his") fullest humanity. Because humans are active, social, and moral beings, concerned with the purpose of life, they seek to attain higher ends and must, in doing so, engage in self-determination. "Therefore, the citizen rules and is ruled; citizens join each other in making decisions where each decider respects the authority of the others, and all join in obeying the decisions . . . they have made" (Pocock 1995, 31). Citizens are more concerned with the "ends" to be attained in social life; they have less concern for the "means" of industry or production. Citizenship is not seen as an instrumental activity (a means to an end). To be an active citizen is an end in itself. It is valued for the freedom that is obtained by participating in the work of the polity.

There is an alternative view, one that Pocock traces to the Roman jurist Gaius, who moved from a concept of the citizen as a *political* being to the citizen as a *legal* being, existing in a world of persons, actions, and things. The concept of "things" is the one that particularly makes a difference. Aristotle's citizens were, of course, concerned with things (such as land or trade), but they did not act through the *medium* of things. Quite to the contrary, "Aristotle's citizens were persons acting on one another, so that their active life was a life immediately and heroically moral" (Pocock 1995, 34).

For Gaius, people acted primarily on things, and indeed most of their actions were focused on taking or maintaining possession of things. The resulting disputes over things were what led most directly to the need for regulation. The individual as a citizen was first concerned with the possession of things and second with legal actions taken with respect to things—authorization, conveyance, litigation, and so on. In this view, the world of things became the reality, the medium through which human beings lived their lives and, indeed, defined their lives. Citizenship then became a legal status, one associated perhaps with certain "rights," especially property rights, but not a moral or political one. "The Greek citizen . . . stepped out of a world of things into a world of purely personal interactions, a world of deeds and words, speech and war. The Roman citizen, subject to both law and prince, was constantly reminded by the Gaian formula that he lived in the world of things, as well as the world of persons and actions" (Pocock 1995, 40).

Much later, Jean-Jacques Rousseau, following in the Aristotelian tradition, basically defined the citizen as one who acts with the good of the community in mind. Citizenship is a way of life that involves a commitment to the community and to its members, a significant level of involvement in public affairs, and an occasional willingness to put one's own interest below those of the broader society, what Alexis de Tocqueville later called "self-interest properly understood" (Tocqueville 1969, 526–27). Others, such as John Stuart Mill, also envisioned citizen participation as a vital and necessary component of democratic government. As Mill stated, "good government . . . depends . . . (on) the qualities of the human beings composing the society over which the government is exercised" (Mill 1862, II, 2).

The legal tradition, which is often skeptical of public participation, was maintained in the writing of the U.S. Constitution. Consistently with the tradition of legalism and jurisprudence, the founding fathers created a government with careful attention to the balance, or one might say the dilution of power, in order to protect the public from governmental tyranny. At the same time, however, the framers were extremely suspicious of rule by the masses. For this reason, suffrage was severely limited. The concept of "citizen" pertained only to white male landowners, who were believed to have enough at stake, and presumably enough knowledge, to participate through voting and public service.

James Madison was particularly concerned about the notion of citizen action. He believed that among the "heaviest misfortunes" of the new republic was the "unsteadiness and injustice [with] which a factious spirit has tainted our public administration" (Madison 1787/1987, #10, 1). To Madison, factions were "a number of citizens, whether amounting to a majority or minority of the whole, who are united and actuated by some common impulse of passion, or of interest adverse to the rights of other citizens, or to the permanent and aggregate interests of the community" (#10, 1). Thomas Jefferson, on the other hand, strongly defended the involvement of citizen in the conduct of government, writing in the Declaration of Independence that "Governments are instituted among Men, deriving their just Powers from the Consent of the Governed" (Declaration of Independence 1776/1970). And so the debate continued.

While the United States constitutional system does not fully support the democratic ideal, having a more legalistic focus designed in part to protect government from excessive intrusions on the part of citizens, there has been a strong informal commitment to the democratic ideal. As an abstract value, the concept of citizen participation is unquestionably accepted as an unmitigated good. Abraham Lincoln in the Gettysburg Address echoed the sentiment in the well-known phrase "government of the people, by the people, for the people." Thus, there is a strong and explicit value placed on the role of the citizen in American democratic ideology.

Moreover, Americans have a strong tradition of *acting* in a way consistent with the ideal of democratic citizenship. Summarizing the history of civic involvement in this country, Terry Cooper writes, "From the covenantal tradition of the early Puritan communal with their forms of participatory self-governance; the New England town meetings; the experience of forming voluntary associations, which captured the attention of Tocqueville; Antifederalist thought; and the cooperative establishment of frontier settlements, there has emerged a set of values, customs, beliefs, principles, and theories which provide the substance for ethical citizenship" (1991, 10). This strong tradition of ethical citizenship stands in contrast to the more formal legal approaches, and provides the basis for an active and involved citizenry in this country.

Earlier we noted a difference between a perspective on governance in which citizens look beyond their self-interest to the larger public interest, and one in which government exists to ensure that citizens can make choices consistent with their self-interest by guaranteeing certain procedures and individual rights. What has now become clear is that theories of citizenship diverge in a strikingly similar way. The democratic ideal of persons actively engaged in the work of the community or nation, benefiting both the society and themselves as they become more complete human beings through their involvement in the political system, is contrasted with the world of jurisprudence and legal rights, both shaped to protect our interest in things, our possessions. In this chapter, we argue that the prevailing view in both politics and administration is associated with self-interest, but that a resurgence of democratic spirit might have great benefits for society and for its members.

The Role of the Citizen

Unfortunately, in recent times, the ideals of citizenship have been largely overwhelmed by increased power, professionalism, and complexity. Robert Pranger, for example, argues that much of what is termed "politics" today is actually "power politics," largely concerned with the activities of leaders, officials, and other power holders in society. Pranger contrasts this orientation to an alternative, the politics of citizenship or the "politics of participation." In the politics of participation, ordinary citizens engage in dialogue and discourse concerning the directions of society and act based on moral principles such as those associated with the term "civic virtue." A similar distinction has been made between high and low views of citizenship. High definitions of citizenship, associated with such writers as Aristotle, Rousseau, and Mill, assume a wide distribution of power and authority and view citizens as sharing equally in the exercise of authority. Low citizenship, associated with such names as Thomas Hobbes or the more contemporary democratic elitists, assumes a hierarchical distribution of authority, with the greatest power wielded by those "at the top" and little power exercised by others (Cooper 1991, 5). In either case, it appears that, in modern American society, the "politics of power" or "low citizenship" has come to dominate—perhaps not to the exclusion of the "politics of participation" or "high citizenship," but certainly to its disadvantage.

Carole Pateman argues that these "low" theories of citizenship have become self-fulfilling. She is disturbed by the fact that much contemporary theory is not "centered on the participation of 'the people,' or . . . the development of politically relevant and necessary qualities in the ordinary individual." Further, she states that "in the contemporary theory of democracy it is the participation of the minority elite that is crucial and the non-participation of the apathetic ordinary man lacking in the feeling of political efficacy that is regarded as the main bulwark against instability" (Pateman 1970, 104). She suggests that the present institutional setting is hostile to citizen participation, and creates feelings of apathy and low political efficacy. Therefore, the development of a "democratic character" among the citizenry, which she suggests is necessary for participation, is thwarted in the current system.

For whatever reason, as we noted earlier, political participation today is generally down, at least when measured in terms of formal involvement, such as voting or attending meetings. At the same time, trust in government has dropped precipitously and people seem quite cynical about the means and motives of politicians. The gap between leaders and citizens seems substantially greater than before. In fact, Barber points out the irony that while democracy needs both strong leadership and vigorous citizenship, that strengthened leadership, especially when it is associated with the manifest exercise of power, may in fact undermine a more active, participatory citizenship (1998).

Active citizenship may also be discouraged by the professionalization of government and its increasing dependence on "experts." As expert advice is increasingly heralded as essential to solving the problems faced by modern government, the opinions of ordinary citizens are largely devalued. Under these circumstances, officials and administrators may be inclined to disregard views they dismiss as lacking clarity and sophistication. Indeed, having to listen to such views becomes an "annoyance" interfering with the resolution of the technical problems that experts are trained to solve. Moreover, ordinary citizens may themselves become overwhelmed by the intricacies of problems and feel they have nothing to contribute—even though their "common sense" may be extremely valuable.

Finally, the sheer complexity of today's society makes civic involvement difficult. The pressures of making a living, raising children, and meeting all the other demands of modern life mean that many people simply feel they don't have enough energy for politics. Involvement in the public sphere takes time, and many people simply don't feel they can devote the time necessary to make democracy work.

Building Citizen Involvement

For obvious reasons, we might hope for high levels of public participation in a democratic society. All these reasons are based in the notion of democracy as involving the rule of the people carried out in a way consistent with fundamental democratic values. The first reason is our belief that through active participation we can most likely achieve the best political outcomes, outcomes that reflect the broad judgments of the people as a whole or the considered judgments of specific groups *and* are consistent with the norms of democracy. Second, through participation, we might fulfill what Thompson calls the democratic objective, "attaining rules and decisions which satisfy the interests of the greatest number of citizens" (Thompson 1970, 184). Through widespread public participation in civic affairs, citizens can help assure that the individual and collective interests are being heard and responded to by governmental officials. Moreover, they can prevent rulers from violating the interests of citizens. Third, democratic participation enhances the legitimacy of government. People who are involved in decision making are more likely to support those decisions and the institutions involved in making and carrying out those decisions.

These ideas come together in what Emmett S. Redford (1969) calls "democratic morality," an expression of the democratic ideal resting on three premises. First, democratic morality assumes that the individual is the basic measure of human value. Our social and political system can only be considered successful to the extent that it promotes the realization of the fullest potential of the individual. Second, democratic morality means that all persons have full claim to the attention of the system. While some people, for example, may have more wealth than others, that shouldn't give them undue advantage in political affairs. Third, democratic morality assumes that individual claims can best be promoted through the involvement of all persons in the decision-making process and that participation is not only an instrumental value, but is essential to the development of democratic citizenship. The ideal of universal participation may take various forms; however, Redford indicates some basics: "Among these are (1) access to information, based on education, open government, free communication, and open discussion; (2) access, direct or indirect, to forums of decision; (3) ability to open any issue to public discussion, (4) ability to assert one's claims without fear of coercive retaliation; and (5) consideration of all claims asserted" (1969, 8).

Through such processes, advocates of democracy believe the best government will be obtained and maintained. But what about the other side of the equation? From the standpoint of the citizen, what is there to be gained by further involvement in the body politic? Generally speaking, political theorists have come up with three answers, the ethical, the integrative, and the educative. We have already explored the ethical argument—that active involvement in political life is a part of realizing one's fullest potential. To Barber, for example, the aim of participation is to create communities of active, interested citizens "who are united less by homogeneous interests than by civic education and who are made capable of common purpose and mutual action by virtue of their civic attitudes and participatory institutions." (1984, 117). He sees citizens being transformed from having only private, selfish interests to having a regard for the public good. Similarly, Pranger writes that "The conduct of citizens in the culture of power is basically unvirtuous in that it has little to do with the citizen's main duty as an agent responsible for common participation based on independent points of view, eventually fostering that mutual responsibility which alone enriches the commonwealth's life" (1968, 53).

Active participation and the occasional sacrifice of one's own interest that is often involved in a democracy builds "character." Through discipline and self-sacrifice, citizens may become more virtuous. Involvement in the work of the polity teaches responsibility and tolerance. Active citizenship may not lead to spectacular deeds, but, according to Tocqueville, "every day it prompts some small ones; by itself it cannot make a man virtuous, but its discipline shapes a lot of orderly, temperate, moderate, careful, and self-controlled citizens. If it does not lease the will directly to virtue, it establishes habits which unconsciously turn it that way" (1969, 526–27). To put it simply, the person who remains actively involved in civic life will become a better person.

The integrative argument in support of more active citizenship suggests that people play many roles in society—employer, employee, teacher, student, parent, consumer, union representative, churchgoer—but that the citizenship role is one of very few roles that brings these different aspects of our lives together. (Religion might be another.) The political theorist Sheldon Wolin writes, "Citizenship provides what other roles cannot, namely an integrative experience which brings together the multiple role activities of the contemporary person and demands that the separate roles be surveyed from a more general point of view" (1960, 434). My role as a parent may sometimes conflict with my role as an employee. Where this is the case I need a broader way of bringing together the various roles in a synoptic fashion. The citizenship role can provide such integration.

This argument is especially interesting as we consider the question of civil society, because it is those smaller groups, associations, and day-to-day patterns of interactions that provide the "social glue" that holds society together. Michael Walzer points out that citizenship is one of many roles that members play, but the state itself is unlike all the other associations. "It both frames civil society and occupies space within it. It fixes the boundary conditions and the basic rules of all associational activity (including political activity). It compels association members to think about a common good, beyond their own conceptions of the good life" (1995, 169). Through the citizenship role, we may integrate the interests and experiences that we have in other, less comprehensive realms. Moreover, acting as a citizen, exercising the civic virtues brings us into a closer relationship with others. It increases the feeling that people belong to a community. So, "the activity of citizenship performs an integrative function in two respects, first, it enables the individual to integrate the various roles he or she plays; second, it integrates individuals into the community" (Dagger 1997, 101).

The educative argument in support of active and public-spirited participation is especially well developed in Carole Pateman's classic discussion of Rousseau's views on the matter. According to Rousseau, as the individual engages in the political process, he or she learns the importance of taking into account the views of others in order to gain their cooperation. "As a result of participating in decision making the individual is educated to distinguish between his own impulses and desires, he learns to be a public as well as a private citizen" (Pateman 1970, 25). As individuals engage in participation, they begin to learn and develop the skills appropriate to the process of participation, so that the process becomes self-sustaining. That is, the more the individual participates, the better he or she is able to do so. The classical or ideal theory of democratic citizenship, then, has an ambitious agenda—"the education of an entire people to the point where their intellectual, emotional, and moral capacities have reached their full potential and they are joined, freely and actively in a genuine community" (Davis, quoted in Pateman 1970, 21)

The educative argument is, of course, based on a faith in the "improvability" of the ordinary citizen. If there are problems with the involvement of citizens, if their participation doesn't bring about political improvements as well as heightened legitimacy, then the response is not to end participation, but to further educate the citizenry. Thomas Jefferson was clear on this point: "I know of no safe depository of the ultimate power of the society but the people themselves, and if we think them not enlightened enough to exercise their control with a wholesome discretion, the remedy is not to take it from them, but to inform their discretion" (Jefferson 1903, 278). If there are problems encountered in a participatory society, the answer is not to limit participation (the Madisonian response) but rather to further educate and to inform.

Public Service as an Extension of Citizenship

Clearly the idea of civic virtue, at least in the democratic ideal, incorporates the notion of service to the public. For this reason, discussion of democratic theory must attend to the roles and responsibilities or the duties and obligations of citizenship. A part of that discussion of particular relevance to our argument here is related to the idea of service to the community or nation. The virtuous citizen obviously is a citizen engaged in the work of the community, but the virtuous citizen also has a duty or responsibility to serve others. The idea of democratic citizenship has, since the earliest times, implied a certain duty or obligation on the part of the citizen to contribute to the betterment of the community. Many will recognize the Athenian Oath, from ancient Greece:

> We will never bring disgrace on this our City by any act of dishonesty or cowardice.

> We will fight for the ideals and Sacred Things of the City both alone and with many.

> We will revere and obey the City's laws, and will do our bes⸱
> reverence and respect in those above us who are prone to
> them at naught.
>
> We will strive increasingly to quicken the public's sense of civi⸱
>
> Thus in all these ways we will transmit this City, not only not less, bu⸱
> greater and more beautiful than it was transmitted to us. (Quoted in Bennett
> 1993, 217)

Similarly, Thomas Jefferson once wrote to a friend, scolding him for not
being more active in national affairs, saying, "There is a debt of service due
from every man to his country, proportioned to the bounties which nature
and fortune have measured him" (Jefferson, quoted in Staats 1988, 605).
The democratic ideal clearly posits an active and engaged citizen, one pro-
pelled at least in part by a commitment to serve others and to serve the
community. As one contemporary political theorist puts it, "Civic virtue, the
cultural disposition apposite to citizenship was thus two-fold, a willingness
to step forward and assume the burdens of public office; and second, a willingness to subordinate private interests to the requirement of public obedience. What Aristotle called the 'right temper' of a citizen was thus a disposition
to put public good ahead of private interest" (Ignatieff 1995, 56).

For some, the impulse to engage in public processes extends beyond voting,
going to community meetings or public hearings, writing letters or e-mails, or
engaging in focus groups and visioning projects. It leads to a full-time commitment to engage in what we typically call "public service." The call to
public service that many experience is based on the responsibility of all citizens to serve, but it goes far beyond this responsibility, to become a full-time
occupation, even a preoccupation. The public servant may be someone who
runs for and serves in elective public office, perhaps for a short time, perhaps
throughout a career; but he or she may also be someone who works in an
agency of government—in social services, public health, environmental protection, law enforcement, or any one of myriad other public and governmental
agencies. Today the public servant may even be someone who works outside
government, perhaps in a nonprofit organization or in a public advocacy role.
Wherever public servants are found, they are likely to be motivated by the
desire to make a difference, to improve the lives of others, to do something
meaningful with their own lives, to do something "significant."

What we think of as public service, therefore, is an extension of the virtues expected of all citizens in a democracy, a point most eloquently and
thoroughly captured by Terry Cooper in his book *An Ethic of Citizenship for
Public Administration* (1991). Cooper argues for the citizenship role as a

basis for understanding the role of public servant and, more explicitly, the role of public administrator. He begins by noting that, historically, the connection between citizenship and administration was extremely close. For example, the two oldest schools of public administration, Syracuse and the University of Southern California, began as schools of citizenship. While the field of public administration has drifted away from its roots in this regard, Cooper argues that public servants and public administrators still derive their standing and legitimacy from their role as professional citizens. In this view, the public administrator is not merely a technician, a problem solver, or an employee of government. Rather, the public servant or public administrator is best understood as someone who extends the responsibilities of citizenship into his or her life's work. Public administrators are, in the words of Michael Walzer, "citizens in lieu of the rest of us; the common good is, so to speak, their specialty" (quoted in Cooper 1991, 139).

If administrators derive their ethical identity from a base in democratic citizenship, then they assume special roles and responsibilities, including specific understandings of issues such as responsiveness and accountability, which are inherent in the idea of democratic morality. Cooper writes,

> The ethical identity of the public administrator then, should be that of the citizen who is employed *as* one of us to work *for* us; a kind of professional citizen ordained to do the work which we in a complex large-scale political community are unable to undertake ourselves. Administrators are to be those "especially responsible" citizens who are fiduciaries for the citizenry as a whole. (Cooper 1991, 139)

As such, administrators will naturally be held to a set of ethical standards appropriate to the conduct of public affairs. Indeed, a substantial literature on the ethics of public service has developed. Without going into the details of that material, we should mention several important components of ethical concern in the public service. Some years ago, Paul Appleby urged that administrators attain a "special attitude of public responsibility" and that, in addition to learning the skills of management, they would be imbued with the "democratic spirit" (1945, 4).

Stephen K. Bailey interpreted Appleby's remarks to mean that administrators needed an understanding of the moral ambiguity of public policies, a recognition of the moral priorities and paradoxes of the public service, and the moral qualities of "(1) optimism, (2) courage, and (3) fairness tempered by charity" (1966, 24). Many more recent writings have followed in this tradition of elaborating the administrator's sense of democratic responsibility. For example, Patrick Dobel (1990) suggests that the administrator's integrity involves several different justifications for the exercise of discretion.

These include regime accountability, personal responsibility, and prudence, justifications that in practice must be balanced and integrated:

> First, be truthfully accountable to relevant authorities and publics. Second, address the public values of the regime. Third, respect and build institutions and procedures to achieve goals. Fourth, ensure fair and adequate participation of relevant stakeholders. Fifth, seek competent performance in the execution of policy and program. Sixth, work for efficiency in the operation of government. This builds up the legitimacy of the regime, is true to the basic purposes and genealogy of public funds, and buttresses concerns with conscientiousness and competence. Seventh, connect policy and program with the self-interest of the public and participants in such a way that the basic purposes are not subverted. (Dobel 1990, 363)

If, as Cooper argues, the administrative role derives from the role of the citizen, then surely a part of the administrator's responsibility is to assist citizens in fulfilling their own civic duty to be fully engaged and involved in the work of the polity. While administrators oriented toward efficiency and productivity may find the involvement of citizens awkward and time consuming, encouraging that involvement is nonetheless an essential element of the public servant's role. Dennis Thompson points out that the demand that citizens take a significant role in the political process means that leaders, and here we would include all public servants, such as public administrators, should "not only share the values and beliefs of the ordinary citizen, not only that they remain sensitive to his needs, but also that *leaders strive to activate the inactive citizen*" (1970, 26).

We argue here that public servants, especially including public administrators, have an ethical obligation to extend the boundaries of public participation in the political process in whatever way they can. Often, such an effort will be uncomfortable for administrators. In many cases, "unwarranted" delays and confusion may result. Frequently, the time involved in engaging citizens will be maddening for administrators; but this will be the case only if administrators see their role as a primarily technical one focused on efficient problem solving. If they see their role as engaging citizens in the work of democracy, then such efforts will hardly be confounding. As difficult as they may be, the efforts will be a source of exhilaration and joy.

The Old Public Administration and Client Service

Traditional public administration or the Old Public Administration was largely concerned with either the direct delivery of services or the regulation of individual and corporate behavior. Those on the "receiving" end were generally referred to as "clients." The word "client," of course, means "a party for which professional services are rendered" (*American Heritage Dictionary* 2000). What is interesting is that the word "client" is derived from the Latin *cliens*, which means "dependent" or "follower." In many cases, public agencies operating under the Old Public Administration dealt with their clients in just such a manner. Clients were seen as in need of help and those in government made honest efforts to provide the help that was needed through the administration of public programs. Inevitably those in the agency came to be seen as being "in control" of those dependent on the agency. For many clients, the agency's view appeared to be quite patronizing and even dismissive. The stereotype of the thoughtless, uncaring bureaucrat is surely overdone but perhaps contains a modicum of truth.

The New Public Management and Customer Satisfaction

The New Public Management addresses the relationship between government and citizens, not just a practical concern, but from a distinct theoretical position. Earlier in this chapter we examined in detail the ideal concept of citizenship as being active, involved, and public spirited. We also pointed out the alternative legal definition of citizenship—a view we find to be based not only on legalism but also on self-interest. This theoretical viewpoint so clearly underlies the way in which the New Public Management views the relationship between those in government and those served or regulated by government that is worthwhile to elaborate the theoretical notion of citizen as *consumer.* This view is largely derived from the so-called economic theory of democracy, a theory that explains political behavior in terms of economic competition. Political parties, for example, are seen as competing for votes just as corporations are seen as competing for profits. Citizens, in turn, are seen as consumers for whose votes the parties compete. These citizen/consumers make decisions based on their efforts to maximize their own utilities, casting their votes for one or the other party, or simply turning away from politics and seeking great utilities by spending their time and energy elsewhere (Dagger 1997, 105).

This view of citizens as consumers is certainly consistent with the self-interested interpretation of political life we examined earlier: the view that government ultimately reflects the accumulated self-interests of largely disconnected and utility-maximizing individuals. This interpretation is also consistent with the legal definition of citizenship, since the citizen/consumer enjoys certain rights and liberties protected by the state's system of jurisprudence. Finally, this view is consistent with an economic interpretation of political life. Proponents of this view "conceive of citizenship in economic terms, so that citizens are transformed into autonomous consumers, looking for the party or position that most persuasively promises to strengthen their market position. They need the state, but have no moral relation to it, and they control its officials only as consumers control the producers of commodities, by buying or not buying what they make" (Walzer 1995, 160).

The New Public Management brings this idea of consumerism directly into the debate about the appropriate relationship between public administrators and citizens by conceiving of the recipients of government services (or delivered by contracted agencies) as consumers or "customers." Like other elements of the New Public Management, the customer service orientation is clearly related to the experience of business, in this case the customer service movement of the last twenty years. In such books as *In Search of Excellence* (Peters and Waterman 1981) and *Service America* (Albretch and Zemke 1985), management consultants made the argument that if businesses are fully attentive to customers, then everything else, including profits, will fall into place. The customer is conceived as constantly calculating satisfaction utilities: "We can think of the customer as carrying around a kind of 'report card' in his or her head, which is the basis of a grading system that leads the customers to decided whether to partake of the service again or go elsewhere" (Albretch and Zemke 1985, 32). The customer is clearly a construct derived from the classic model of economic man.

Osborne and Gaebler argue that customer-driven government is superior to bureaucratic government, having the advantages of greater accountability, greater innovation, the possibility of generating more service choices, and less waste (1992, 180–85). Similarly, Barzelay contends that thinking in terms of customer service helps public managers articulate their concerns about performance and come up with innovative solutions to problems that arise (Barzelay 1992, 6–7). For those agencies that interact directly with the public, the recipient of the service is the "customer." For some staff agencies (such as budgeting or purchasing), there is rather an internal customer, the agencies whose work they support.

The language of customer service has become central to the New Public Management. The National Performance Review, for example, had a goal of "providing customer services *equal to the best in business*" (Gore 1993, 44). Noting that government's customers often face long lines, busy signals, inadequate information, and indifferent employees, the report urged "entrepreneurial" federal agencies to assess the needs of customers, to set standards for the delivery of services, and to take those steps necessary to meet those standards. Similar language and approaches were taken at the state and local level, as governments and their agencies sought to "reinvent" themselves as customer-driven operations. In other countries, comparable efforts were undertaken, actually in many cases predating the United States' efforts in this regard. The British "Citizen's Charter" movement set minimum standards of service, backed by ministerial authority, and in some cases even provided redress when those standards were not met. Similar efforts were undertaken in other countries, including Australia, New Zealand, France, and Belgium.

While improving the quality of governmental services is an idea no one would dispute, using the rhetoric and approach of "customer service" has both practical and theoretical difficulties. In the first place, the notion of choice is essential to the economic concept of the customer. Generally, in government, there are few if any alternatives. There is only one fire department, for example (and the fire department cannot choose to go into another line of work). Moreover, many services provided by government are services the specific recipient may not want—receiving a speeding ticket, being held in jail, and so on. Even identifying the customers of government is problematic. Who are a local health department's customers? People who visit a clinic? Citizens who might be concerned about a particular health hazard? Doctors and nurses? Local hospitals? The general public? All of the above? Even listing all the potential customers points out another dilemma: All the customers of government seem to have different interests. For example, often there is a conflict between the interests of the immediate recipient of government services and the taxpayers who must pay the bill. And, of course, some government services—foreign policy or environmental protection, for example—do not connect with individual customers; once they are provided, they are provided for all, whether you want them or not.

Perhaps the most important objection to the customer orientation has to do with accountability. In government, citizens are not only customers; they are "owners" (Schachter 1997). As George Fredrickson puts it, "Customers choose between products presented in the market; citizens decide what is so important that the government will do it at public expense" (1992, 13). Further, the interests of customers and owners do not always coincide—in business or government. While businesses may benefit in the long term from satisfying the immediate customer, government may not. A state motor vehicle division made important efforts to improve customer satisfaction—brightening their waiting areas, cutting down on waiting time, even making the pictures better. But a statewide commission questioned whether these changes were made at the cost of safety on the highway. Similarly, Tom Peters supposedly tells a story of getting a building permit. "I don't want some bureaucrat at City Hall giving me a hard time. I want proper, quick, businesslike treatment. But what if my neighbor wants a permit to enlarge *his* house? Who's City Hall's customer then?" (quoted in Mintzberg 1996, 77). Government must be accountable to the larger public interest—not merely the self-interests of individual customers or consumers. In any case, the issue of accountability is critical. "The bottom line for democratic government is accountability—not profits or citizen satisfaction—and customer service does not provide a good proxy measure for accountability" (Kettl 2000a, 43).

The New Public Service and Quality Service for Citizens

The New Public Service recognizes that those who interact with government are not simply customers but rather citizens. Henry Mintzberg, the Canadian management theorist, has pointed out that there are actually several types of relationships that we have with government. "I am not a mere customer of government, thank you. I expect something more than arm's length trading and something less than the encouragement to consume" (1996, 77). Someone engaged in a direct transaction with government—buying a lottery ticket—might indeed be considered a *customer*. However, someone receiving a professional service from government—education, for example—might more appropriately be called a *client*. Of course, we are also *subjects* of government—required to pay taxes, respect regulations, and obey the laws. Most important, we are *citizens* and a large part of the services of government provides would seem to fall under this category, "social infrastructure (such as museums), physical (such as roads and ports), economic (such as monetary policy), mediative (such as civil courts), offshore (such as embassies), and the government's own support infrastructure (such as election machinery)" (77).

There is certainly no question but that government agencies should strive to offer the highest quality service possible, within the constraints of law and accountability—and, indeed, many agencies are doing so. One of the most sophisticated efforts to improve service quality begins with a recognition of the differences between customers and citizens (Schmidt with Strickland 1998). Citizens are described as bearers of rights and duties within the context of a wider community. Customers are different in that they do not share common purposes but rather seek to optimize their own individual benefits. The distinction then is made between citizens and clients, the latter either internal or external: "The following example may serve to illustrate these definitions. A citizen may not collect employment insurance and yet has an interest in how the system functions; the actual recipient of an employment insurance payment would be an external client. A regional employment insurance office that depends on a central agency to distribute the employment insurance payments to their office would be an internal client" (3). It is important to recognize that public servants rarely deal with a single client or citizen. The front-line employee may be assisting someone sitting across the table, but he or she is simultaneously serving the citizen by ensuring that the process meets legal requirements. The complexity of government's interactions with citizens and clients marks all efforts to improve service quality in government

Despite this complexity, there have been a variety of efforts to define public sector service quality. One especially comprehensive list developed for local government includes the following:

1. *Convenience* measures the degree to which government services are easily accessible and available to citizens.
2. *Security* measures the degree to which services are provided in a way that makes citizens feel safe and confident when using them.
3. *Reliability* assesses the degree to which government services are provided correctly and on time.
4. *Personal attention* measures the degree to which employees provide information to citizens and work with them to help meet their needs.
5. *Problem-solving approach* measures the degree to which employees provide information to citizens and work with them to help meet their needs.
6. *Fairness* measures the degree to which citizens believe that government services are provided in a way that is equitable to all.
7. *Fiscal responsibility* measures the degree to which citizens believe local government is providing services in a way that uses money responsibly.
8. *Citizen influence* measures the degree to which citizens feel they can influence the quality of service they receive from the local government (Carlson and Schwarz 1995, 29).

What is especially interesting about this list is not only that citizens expect public services to meet such standards as timeliness and reliability, but that they should and do expect that services be delivered fairly and with attention to fiscal responsibility as well; citizens expect to have the opportunity to influence the services they receive as well as the quality of those services.

This same point can be made more theoretically. According to Jenny Potter (1988), the theory of consumerism suggests that there is an imbalance of power between those who provide services and those who receive services. The latter carry weight only as a result of their accumulated choices. To shift greater power toward consumers, theorists have identified five key factors: access, choice, information, redress, and representation. While these factors were originally developed in relation to private goods and services in the marketplace, they can be adapted to the public sector, providing guidance on how the interests of citizens, both individually and collectively, might be enhanced. *Access*—deciding who will have what—is not strictly a matter of individual right; rather, it is a matter of political responsibility. However, citizens should expect to be engaged in that decision. *Choice* also is not a matter of right, but citizens should expect to be involved in shaping and extending choices available to them. They should also expect to have full *information* about goals and objectives, standards of service, their rights to service, alternatives being debated, why decisions are made, and what those decisions are. Citizens should also expect to have some means of communicating their grievances and complaints, and to receive *redress* where appropriate. *Representation* opens up wider questions of consultation and ultimately participation by citizens in making decisions.

Potter concludes that the theory of consumerism can certainly point citizens in the right direction with respect to improving service quality; however, ultimately, as an economic concept, the theory of consumerism cannot address the political question of how power might be more extensively shared between the governors and the governed, the administrators and the administrated" (1998, 156). As already noted, the theory of consumerism starts with an imbalance of power. The key question for government is how far government is willing to go in redressing that imbalance of power between providers and users or citizens.

In contrast to concentrating solely on the "charm school and better wallpaper" (Pollitt 1988, 125) approach taken by many public agencies in their efforts to improve customer service, the real issues that must be addressed as the New Public Service evolves will be those that deal with information and power. The customer orientation treats the provision of information as providing better signposts or schedules. A more complete approach to the provision of information would likely include having agencies publish performance data so that citizens can make informed decisions about choices that are available to them. It would also mean providing detailed information about standards of service and the agency's success in meeting those standards. Finally, agencies should consult and involve their users in these tasks and should provide effective remedies if things go wrong. Ultimately, those in government must recognize that public service is not an economic construct, but a political one. That means that issues of service improvement need to be attentive not only to the demands of "customers" but also to the distribution of power in society. Ultimately, in the New Public Service, providing quality service is a first step in the direction of widening public involvement and extending democratic citizenship.

Conclusion

Despite the obvious importance of constantly improving the quality of public sector service delivery, the New Public Service suggests that government should not first or exclusively respond to the selfish, short-term interests of "customers." The New Public Service suggests instead that people acting as citizens must demonstrate their concern for the larger community, their commitment to matters that go beyond short-term interests, and their willingness to assume personal responsibility for what happens in their neighborhoods and the community. After all, these are among the defining elements of effective and responsible citizenship. In turn, government must be responsive to the needs and interests of citizens. In any case, the New Public Service seeks to encourage more and more people to fulfill their responsibilities as citizens, and in turn, to be especially sensitive to their voices.

Chapter 4

Seek the Public Interest

Seek the public interest. Public administrators must contribute to building a collective, shared notion of the public interest. The goal is not to find quick solutions driven by individual choices. Rather, it is the creation of shared interests and shared responsibility.

One of the core principles of the New Public Service is a reaffirmation of the centrality of the public interest in government service. The New Public Service demands that the process of establishing a "vision" for society is not something merely to be left to elected political leaders or appointed public administrators. Instead, the activity of establishing a vision or direction, of defining shared values, is something in which widespread public dialogue and deliberation are central (Bryson and Crosby 1992; Luke 1998; Stone 1988). Even more important, the public interest isn't something that just "happens" as a result of the interaction between individual citizen choices, organizational procedures, and electoral politics. Rather, articulating and realizing the public interest is one of primary reasons government exists.

The New Public Service sees a vital role for government in the process of bringing people together in settings that allow for unconstrained and authentic discourse concerning the directions society should take. Based on these deliberations, a broad-based vision for the community, the state, or the nation can be established and can provide a guiding set of ideas (or ideals) for the future. It is less important that this process result in a single set of goals than it is to engage administrators, politicians, and citizens in a process of thinking about a desired future for their community and their nation.

In addition to its facilitating role, government also has a moral obligation to assure that any solutions that are generated through such processes are fully consistent with norms of justice and fairness, and are arrived at through a process that is fully consistent with the norms and ethics of democracy. Government will act to facilitate the solutions to public problems, but it will also be responsible for assuring that those solutions are consistent with the public interest—both in substance and in process (Ingraham and Ban 1988; Ingraham and Rosenbloom 1989). In other words, the role of government will become one of assuring that the public interest predominates: that both the solutions themselves and the process by which solutions to public problems are developed are consistent with democratic norms and the values of justice, fairness, and equity.

In the New Public Service, government plays an important and active role in creating arenas in which citizens, through discourse, can articulate shared values and develop a collective sense of the public interest. Rather than simply responding to disparate voices by forming a compromise, public administrators will engage citizens with one another so that they come to understand each other's interests and ultimately adopt a longer-range and broader sense of community and societal interests. Moreover, doing so is vitally important to the realization of democratic values in the governance process. The issue is complex, involving not only the nature of citizen trust and governmental responsiveness but the purposes and responsibilities of government itself. At stake is the question of whether or not citizens trust their government to act in the public interest. As Kenneth Ruscio states, "Prescriptions for establishing trust—and indeed our understanding of why it is even necessary—require staking out positions on human nature, the meaning of public interest, and the reasons for engaging in political life" (1996, 471).

This chapter will explore the concept of the public interest. We will begin with a look at the various ways the public interest has been defined, noting competing ideas about what purpose, if any, the concept serves in governance. We will then review how the notion of public interest was understood at the time the field of public administration was founded in the United States, and trace some of the reasons for its decline as a central component of public administration theory and practice. We will then ask how conceptions of the public interest have changed over time and what are the controversies and issues regarding its existence and meaning. We will also ask about the importance of the public interest from an administrative perspective. We will then discuss how the public interest has been conceived in the Old Public Administration and the New Public Management, concluding with some thoughts about how the search for the public interest shapes the New Public Service.

What Is the Public Interest?

In the last one hundred years, the concept of the public interest has been variously derided, applauded, dismissed, and revived—leaving little consensus on what it means or if it is even a useful concept. Walter Lippman defined the public interest as "what men would choose if they saw clearly, thought rationally, and acted disinterestedly, and benevolently" (1955, 42). But Glendon Schubert suggested that the concept of the public interest "makes no operational sense. . . . Political scientists might better spend their time nurturing concepts that offer greater promise of becoming useful tools in the scientific study of political responsibility" (1962, 176). Likewise, Frank Sorauf stated that the term is "too burdened with multiple meanings for valuable use" (Sorauf, 1957, 624). Howard Smith, on the other hand, said that while the public interest is a myth, it is a useful myth (1960). Still others have pointed out that, regardless of its ambiguity, "there has never been a society which was not, in some way, and to some extent guided by this ideal" (Bell and Kristol 1965, 5). Despite this disagreement, the concept of the public interest has remained important in public discourse and academic literature.

In one sense, attempting to define "the public interest" is a little like trying to define "love." It is clear that *love* means different things to different people under varying circumstances. It can change over time in both form and substance. It also changes us—how we think and behave. Although seeing its effects is often possible, it is difficult to observe directly. It can be simultaneously seen as both a state of being and an ongoing process. Its quality and significance are bound up in both the process of seeking it and in the realization that it must always be pursued. As a result, it defies quantification and meaningful measurement and is, therefore, difficult to use in certain kinds of analyses. Some conclude from this complexity, fluidity in meaning, and difficulty in measurement that love isn't a very useful concept. Others may question whether it even exists. Still others might readily admit that love may exist, but argue that it cannot and should not be the subject of empirical study and social science because it cannot be appropriately operationalized. Yet, most of us would agree that any explanation of the human experience—be it personal, social scientific, philosophical—would be sorely lacking without the use of the concept of love.

The public interest, like love, means different things to different people, changes over time, motivates behavior, frames our thinking, defies measurement, and involves both substance and process. Just as understanding the human experience virtually requires a recognition of the role of love, it is difficult if not impossible to understand the depth and breadth of public service without a recognition of the role of the public interest. Accordingly, the difficulties and ambiguities encountered in attempts to define and place conceptual boundaries around the public interest are more than outweighed by the richness it brings to our understanding of citizenship, governance, and public service. We acknowledge that the public interest is ambiguous and fluid at the same time that we advocate for its centrality to democratic governance.

We should point out that exploring the idea of the public interest is not just an interesting academic pursuit. The way we think about governance and the public interest defines how we act. Depending on which view of the public interest we take, our actions will be directed in different ways. Here we will approach the task of defining the concept of the public interest by examining four approaches to the idea. While these categories are not entirely mutually exclusive, they us a reasonable starting point for our discussion. In part using Clarke Cochran's (1974) schema for the different schools of thought with regard to the public interest, we will classify models of the public interest as being primarily either: (1) normative, (2) abolitionist, (3) political process oriented, or (4) based on shared values.

Normative Models

Normative models are used by social scientists not to describe what is, but rather what ought to be. In normative models of the public interest, the "public interest becomes an ethical standard for evaluating specific public policies and a goal which the political order should pursue" (Cochran 1974, 330). In this view, the *public interest* is a moral and ethical standard for decision making. For example, C.W. Cassinelli (1962) writes that the public interest is a standard of goodness by which political acts can be judged. In other words, actions that can be taken in the public interest deserve approval because they meet this standard of goodness. Because Cassinelli defines the public interest as an ethical standard, he dismisses the claim that the public interest is useless as a "tool of analysis" or an "aid to scientific study" as irrelevant. He argues instead that the public interest, as an ethical concept, has functions different from those of analytic models. "Social scientists cannot ignore the fundamental issue of the final political good: this is the principal lesson to be learned from examining the concept of the public interest" (1962, 47).

To Cassinelli and other advocates of the normative model, the public interest is the "highest ethical standard applicable to political affairs" (1962, 46). In this view, when something is good for the public, that is a higher level of good than when something is good for only part of the public.

Accordingly, the political system should seek a fair distribution of advantages across a community. This does not mean that all people are entitled to identical or equal benefits, but suggests that, on balance, everyone be treated fairly.

An early public administrationist, E. Pendleton Herring, for example, wrote about the public interest from a normative perspective. In his 1936 book, *Public Administration and the Public Interest*, Herring argued that laws were, by necessity, at least somewhat vague and that the bureaucrat's job was to reconcile competing group pressures in order to interpret the statute ethically. Administrators could best meet their ethical and legal obligation to resolve these conflicts, he said, according to the ideal of the public interest. He wrote, "Under democracy the public interest is based not upon the welfare of one class but upon a compounding of many group interests. We assume the possibility of achieving a balance of forces, social and economic" (1936, vii). More succinctly, he stated, "The public interest is the standard that guides the administrator in executing the law" (23).

Similarly, Emmette Redford also defined the public interest in a normative manner: "[The public interest] may be defined as the best response to a situation in terms of all the interests and of the concepts of value which are generally accepted in our society" (1954, 1108). Likewise, Philip Monypenny's code of ethics for public administration included a section called "The Public Interest" which stated that the administrator "should follow the public interest as he understands it rather than his personal convenience or any private aim or goal" (1953, 441). This view of the public interest as a normative, ethical standard has remained important in the field of public administration to the present. In fact, the American Society for Public Administration (ASPA), in its code of ethics for its members, states as the first principle, "Exercise discretionary authority to promote the public interest" (2001).

Abolitionist Views of the Public Interest

In contrast to the normative theorists discussed above, those who subscribe to the abolitionist view of the public interest argue that the concept of the public interest is neither meaningful nor important. These scholars tend to take one of two lines of reasoning, either (1) the public interest can't be measured or directly observed, so isn't valid, or (2) the concept of the public interest or collective will isn't necessary because individual choices are the best way to understand the policy process and set policy. For example, while Glendon Schubert acknowledged that people talk about the public interest, therefore making it a part of the study of political behavior, it remained an ill-defined and scientifically irrelevant idea. He claimed that despite considerable effort:

> American writers in the field of political science have evolved neither a
> unified nor a consistent theory to describe how the public interest is defined in governmental decision-making; they have not constructed theoretical models with the degree of precision and specificity necessary if
> such models are to be used as description of, or as a guide to, the actual
> behavior of real people. (Shubert 1960, 220)

In order to be useful, Schubert wrote, a theory of the public interest would have to be able to describe the relationship between the public interest and behavior in a way that can be empirically validated. He concluded that, because theories regarding the public interest cannot do so, "it is difficult to comprehend the justification for teaching students of political science that subservience to the public interest is a relevant norm of official responsibility" (1960, 220).

Political Process Theories

Cochran describes process theorists as those who "define the concept by reference to the political processes through which policy is made" (1974, 331). In this view, the public interest is realized through a particular process that allows interests to be aggregated, balanced, or reconciled. For example, Howard Smith states clearly that "The Public Interest is most properly identified with, not concrete politics as such, but rather a particular kind of a process by means of which it is decided what should be done" (1960, 159). In other words, advocates of this view suggest that it is less important what the public interest *is* than how we arrive at it. Because process theorists are concerned primarily with the process, many can be considered to be analyzing the public interest as the logical extension of a longstanding and ongoing debate among political scientists about the best way to understand the political process per se. A key point of contention in this debate is whether political parties or interest groups are considered to be the preferred mechanism for the representation of interests in a democracy.

As evidenced by James Madison's early references in the Federalist Papers Number 10, factions have long been considered to be natural to the American system of government (Hamilton, Madison, and Jay 1982/1787). While Madison and others have debated the "misfortunes" and disadvantages of politics based on interest group activity, those views were reflected more recently in Robert Dahl's A *Preface to Democratic Theory* (1956) and in his

Who Governs? (1961). Pluralist views of democracy are based on the idea that interest groups, rather than individual citizens or the people as a whole, are the best vehicle for representing and defending the interests of citizens in the policy process. Pluralists argue that direct participation is impractical and unworkable, and that by forming groups, like-minded individuals can have a greater voice in policymaking than they can as individuals. Dahl suggested that interest group pluralism was not only the best way to describe American politics as it currently operated but also the best way to maximize democratic principles.

The dominance of pluralism as the model for American democracy strongly influenced those who defined the public interest from the standpoint of process. Pluralists were certainly not without their critics, however, who claimed that democracy and the public interest were better served by other processes. E.E. Schattschneider, for example, was a vocal proponent of majoritarian party politics as the best way to serve the public interest. He argued that private, special and local interests are enemies of the common interest, but political parties can synthesize and transcend special interests. Rejecting the idea that the compilation of the special interests would equal the public interest, he stated, "The public interest is not the mere sum of the special interests, and it is certainly not the sum of the organized special interests" (1952, 23).

In either case, whether advocating for interest group politics or party politics, these scholars largely ignore the role of citizens. The assumption is that citizens will be adequately represented by either interest groups or parties, and if we let one of these mediating institutions be the primary voice of the people in the policy process, that will approximate the public interest.

Shared Values

Cochran called models of the public interest based on shared values "consensualist." Consensualists view the public interest as a vague, but valuable, term that refers to policy debate to achieve a public value consensus. We have broadened this category to include notions of the public interest based on shared values that guide both the process for articulating these interests and the substance of the public interest itself. This shared value model was evidenced in the early writings of Paul Appleby, who stated:

> The public interest is never merely the sum of all private interests nor the sum remaining after canceling out their various pluses and minuses. It is not wholly separate from private interests, and it derives from citizens with many private interests; but it is something distinctive that arises within,

among, apart from, and above private interests, focusing in government some of the most elevated aspiration and deepest devotion of which human beings are capable. (Appleby 1950, 34–35)

This idea of the public interest as referring to the broad, shared interests of society is consistent with how Deborah Stone (1988) defines the public interest in what she calls the "polis," or political community. The public interest in Stone's view is based on the active and conscious pursuit of collective values. She defines the polis in part by contrasting it with the market or aggregation of individual interests model (described above in the section on abolitionist views). The market view, she says, is based on the idea that public policy or the public interest is the net result of all individuals pursuing their self-interest. Thus, the public interest in the market model is the by-product of individual choices.

In the polis or collective model, on the other hand, building a society in the collective interest is the aim, not the by-product. Stone suggests that:

> Public policy is about communities trying to achieve something *as communities*. This is true even though there is almost always conflict within a community over what its goals should be and who its members are, and even though every communal goal ultimately must be achieved through the behavior of individuals. Unlike the market which starts with individuals and assumes no goals, preferences, or intentions other than those held by individuals, a model of the polis must assume both collective will and collective effort. (Stone 1997, 18, emphasis added)

Rather than beginning with the market assumption that people are only self-interested, she suggests that values such as sharing, caring, and maintaining relationships are at least as strong in motivating behavior as competition, separation, and promotion of self-interests. While history, loyalty, and leadership are important factors in the polis, the market does not give us any way to talk about such influences. Further, in the market model, "commons" problems are considered to be the exception. "Commons" problems refer to situations in which self-interest and the public interest are in conflict. The example often used is of a pasture that is available to all cattle owners. Self-interest dictates that each person will seek to maximize his or her individual gain by keeping as many cattle as possible on this common land. But because each person sharing the common land makes this same decision, the commons are depleted and of no use to anyone. Thus, by pursing their individual interests, the shared interests of the cattle owners are lost.

As suggested above, commons problems are considered to be an unusual occurrence in the market. In the polis, on the other hand, commons problems are considered to be, well, common. Not only do they occur frequently; the most significant policy problems *are* commons problems. In the polis it is assumed that policies will rarely affect only one or two individuals. The purpose of political dialogue, then, is to encourage people to articulate shared interests and to give primacy to the broader consequences of policy choices. People are encouraged to do so based on influence, cooperation, loyalty, and the connections that bond people together over time.

Further, the search for the public interest in the polis is ongoing. It is, as the saying goes, more a journey than a destination. Problems in the polis are not "solved" in the way that economic needs are met in the market model. "It is not as though we can place an order for justice, and once the order is filled, the job is done" (Stone 1997, 34). Moreover, there is never full agreement on what the public interest is. Instead, the search for its meaning is the raison d'être of public life, much as choice based on self-interest is the cornerstone of the market. As Stone puts it, "The concept of public interest is to the polis what self-interest is to the market. They are both abstractions whose specific contents we do not need to know in order to use them to explain and predict people's behavior. We simply assume that people behave as if they were trying to realize the public interest or maximize their self-interest" (1997, 21).

In the polis, the development of shared values and a collective sense of the public interest is the primary aim. Stone suggests that the public interest can be understood as those things desired by the "public-spirited side of citizens" such as good schools and clean air, even if it interferes with their right to burn trash or have lower taxes. The public interest can also be expressed as those "goals on which there is a consensus" and/or "things that are good for a community as a community" such as the preservation of order, maintenance of governing processes, and defense against outsiders. There is never complete agreement on the public interest. In fact, Stone says, "Let it be an empty box, but no matter; in the polis, people expend a lot of energy trying to fill up that box" (1997, 21).

So, the public interest based on shared values suggests a process that goes beyond the interplay of special interests to include shared democratic and constitutional values. More importantly, shared interest theorists argue that not only are people capable of more than self-interest, but also government should work to nurture and develop that capacity. In part, that capacity depends on trust. Citizen trust and confidence are built on the belief that government is acting in response to the public interest and the shared values of the community. Trust and acting in the public interest become mutually reinforcing—as the government acts in the public interest, citizen trust is enhanced. Conversely, when citizen trust is enhanced, citizens may experience an increase in their capacity to see and act on shared interests.

Given this evolution in thought, what views of the public interest and what assumptions for the role of public servants are associated with the Old Public Administration, the New Public Management, and the New Public Service? As should be clear from the preceding discussion, ideas and arguments about the public interest have not unfolded in a neat, linear fashion. However, we can identify certain dominant themes associated with the Old Public Administration, the New Public Management, and the New Public Service.

The Old Public Administration and the Public Interest

In the Old Public Administration, public service was thought to be a value-neutral technical process and the authority of the administrator was the authority of expertise. As Schubert put it, "The public interest is found in the rationalization of the decisional process so that it will automatically result in the carrying out of the Public Will. Human discretion is minimized or eliminated by defining it out of the decisional situation; responsibility lies in autonomic behavior" (1957, 347). This perspective was closely connected with the emphasis on neutrality and efficiency that we saw earlier associated with the progressive reform movement and the scientific management movement. In one sense, then, the Old Public Administration didn't have a theory of the administrative responsibility to defend and protect the public interest. The public interest was to be determined by elected officials. In the Old Public Administration it was implicit, however, that focusing on neutrality, efficiency, and a strict separation between politics and administration was the best way for public servants to serve the interests of the public. Thus, there was a subordination of administrative activities and discretion to hierarchical controls, legislation, and the interplay between special interests.

When writers like Woodrow Wilson and Frank Goodnow first attempted to define the field of public administration at the turn of the century, the concept of the public interest was important, but was considered to fall solely within the province of politics. Wilson wrote: "[P]olicy will have no taint of officialism about it. It will not be the creation of permanent officials, but of statesmen whose responsibility to public opinion will be direct and inevitable" (quoted in Shafritz and Hyde 1997, 22). Likewise, Goodnow defined politics as the "expression of the will of the state" with administration serving a subordinate role in executing that will (quoted in Shafritz and Hyde 1997, 28).

The role of public administration in relationship to the public interest remained a passive one into the mid-1930s: a view that was articulated in the work of E. Pendleton Herring. In this era of the New Deal, Herring found that administrators often had to interpret and define vague legislation. He wrote, "Upon the shoulders of the bureaucrat has been placed in large part the burden of reconciling group differences and making effective and workable the economic and social compromises arrived at through the legislative process" (1936, 7). Herring did not reject the notion of neutral expertise; he merely suggested that some level of discretion was needed to deal with the demands of special interests. In exercising this discretion, Herring argued that "the public interest is the standard that guides the administrator in executing the law" (23). Again, the assumption was that the public interest could be found in the interplay of special interests. Therefore, in this model, the administrator facilitates the "reconciliation of group interests," using the public interest as a "verbal symbol designed to introduce unity, order, and objectivity"(23). While accountability to the public interest was emphasized, Herring's model assumed that no direct citizen involvement was necessary.

Further, the role of the administrator was clearly a passive one. For example, Herring stated, "The task of government in a democracy, we assume, is the adjustment of warring economic and social forces. The public interest is the standard that supposedly determines the degree to which the government lends its forces to one side or the other. Without this standard for judgment between contenders, the scales would simply be weighted in favor of victory for the strongest" (1936, 23). In effect, Herring was describing the public administrator as a last resort "tie breaker" when the conflict between interests leads to an unclear outcomes or seems to exclude certain important interests.

Others also suggested a relatively modest role for administrators, a role subordinate to other participants in the process. From this perspective, the public administrator becomes the voice of the underrepresented and unorganized, but that voice is subordinated to the forces or hierarchy and the political process in most cases. Monypenny, for example, advises administrators on how to serve the public interest by stating:

> The primary determination of the public interest for public servants is by the action of his political and hierarchic superiors, acting through the conventional channels, by legislation, and court decisions where applicable. However there will be areas of discretion still, and in the use of these the public servant will be exposed to a relatively small group of persons immediately affected by a proposed action. The public servant must accept their right to speak and even to be consulted, must consider the consequences, which they present. But he must remember that there are others

unorganized and not directly represented, and as far as he can perceive the consequences to them, he must be their representative also in considering this discretionary action. (Monypenny 1953, 441)

In short, in the Old Public Administration, the public interest was defined by popularly elected policymakers. It was assumed that administrators could best serve the public interest by implementing laws in the most efficient, scientific, politically neutral manner possible. Although the need was for administrators to be mindful of the public interest in working through conflicts among special interests in the implementation of legislative policy, the idea was that their discretion should be limited. Public administrators would play a largely passive role in reconciling special interests and only when necessary to allow administrative action.

The New Public Management and the Public Interest

With the ascendancy of the New Public Management in the 1980s and 1990s, the ideal of the public interest as based on shared values lost currency and relevancy. As we noted earlier, the New Public Management is predicated on the notion government should create marketlike arenas of choice in which individuals, as customers, can make decisions based on their own self-interest. In the role of customers, individuals do not need to be concerned with the interests of their fellow customers. As we begin to think about citizens as being analogous to customers, and government as analogous to a market, the need to talk about or act upon the "public interest" largely disappears.

In this way, questions about the administrative responsibility with regard to the public interest are rendered largely irrelevant in the New Public Management. Public choice theorists, for example, would deny that the "public interest" as a concept or ideal is meaningful, and would in fact, question whether it even exists. Their reasoning is that individual choices in a marketlike arena are superior to collective action based on shared values. Because of their reliance on the market metaphor, and the assumption that self-interest is the primary and most appropriate basis of decision making, the shared public interest becomes both irrelevant and a definitional impossibility. Their perspective on the public interest would clearly be defined as abolitionist.

As Stone (1997) explains, when society is viewed as a market, it is assumed that individuals have relatively fixed, independent preferences for goods, services, and policies (9). "The market model therefore gives us no way to talk about how people fight over visions of the public interest or the nature of the community—the truly significant political questions underlying policy choices" (10). People are considered to be the best judges of their own interest. The public interest, if it exists at all, is simply the by-product of citizens (as customers) making individual choices in a market-like arena.

In the recent past, a shared view of the public interest has been largely been overshadowed by the ascendancy of the New Public Management. According to Trudi Miller (1989), the negation of the concept of the public interest, coupled with a reliance on market models of choice and the pluralist model of politics, has far-reaching and damaging effects on democratic governance and the field of public administration. In fact, she argues that, to the extent that public servants adhere to the pluralist view of politics, they actually contribute to undermining and corrupting liberal democracy. In a liberal democracy, the institutions of government respond to "shared popular views of the public interest [while respecting liberties that are beyond the reach of government] and works to "block efforts by narrow factions to coerce and tax the public for reasons not warranted by the public interest" (511). She points out that liberal democracy is based on a value system that embraces the idea of reciprocity, morality, and populism. Accordingly, one of the functions of a democracy is to correct the market imperfections of capitalism.

Miller then argues that the ascendancy of the pluralist model of politics turns liberal democracy "on its head" by rendering "shared views of the public interest meaningless and unimportant" and negated the values that form the foundations of democracy" (1989, 511). In the pluralist model, democracy responds to the interplay of special interests, but does not respond to or recognize shared views of the public interest. In other words, government in the pluralist model, she says, "does not respond to what the citizens collectively say they want" (515). Instead, it substitutes the will of the winning coalition of special interests.

Miller cautions that, to the extent that public servants adhere to a restricted notion of politics and of social science, they in fact contribute to the demise of democracy based on a shared view of the public interest. This is so, she says, simply because our way of thinking and methods of analysis negate its possibility. When we assume that are responsibilities are defined as responding to the demands of special interests is enough, when we act on behalf of "winning coalitions" of narrow interests rather than trying to discover shared values, when we rely solely on quantitative analysis to determine the "right" course of action, our behavior reinforces the idea that shared public preferences either do not exist or are irrelevant.

The New Public Service and the Public Interest

In contrast, the New Public Service rejects the views of the public interest implicit in both the Old Public Administration and the New Public Management. In fact, it is the rejection of those perspectives that is a defining feature of the New Public Service. We argue that public servants have a central and important role in helping to citizens to articulate the public interest, and, conversely, that shared values and collective citizen interests should guide the behavior and decision making of public administrators. This is not to say that the outcomes of the political process are wrong, or that public administrators should substitute their own judgments for policies with which they disagree. Rather, it is that public administrators must work to ensure that citizens are given a voice in every stage of governance—not just in electoral politics. Public servants have a unique and vitally important responsibility to engage with citizens and create forums for public dialogue.

Interestingly, glimpses of this viewpoint can be found in some of the early voices in the field of public administration. Although these ideas were soon overshadowed by the views of interest group pluralists, it is interesting to note some of the early references to the public interest as based on shared values and long term and common interests of the people. For example, although Paul Appleby would later come to see the public interest as the interplay of special interests, in 1950 he said that the job of the administrator was "to bring into focus—to resolve and integrate—these popularly-felt needs; to give specific form to responses of the government designed to meet the needs; to inject foresight and concern for factors not readily visible to citizens at large; to try so to organize governmental responses as to secure at least majority consensus or consent" (155). Here, he seems to recognize that there is a need to think not only of special interests, but also of larger questions of the public interest and the need to build consensus.

Likewise, in 1954 Emmette Redford wrote that administrative decisions are based on "common interests and ideas" and that the administrator acting to "look for common and enduring interests is an essential safeguard for the public interest" (1107). He made a case for the administrator's attention to the underrepresented, but he talked about the importance of future and shared interests as well: "the real danger is that the interest of the unorganized and weak, the shared interests of men generally, and the interest of men for tomorrow will not have proper weight in government councils" (1109).

Despite the early voices calling for administrative attention to the public interest, the criticisms of such views were insistent and largely successful. Schubert, for example, dismissed the idea of the public interest as a guiding force in administrative decision making, deriding the idea of "benevolent bureaucrats, who are the Guardians of the democratic state" (1957, 349). He questioned, even ridiculed the appropriateness and reasonableness of what he argued was the premise of such views, that "the public interest would be realized if bureaucrats . . . obeyed the exhortations . . . of moralists . . . [to] Be clever! Be wise! Be good!" (354).

The New Public Service regards these criticisms as simplistic and misplaced. Administrators need not simply be admonished to be clever or wise and to act as guardians in judging what is to be considered moral. Instead, the New Public Service advocates an active and positive role for administrators in facilitating citizen engagement in defining and acting on the public interest. The New Public Service also rejects the idea that the public interest can be understood as the aggregation of individual self-interests. In the New Public Service, the goal is to move beyond self-interest to discover and act upon shared interests—the public interest.

This view also affects how we look at trust in government. Ruscio, for example, argues that in government, "the decline in trust is due to the growing perception that elected officials, administrators, and citizens seek to maximize their self interest" (1996, 464). He goes on to emphasize that "[g]enuine trust depends on an assumption not easily accommodated by rational choice theorists: Individuals can act on some basis other than their private interest" (464). This means that trust is does not rely on self-interest. Rather, it is based on norms and values, and assumes that behavior can be influenced by the shared public interest. In other words, trust will decline if people believe that the demands of self-interested citizens drive governmental responses. Citizen trust and confidence in government are built on the perception that governmental policy is focused on the public interest. Recent research by Glaser, Parker, and Payton (2001) and Glaser, Denhardt, and Hamilton (2002) supports this contention; when government agencies visibly concentrate their efforts on increasing the well-being of community, it appears they can begin to close the gap between citizens and government.

The New Public Service suggests that government should encourage citizens to demonstrate their concern for the larger community, their commitment to matters that go beyond short-term interests, and their willingness to assume personal responsibility for what happens in their neighborhoods and the community. In this view, as suggested in Chapter 2, citizens adopt a broader and more long-term perspective based both on their knowledge of public affairs and a sense of belonging, a concern for the whole, and a moral bond with the community (Sandel 1996).

This is not to suggest that determining what governmental action will best serve the public interest is a simple or straightforward proposition. As Edward Weeks points out, "any solutions to a significant public problem will likely displease some segment of the community" (2000, 362). Seeking the public interest does not mean that governmental decision makers will somehow develop policy with which all citizens will agree. Rather, the public interest is best thought of as a process of community dialogue and engage-ment. This process both informs policymaking and builds citizenship. "By requiring that we interact—that is engage in democratic discourse—with others, participation broadens our perspectives and helps us see beyond our own narrow interests" (deLeon and Denhardt, 2000, 94). Or as Berry, Portney, and Thomson put it, "People who participate in the life of the community share a strong appreciation of its riches" (1993, 239). It is the ability to transcend narrow interests and recognize shared community interests and "riches" that is at the core of citizenship in a democracy. Government can play a central role in facilitating such a process and elevating the discourse to focus on long-term community interests. As Weeks (2000) found, such pro-cesses may not be quick or easy, but they can be powerful instruments in engaging citizen dialogue and creating the public will to act.

What we seem to be witnessing is a renewed emphasis on the public interest and shared values as the basis for the field of public administration. In fact, several contemporary public administration scholars have used the concept of the public interest as a means to explain and legitimate the role of public administration in a democracy. John Rohr (1986), for example, as-serted that the constitutional legitimacy of public administration rests upon a charge to uphold constitutional values in the public interest. In a similar vein, Charles Goodsell argued that "public bureaucracy is . . . the leading institutional embodiment and proponent of the public interest in American life" (1994, 107).

Similarly, Gary Wamsley and his coauthors (1990) reconceptualized bu-reaucracy as "the Public Administration" and argued that the Public Admin-istration is an institution of government rather than an organizational form. As such, administration should be defined in large part as competence di-rected toward the public interest. In this view, the role of the public admin-istrator is about both responsiveness and responsibility (1990, 314). Wamsley and his coauthors suggested that characterizations of civil servants as seeking status and power are erroneous and harmful. Instead, we should affirm a more "transcendent" role based on a commitment to the amelioration of soci-etal problems and improving the quality of citizens' lives. Citizens should play a crucial role in public administration and in the shift of the American political dialogue. "Administrators must seek to expand opportunities for direct citizen involvement in governance, so that citizens develop the practical wisdom that is the ultimate basis of trust in administrative good faith" (315).

The idea is not that public administrators become the guardians of de-mocracy by substituting their superior vision of the public interest for the will of, for example, the legislative or judicial branches. For public ser-vants to act as if their version of the public interest is somehow superior to the perspectives and values of citizens, elected officials, interest groups, and political parties is at least undemocratic if not outright unethical. Rather, public servants play a role in facilitating dialogue about the public interest and in acting to realize those values, within the larger system of political discourse and governance. In other words, public administrators do not and cannot act as the "administrative Platonists" that Schubert feared. Acting to single-handedly define the public interest, in the style of administrative "Lone Rangers," completely ignores the active role played by elected officials, citizens, the courts, and the myriad other participants in the governance process.

Conclusion

In the New Public Service, the public administrator is not the lone arbiter of the public interest. Rather, the public administrator is seen as a key actor within a larger system of governance including citizens, groups, elected representatives, as well as other institutions. As Frederickson states:

> The pursuit of self-interest through government, while commonplace, must be resisted when either citizen or public servant self-interest erodes the general interest. Rather than merely facilitating the pursuit of self-interest, the public administrator will continually strive, with elected representatives and the citizens, to find and articulate a general or common interest and to cause the government to pursue that interest. (Frederickson 1991, 415–16)

This argument, of course, has important implications for the roles and responsibilities of public administrators, emphasizing that the role of government becomes one of assuring that the public interest predominates, that both the solutions themselves and the process by which solutions to public problems are developed are consistent with democratic norms of justice, fairness, and equity (Ingraham and Ban 1988; Ingraham and Rosenbloom 1989). One of the most important implications of viewing government as the vehicle for achieving values such as fairness and equity is that the purpose of government is fundamentally different from that of business. These differences make the exclusive use of market mechanisms and assumptions about trust as a self-interested calculation at least suspect. Although there are many characteristics that distinguish business from government, government's responsibility to enhance citizenship and serve the public interest is one of the most important differences—and is a cornerstone of the New Public Service.

Chapter 5

Value Citizenship over Entrepreneurship

. Value citizenship over entrepreneurship. The public interest is better advanced by public servants and citizens committed to making meaningful contributions to society than by entrepreneurial managers acting as if public money were their own.

While, in the past, government played a central role in what has been called the "steering of society" (Nelissen et al. 1999), the complexity of modern life sometimes makes such a role not only inappropriate, but impossible. Those policies and programs that give structure and direction to social and political life today are the result of the interaction of many different groups and organizations, the mixture of many different opinions and interests. In many areas, it no longer makes sense to think of public policies as the result of governmental decision-making processes. Government is indeed a player—and in most cases a very substantial player. But public policies today, the policies that guide society, are the outcome of a complex set of interactions involving multiple groups and multiple interests, ultimately combining in fascinating and unpredictable ways. Government is no longer "in charge."

In this new world, the primary role of government is not to direct the actions of the public through regulation and decree (though that may sometimes be appropriate), nor is the role of government to simply establish a set of rules and incentives (sticks or carrots) through which people will be guided in the "proper" direction. Rather government becomes another player, albeit an important player, in the process of moving society in one direction or another. Government acts, in concert with private and nonprofit groups and organizations, to seek solutions to the problems communities face. In this process, the role of government is transformed from one of controlling to one of agenda setting, bringing the proper players "to the table" and facilitating, negotiating, or "brokering" solutions to public problems (often through coalitions of public, private, and nonprofit agencies). Whereas traditionally government has responded to needs by saying, "yes, we can provide that service" or "no, we can't," the New Public Service suggests that elected officials and public managers should respond to the requests of citizens not just by saying yes or no, but by saying such things as "Let's work together to figure out what we're going to do, then make it happen."

In a world of active citizenship, the role of the public servant changes. Public administrators will increasingly play more than a service-delivery role—they will play a conciliating, a mediating, or even an adjudicating role. And they will no longer rely on the skills of management control, but rather on the skills of facilitating, brokering, negotiating, and conflict resolution.

A Governance Perspective

One of the most important developments in political life today, and one recognized by the proponents of both the New Public Management and the New Public Service, is a dramatic change in the way that the rules and regulations, the programs and processes that guide society are being developed—or, to put it slightly differently—a change in the way public policy is being developed. As we noted earlier, in the past, government played a predominant role in the "steering of society" (Nelissen et al. 1999). That is not to say that other interests were not represented, but that government played a decisive role.

To use a sports analogy, the playing field on which the game of public policy formation occurred was one prescribed by government, and the primary players were elected public officials and policy advisors throughout government agencies. In turn, public administrators, playing on the same field, though often somewhere near the sidelines, were largely concerned with the implementation of public policies. They were concerned with managing their organizations so that the proper things would get done. But time and circumstances have changed. The game of public policy formulation is no longer played primarily by those in government. You might even say that now the audience is no longer in the stands, but right there on the field, participating in every play. To put this more formally, there has been a reformulation of the steering mechanisms of society. Today many groups and many interests are directly involved in the development and implementation of public policy. "This means that steering goes through channels other than the controlled hierarchical structures of central government" (Nelissen 2002, 6).

There are several reasons this has occurred. First, the more fluid character of the market, especially the expansion of international or global markets, has opened new issues to public concern. Governments are engaging more extensively with other governments and with organizations like the World Trade Organization (WTO), to say nothing of multinational corporations and similarly large and complex nongovernmental organizations. Second, the welfare state has been reconfigured so that government itself is no longer the primary actor in the delivery of services. Especially in this country, welfare and other governmental responsibilities have been pushed down to lower levels of government and out to for-profit and nonprofit organizations.

Donald Kettl has commented on these trends in globalization and devolution as follows:

> In short, America's preeminent policy strategies have tended to grow beyond the nation-state, to linkages with international organizations, and to focus below it, to partnerships with subnational, for-profit, and nonprofit organizations. Supranational organizations have grown to new but poorly understood functions. Subnational organizations have transformed the role of state and local governments. As we have debated privatizing government, they have paradoxically also governmentalized a substantial part of the for-profit and nonprofit sectors. The federal government's institutions, political and administrative, find themselves with yet more challenges, from orchestrating these partnerships to shaping the national interest. The roles of all these players have changed dramatically. Managing these roles requires capacity that lies far beyond the standard responses, structures, and processes that have gradually accumulated in American government. (Kettl 2000b, 489–90).

Third, technology has made possible greater and greater public access to the policy process, not only in the sense that people can access information more easily and can use that information to greater impact. Whereas in the past government had somewhat of a monopoly on the collection and dissemination of large amounts of data—and enjoyed a unique position because of this—today that capacity is widely distributed. As a result, government's role in the policy process has been diminished. In this sense, Harlan Cleveland was correct in predicting that the global information explosion would lead to the "twilight of hierarchy" (1985).

Similarly, H. Brinton Milward has suggested several related factors that have caused the dispersion of power and responsibility that characterizes the contemporary policy process, (1) institutional overlap, (2) overlapping authority among levels of government, (3) the fact that particular organizations have only limited responsibility for program implementation, and (4) public policy instruments that cause fragmentation (e.g., grants, contracts, and subsidies) (1991, 52). These factors have led to the development of what have been called "policy networks," networks composed of businesses, labor unions, nonprofit organizations, interest groups, governmental actors, and ordinary citizens. These policy networks now constitute the main arenas in which the game of public policy is played out.

In fact, what we are witnessing is the development of many different policy networks—each serving its own substantive interests, whether transportation, social welfare, education, or another area. Each network focuses on its own policy area and, in many ways, defines the way in which policies will be developed in that area. That is, one set of rules might define the way the "defense" game is played, while another set of rules might define how the "social welfare" game is played. In each arena, major developments in public policy, and major developments in the steering of society, are likely to occur through a difficult and convoluted process of bargaining and negotiation within that particular policy network.

Under these circumstances, the role of government is changing. As we witness a fragmentation of policy responsibility in society, we must also recognize that the traditional mechanisms of governmental control are no longer workable—or even appropriate. Traditional hierarchical government is giving way to a growing decentralization of policy interests. Control is giving way to interaction and involvement. Today, national, state, and local governments are involved in governance *along with* thousands of citizens, other public institutions, private companies, and nonprofit organizations. For this reason, it increasingly makes sense to talk not just about government, but about the process of governance.

We define governance as the exercise of public authority. The word "government" is usually used to refer to the structures and institutions of government and of those public organizations formally charged with setting policy and delivering services. Governance, on the other hand, is a much broader concept. *Governance* can be defined as the traditions, institutions, and processes that determine the exercise of power in society, including how decisions are made on issues of public concern and how citizens are given voice in public decisions. Governance speaks to how society actually makes choices, allocates resources, and creates shared values; it addresses societal decision making and the creation of meaning in the public sphere. As John Kirlin argues, existing conceptions of government which emphasize service delivery "undervalue the large role governments must successfully perform in providing the institutional framework for all human activity" (1996, 161). Governments exist, he says, to create value, including the value of place and the character of community.

In the overall scheme of governance, then, what role will formal government play? First, government will continue to play an overall role in establishing the *legal and political* rules through which various networks will operate. We might say that government will operate at the "meta-level," that is, government will help in ratifying, codifying, and legitimizing decisions that arise from within the various policy networks. Moreover, government will continue to establish broad principles of governance that apply to all, for example, setting the overarching rules of the game. Second, government will likely help in resolving resource distribution and dependency issues within various networks, but especially between and among those networks. Government will aid in protecting *economic interests* that are played out in the relationships between different sectors or policy networks; it will play a role of balancing, negotiating, and facilitating relationships across network boundaries (often through the use of incentives rather than directives), and assuring that one sector doesn't come to dominate others. Third, government will be required to monitor the interplay of networks to assure that principles of *democracy and social equity* are maintained within specific networks and in the relationships between and among the different networks. Government must make sure that democratic processes are maintained and that ultimately the public interest is served.

Just as the steering of society is changing, so are the roles and responsibilities of elected and appointed public officials changing—and changing in exactly parallel ways. Not surprisingly, each of the three roles we have just described—those associated with *legal or political* standards, those associated with *economic or market* considerations, and those associated with *democratic or social criteria*—are reflected in popular approaches to understanding the role of government and especially public administration today. As the steering of society has changed, the roles of public officials and the standards by which administrative performance will be judged have also changed.

How have these three new roles of government been translated into schools of theory and practice, and how do they affect the standards or expectations for assessing governmental performance? The first of these schools of theory and practice is the most familiar and most easily characterized. Attention to the development of legal and political standards will continue to be important in the field of public affairs. According to this school, public officials are involved in designing and implementing policies focused on limited, politically defined objectives. They are bound by the law and by political realities. They are concerned with developing programs through the traditional agencies of government. In turn, these policies are carried out by administrators in the various agencies of government. The question of accountability—the question of how administrators know that their work is consistent with the wishes of the people—is answered by the accountability of administrators to democratically elected political leaders. The school of theory and practice associated with this approach is simply traditional public policy and public administration, the Old Public Administration.

The next two approaches have emerged much more recently. The second, which has to do with *economic and market* considerations, is based in a view of political life which sees the role of government as continuing to steer, at least in the sense of acting as a catalyst to unleash the forces of the market and in creating mechanisms and incentive structures to achieve policy objectives through private and nonprofit agencies. The approach to accountability reflected in this viewpoint suggests that ultimately the accumulation of individual self-interests will result in outcomes desired by broad groups of citizens, which, as we saw earlier, this approach calls "customers." The school of public administration theory and practice associated with this approach is, of course, the New Public Management.

The third emerging (or perhaps reemerging) role of government focuses on *democratic and social criteria*. This view suggests that the public interest is paramount and that the public interest is the result of a dialogue about mutual or overlapping interests. It sees the role of government as brokering interests among citizens and other groups so as to create shared values. This might mean, for example, building coalitions of public, private, and nonprofit agencies to meet mutually agreed upon needs. John Hall states the challenge facing public administration well: "Public management that embraces the power and refines the craft of collaboration, facilitative leadership, public-private partnerships, and 'catalytic governance,' is the new formula. . . . In that spirit, . . . proactive public management will need to sharpen its *capacity to listen*" (Hall 2002, 24 italics added). The understanding of accountability (which will be addressed more fully in Chapter 7) reflected in this approach suggests that public servants must attend to law, community values, political norms, professional standards and citizen interests. The school of public administration theory and practice most clearly associated with this approach is, of course, the New Public Service.

The Old Public Administration and the Administrator's Role

As we saw earlier, public administration has always struggled with the question of the administrator's role in developing policy and with the relationship between administrators and other policy makers. The earliest statements on this issue suggested a separation of policy and administration. Elected political leaders were charged with making policy and administrators were charged with carrying out policy. The administrator, though insulated from the citizenry, was accountable to elected political leaders who were in turn accountable to the electorate, who could vote them out of office, thus maintaining a "chain" of democratic control by citizens over administrators.

The dichotomy of policy and administration, if it was ever fact, came quickly to be regarded as fiction. Administrators came to play an increasingly important though often reluctant role in the policy process. Their reluctance was understandable. If administrators came to substantially influence the policy process, one might ask whether the notion of democratic accountability envisioned under the policy-administration dichotomy would still be sufficient. Where the administrator's role only had to do with implementation, the major choices about societal direction were still being made by elected political leaders who would be held to account every two, four, or six years. But as the administrator's influence in the policy process grew, that chain of accountability came into question. How could citizens be sure that administrators were making policy choices responsive to the public interest?

Administrators were also reluctant to engage in the policy process because they were unclear about their relationship with elected leaders. Traditional public administration, for various reasons, conceived of elected political leaders as having far greater prestige and standing than appointed officials. Administrators engaging in policymaking might be taken as an affront to the authority of elected leaders. It might be seen as taking some of the rightful power away from the people's representatives. Certainly if power were seen as a zero-sum game, there could be no other explanation. Given that circumstance, combined with the fact that the elected leaders could still fire appointed officials, it just didn't seem like a good idea to "challenge" the elected leadership by overt involvement in the policy process.

For these reasons, when public administrators reluctantly moved into making public policy, they did so only under several "cloaks." There was, for example, the cloak of discretion. Administrators could justify their policy role by pointing out that legislation is often, even necessarily broad and requires administrators to define more carefully what legislated policies mean. Administrators exercising discretion are, of course, making policy, but they are required to do so by the breadth of legislation. There was also the cloak of expertise. The argument was that administrators have special knowledge and expertise in the areas of their particular interest and that their expertise needed to be brought into the policy process. Legislators, as generalists, could not be expected to know as much about any particular policy area as administrators who had spent their careers working on those specific problems. So, under the Old Public Administration, administrators were reluctant participants in the policy process, maintaining their neutrality long after it was evident that they substantially influenced public policy.

Beneath the cloaks of justification for the administrator's involvement in policy making, there were occasional hints of something broader—a philosophy that put administrators much more at the center of the governmental process. Theorists recommended creating single centers of administrative responsibility and control through which administrators could influence the rational development of plans to meet societal goals. Specific analytic tools could be developed to calculate optimum policy choices. The result was a shift from dealing with problems through politics to dealing with problems through management. While playing this role, albeit carefully and in silence, administrators could employ their expertise and experience in order to make more rational controlled plans and decisions for (not by) citizens. As Schneider and Ingram remark, "Carried to its extreme, public policy becomes a scientific enterprise dominated by experts who discover the public interest, find optimal policies to achieve it, and develop decision instruments to ensure control over the implementation process. People are simply the targets of policy, available to be manipulated through inducements or penalties to achieve policy goals, rather than citizens who are integral to the democratic process and to the production of socially desirable results" (1997, 38).

The New Public Management and the Administrator's Role

The New Public Management's approach to the question of the administrator's role in policy development has two distinct faces. On one hand, the New Public Management conceives of a much more active role for the administrator in the policy process, the role of policy entrepreneur. On the other hand, the New Public Management urges managers to respond to "customer" demands and, wherever possible, to structure policies so that "customers" can choose, that is, to move as many choices as possible even further out of the political arena by converting those policy alternatives into market choices. In either case, the New Public Management even further extends the rational calculus of costs and benefits in its examination of policy alternatives.

Establishing public managers as "entrepreneurs" is an essential element of the New Public Management. Indeed, the subtitle of the "bible" of the New Public Management, the book *Reinventing Government*, is *How the Entrepreneurial Spirit Is Transforming the Public Sector* (1992). Its authors, Osborne and Gaebler, describe entrepreneurship as maximizing productivity and effectiveness, but entrepreneurship embraces more than mere resourcefulness. First, there is the basic concern for "letting managers manage," giving managers wide latitude to conduct their affairs without the constraints of typical modes of accountability, such as budget restrictions or personnel policies (Pollitt 1993). An example from Gaebler's experience as a city manager is used by Osborne and Gaebler to elaborate this point, "The idea was to get them [the city's management team] thinking like owners, 'If this were my money, would I spend it this way?'" (1992, 3)

More important, the manager is urged to take an active role in promoting policies, "arrangements" or "deals" that he or she thinks would benefit their community or agency. Moreover, the entrepreneurial public manager is encouraged to assume risks wherever necessary in order to arrive at more creative and innovative solutions to public problems. Eugene Lewis described three entrepreneurial "giants" of public management (Hyman Rickover, Herbert Hoover, and Robert Moses) in this way: they were not "criminals in any conventional sense; rather, they were 'rule benders.' They were crafty, and they pushed the limits of what was legal and permissible time after time without getting caught or, when caught, without serious punishment" (1980, 243). In sum, as Larry Terry puts it, the New Public Management supports a position in which "public managers are (and should be) self-interested, opportunistic innovators and risk-takers who exploit information and situations to produce radical change" (1998, 197).

The policy role of the public entrepreneur has been called into question by several writers. First, policy entrepreneurs may be creative and innovative, but they can also be opportunistic and uncompromising. "As a practical matter, in real organizations, entrepreneurial managers pose a difficult and risky problem, they can be innovative and productive, but their single-mindedness, tenacity, and willingness to bend the rules make them very difficult to control. They can become "loose cannons" (deLeon and Denhardt 2000, 92). Second, there is the question of accountability. The idea of public managers independently making policy choices in the guise of "getting the best deal" and, even more important, acting as if the public's money were their own flies in the face of a long tradition of democratic accountability and fiscal integrity in government. The public's business and the public's money, many would argue, should be treated as the *public's*.

In addition to recommending a more entrepreneurial role for public managers, the New Public Management also recommends structuring choices so that they can be made by "customers" in a market rather than by actors in the political sphere. The key, according to Osborne and Gaebler, would be to create market incentives where now there are political choices:

In education, this might mean moving to a competitive market in which customers have choices and key stakeholders (parents and teachers) have genuine control. In job training, it might mean injecting information about the quality of all training providers into the system, putting resources directly into customers' hands, providing them with accessible brokers, and empowering them to choose between competing providers. In unemployment insurance, it might mean creating a financial incentive for corporations to retrain employees rather than lay them off, or creating an incentive for those collecting unemployment to seek retraining. (Osborne and Gaebler 1992, 308)

Again, recommendations such as these are consistent with the New Public Management's dependence on public choice theory and its assumption that the market is the central institution in society and can be relied on, more than other institutions (certainly more than government), to provide for free and fair choices. Through market mechanisms individuals can pursue their own best interests with minimal constraint. Markets, it is argued, are free and without coercion, where government and public policy are coercive. In this view, the only role for government is to correct for market failures and provide goods and services that the market is not able to convey.

This argument is related to public choice theory's more general critique of the policy process. Roughly, that critique first suggests that government provides certain goods or services that could be better handled through the market and that government is not efficiently organized to deliver many services. For example, advocates of this position argue that if education were provided on the basis of consumer choice, say, through vouchers, the competition for students would increase the quality of the service being delivered. Schools would have to improve to attract students, their "customers." Competition would require schools to act more efficiently than if they remained under the aegis of government.

Moreover, proponents of public choice theory argue that political leaders and "bureaucrats," motivated by self-interest, seek excessive increases in programs and budgets, beyond what the public really wants. Finally, they argue that government programs breed "dependency," since recipients of services find it in their self-interest to partake of those programs rather than being self-sufficient. This argument is often made with respect to welfare, where it may appear that having a second child would increase the size of the welfare payment and therefore be an incentive to do so. The same argument might also be made with respect to farmers who received subsidies for growing or even not growing specific crops.

In contrast to centralized government programs, public choice theory recommends decentralization, privatization, and competition. Recommen-

dations flowing from this position include privatizing government functions wherever possible, contracting with private firms (selected through a
competitive bid process) in other cases, creating competitive arrangements
within those government agencies that remain, and charging full market
value for public goods. Specific programs might include the movement to
"choice" in educational policy, contracting for social services, and the development of water policy based on market prices (Schneider and Ingram
1997, 46). Again, the effect of the New Public Management or the public
choice position is to drive public policy out of the political arena and into
the market, where the decisions of self-interested parties, "customers," will
drive policy choices.

We should point out that the New Public Management gives the manager considerable independence with respect to policy development. On
the one hand, administrators (as "entrepreneurs") are urged to act independently to move their own preferred policies or "deals" forward. At the
same time, the manager must try to assess consumer preferences, then,
based on that assessment, to pursue his or her own interpretation of the
public's desires largely unconstrained by external mechanisms of accountability (see Chapter 7). What is, of course, missing in all this is the involvement of citizens in the process of democratic governance. If you
look, for example, at the index of *Reinventing Government,* you won't
find terms such as "equity" or "justice." Nor will you find "citizens" or
"citizenship." It's really quite remarkable that a reform movement as significant as the New Public Management could move forward with such
sparse attention to democratic citizenship.

The New Public Service and the Administrator's Role

The New Public Service, unlike the New Public Management, is distinguished by the involvement of citizens in the administrative process. In
Chapter 3, we examined various dimensions of citizenship and began to
build the case for a richer and fuller engagement of citizens in the policy
process. The New Public Service builds on the tradition of democratic
citizenship described in that chapter, especially as it urges extensive and
authentic citizen involvement in the development of public policy. Here
we review some of the reasons that governments are increasingly involving citizens in the process of making public policy and why public administrators might find greater citizen involvement attractive. Then we
will review a number of different approaches to structuring more extensive programs for civic engagement.

Citizen involvement in government is certainly not a new concept. Indeed, some level of citizen involvement is essential to democratic governance—by definition. However, historically, our representative democracy has largely confined the role of the citizen to voting every few years and occasionally communicating with elected officials. More recently, the rise of special interest groups has restructured the relationship between citizens and their government.

At the same time, government has opened new avenues for more direct citizen involvement. Beginning with the War on Poverty in the 1960s, governments have designed opportunities for "maximum feasible participation" into their processes of policy design and implementation. Consequently, dozens of approaches to soliciting citizen input into the policy process have been tried, ranging from public hearings to citizen surveys, and from planning boards to community panels. While many of these efforts have failed to produce what King, Feltey, and O'Neill (1998) call "authentic participation," and while there is clearly a need to continue to refine the process of citizen involvement, there is no question but that public managers will need to be attentive to the question of participation. As John Clayton Thomas indicates, "the new public involvement has transformed the work of public managers . . . public participation in the managerial process has become a fact of life. In the future, this may become the case for even more managers, since the public's demand for involvement does not seem to be abating" (1995, xi).

There are a variety of both theoretical and practical reasons why public administrators should encourage great citizen involvement in the policy process. At the theoretical level, as we saw earlier, the ethical posture of the public administrator requires an attitude of caring and involvement. David K. Hart (1984) points out that the professional obligation of administrators begins with their duties as virtuous citizens, and that creates an essential link to other citizens. In exercising their public trust, not only must administrators maintain adherence to "regime values," they should be expected to care for their fellow citizens and interact with them on the basis of trust. He suggests that administrators must learn to trust that citizens, given the opportunity, will make the right choices. Interestingly enough, given our earlier discussion of "entrepreneurial government," Hart uses the term "moral entrepreneur" to describe the administrator who is obligated to conduct public affairs on the basis of trust rather than compulsion, something that may require a certain moral "risk-taking" that is even more significant than economic risk-taking. As Louis Gawthrop states, "to commit oneself to the service of democracy requires, at least, a conscious and mature awareness of (1) the ethical impulses of democracy, (2) the transcendent values of democracy, and (3) the moral vision of democracy" (1998, 24).

Others have pointed out that the administrator bears a responsibility to help educate citizens. We noted earlier the argument that participation in the activities of citizenship can serve an educative function, helping people to entertain broader interests than their own and to understand the complexities of the governance process. Participation in democratic governance builds moral character, an empathetic understanding of the needs of others, and the skills to engage in collective action. In that process of education, some have argued, administrators are in a unique position, that of being "civic educators." "Because they comprise that segment of the expert realm that is most insulated from the adversarial process, they are best situated to take the lead in framing questions so that public debate can be made intelligible. They have the prime responsibility for teasing out the essential social and ethical issues at stake from the welter of scientific data and legal formalisms in which those issues are enveloped" (Landy 1993, 25). Importantly, in this context, the educative role of the administrator is not merely that of "giving advice," but rather that of creating circumstances of dialogue and engagement where mutual learning can take place.

Finally, and most basically, as Bellah et al. write, "democracy is paying attention" (1991, 254). As an active participant in democratic governance, the administrator bears a responsibility to listen to the voices of citizens and to be responsive to what is said. In the process of listening, carefully and clearly, the administrator joins self and society in a reflexive relationship. Stivers puts it this way, "As we improve our ability to listen, we increasingly understand the extent to which we hear ourselves in others and they in us; this reciprocity is evoked in our theories and practices of justice. Instead of stripping away the qualities of unique individuals in favor of the ideal of universality, listening expands justice to include the details of the situation and the significant differences among human beings" (1994b, 366).

In addition to these theoretical considerations, there are several more practical reasons for involving citizens in the process of policy development. First, greater participation can help meet citizens' expectations that they are being heard and that their needs and interests are being pursued. Second, greater participation can improve the quality of public policy, as governments tap wider sources of information, creativity, and solutions. Third, greater participation in the policy process aids implementation, as participants have more of a stake in the outcomes. Fourth, greater participation responds to calls for greater transparency and accountability in government. Fifth, greater participation is likely to increase public trust in government. Sixth, greater participation can help meet the challenges of an emerging information society. Seventh, greater participation can create the possibility for new partnerships being developed. Eighth, greater participation can result in a better informed public. Ninth, in a democracy, it's simply the right thing to do.

Robert Reich sums up the position of the public manager nicely when he writes:

> But sometimes, I believe, higher-level public managers have an obligation to stimulate public debate about what they do. Public deliberation can help the manager clarify ambiguous mandates. More importantly, it can help the public discover latent contradictions and commonalities in what it wants to achieve. Thus the public manager's job is not only, or simply, to make policy choices and implement them. It is also to participate in a system of democratic governance in which public values are continuously rearticulated and recreated. (Reich 1988, 123–24)

Unfortunately, in many cases, policy makers have failed to involve citizens in the policy process. Peter deLeon has examined this issue in detail and finds numerous flaws in the current approach to policy development. As opposed to Harold Lasswell's ideal of policy sciences that would "improve the practice of democracy" (quoted in deLeon 1997, 7), policy research today is largely carried out by technically trained policy analysts engaged in detailed policy studies and cost-benefit analysis. In deLeon's words, these analysts are "effectively sequestered from the demands, needs and (most critically) values of the people they are reputed to be helping" (1997, 8). Without the involvement of the people in the process of policy development, the policy sciences may be in danger of becoming what Lasswell feared, the "policy sciences of tyranny." In contrast to a policy science dominated by technical expertise, engaging ordinary citizens in the process of policy development seems most consistent with the democratic dream.

While citizens have sometimes been simply ignored in the process, in other instances they have been involved for the wrong reasons and with poor results. For example, participation has been used to put off decisions by engaging in endless discussions or it has been undertaken with no real commitment on the part of the administrator to use the information and advice that is developed. Even worse, as we have often seen, the decision has already been made, making the involvement of citizens a mere pretense. These "cosmetic" efforts at participation constitute failures from which we can learn as we think about ways to more fully engage citizens in the process of governance.

There have been much more positive experiences with citizen involvement as well—in this country and around the world. These examples have been documented in numerous publications (for example, see OECD 2001; Sirianni and Friedland 2001; Thomas 1995). Based on a comprehensive worldwide survey of these activities, the Public Management Service Working Group on Government-Citizen Connections of the Organization for Economic Cooperation and Development (OECD) defines three levels of involvement, information, consultation, and active participation:

> *Information* is a *one-way relationship* in which government produces and delivers information for citizens. It covers both "passive" access to information upon demand by citizens and "active" measures by government to disseminate information. Examples include, access to public records, official gazettes, government websites.

> *Consultation* is a *two-way relationship* in which citizens provide feedback to government. Governments define the issues for consultation, set the questions and manage the process, while citizens are invited to contribute their views and opinions. Examples include, public opinion surveys, comments on draft legislation.

> *Active participation* is a *relation based on partnership* with government, in which citizens actively engage in defining the process and content of policy-making. It acknowledges equal standing for citizens in setting the agenda, proposing policy options and shaping the policy dialogue– although the responsibility for the final decision or policy formulation rests with government. Examples include, consensus conferences, citizens' juries. (OECD 2001, 23)

Rather than reviewing the practical experiences of public participation in the past, which has been done elsewhere, we would will instead review the contemporary debate concerning how to bring about active, authentic participation. As important as practical designs for participation are, there are significant conceptual difficulties in structuring processes of civic engagement. Interestingly, most of these concerns center on the question of dialogue, debate, deliberation, or discourse—that is, how citizens, politicians, and administrators can engage in a full and complete discussion of the relevant issues facing the polity in a way that is representative of or even inclusive of the citizenry as a whole, that incorporates both technical information and political preferences, and that takes all viewpoints into account through constructive and informed debate.

Obviously, traditional avenues for participation, such as public hearings or advisory boards, involve a limited number of people and typically only those with a special interest in the topic at hand. Moreover, these approaches typically are limited in the amount of informed dialogue that can take place. For these reasons, they present policy makers with a somewhat skewed version of the public's opinion. One way to try to move beyond this limitation is to create more representative bodies and permit them to interact at length around policy issues before arriving at a policy recommendation. James Fishkin, for example, has argued for what he calls a "deliberative opinion poll" as a way of better assessing public opinion (Fishkin 1991, 1995). The deliberative opinion poll brings together a statistically representative group of people in one place for a period of several days, immerses them in the issue through carefully balanced briefing material, allows them to engage in a sustained process of face-to-face interaction and to ask questions of experts and political leaders, then arrive at a conclusion. Through this process of deliberation, it is hoped that the participants will learn from one another and may modify their initial positions, perhaps arriving at a consensus. In any case, a final poll of the participants may then be taken as a "proxy" for the society as a whole.

Fishkin's work is paralleled in some ways by that of Daniel Yankelovich, who begins with another concern raised above—the possibility that expert knowledge will come to dominate the policy process, allowing little room for the public. To offset this tendency, he argues for enhancing the quality of public opinion or what he terms, "public judgment," a particular form of public opinion that exhibits "(1) more thoughtfulness, more weighing of alternatives, more genuine engagement with the issue, more taking into account a wide variety of factors than public opinion as measured in opinion polls, and (2) more emphasis on the normative, valuing, ethical side of questions than on the factual, informational side" (1991). To sharpen public judgment, Yanelovich recommends a structured process of deliberation, through which participants can assess options, develop information needed to make choices, engage in reasoned discussion with their peers, and arrive at a reflective judgment. In this process, participants, indeed, citizens generally, will be aided by creating circumstances for "dialogue," situations in which there is equality and the absence of coercive influences, listening with empathy, and bring assumptions into the open (1999, 41–44). Again, the key is to countering technical expertise (and its potential for unwanted control) is the process of extensive dialogue by citizens. "Information stripped of feelings is not the royal road to public judgment; dialogue, rich in feelings and values, is" (25).

Benjamin Barber takes a similar tack in his argument in behalf of "strong democracy," a form of participatory democracy involving a community of citizens "capable of common purpose and mutual action by virtue of their civic attitudes and participatory institutions" (1984, 117). In Barber's view, the masses become citizens when they deliberate. Citizen participation lacking the quality of deliberation is empty. For this reason, it is important for those involved in designing institutions that would enable great citizen involvement to understand clearly the nature of "democratic talk," which involves listening as well as speaking, feeling as well as thinking, and acting as well as reflecting (178). Again, the qualities of empathy, emotion, and activity come to the fore. Thought of in this way, democratic talk can, in Barber's view, serve many functions. Most often we think of political talk as involving the articulation of interests, persuasion, and bargaining and exchange. Democratic talk can also assist in agenda setting, exploring mutuality, affiliation and affection, maintaining autonomy, witnessing, expressing, reformulating, and reconceptualizing. Most important, democratic talk can assist in community building, creating public interests, common goods, and active citizens (178–98).

A number of theorists have examined the question of deliberative democracy from a more philosophical perspective. Jurgen Habermas, for example, has argued that, while our society operates under a narrow definition of rationality, one consistent with a society dominated by technology and bureaucracy, we maintain an innate capacity to reason in a much larger sense. Moreover, it is this capacity to reason that enables us to communicate across various social and ideological boundaries. But for reason to prevail in any given situation, we must (1) engage in a dialogue, not a monologue, and (2) the dialogue must be free of domination and distortion. Where one party to the communication has more power than another the communication is distorted. Genuine communication in a democracy can only take place where all forms of domination, both apparent and subtle, have been eliminated. A part of our being human is a "gentle, but obstinate, a never silent although seldom redeemed claim to reason, a claim that must be recognized whenever and wherever there is to be consensual action" (quoted in Yankelovich 1991, 217).

In a recent book, *Between Facts and Norms,* Habermas (1996) uses the theory of communicative action (briefly sketched above) as the basis for a form of "deliberative democracy." While Habermas is skeptical of a whole society governing itself through deliberative processes, he feels that within "institutionalized discursive structures" people can in fact reason together. But remember the problem of distortion. Distortion can come about in many ways—through overt exercises of power and influence, through economic pressures and market manipulation, or through the capture of the media for political or economic purposes. Under these circumstances, creating deliberative democracy is very difficult, but at least we have some direction as to what would be required to achieve that objective.

Other efforts to elaborate theories of deliberative democracy have sought to spell out the theoretical considerations concerning the legitimacy of various forms of deliberative democracy—and the resulting debates have been intense. (See, for example, Dryzek 1999; Gutman and Thompson 1996; Macedo 1999.) Some of these have focused on the circumstances under which people would agree that outcomes of a deliberative process are valid. Seyla Benhabib, for example, has suggested three conditions required for such a process to be considered legitimate, "(1) Participation in such deliberation is governed by the norms of equality and symmetry; all have the same chance to initiate speech acts, to question, to interrogate, and to open debate; (2) All have the right to question the assigned topics of conversation; (3) All have the right to initiate reflexive arguments about the very rules of the discourse procedure and the way in which they are applied or carried out" (1996, 70).

Postmodern theorists, including public administration theorists, have also entered into the debate. Charles Fox and Hugh Miller, for example, criticize representative democracy as neither representative nor democratic (1995). Rather, the supposedly legitimizing force of democratic deliberation has been replaced by top down bureaucratic systems and media-infused politics. As an alternative, Fox and Miller offer a set of conditions under which legitimate and "authentic discourse" might take place. Such deliberations would have to occur in a way that would exclude insincere claims, those that are only self-serving, those from persons unwilling to attend to the discourse, and claims from "free-riders." Forums built around norms of inclusion, attentiveness, and understanding may aid in reasserting the democratic ideal. Other theorists, such as Farmer (1995) and McSwite (1997), have taken the issue a step further by arguing that our being limited to "rational" discourse may inhibit our capacity to see beyond our own experience and to engage new ideas and new relationships in a fundamentally different way. "The very essence of the discourse perspective is the idea of creating a kind of relationship among people such that when they engage in dialogue, the *source of the fundamentally new* will come into play" (McSwite 2000, 60).

Conclusion

In this chapter, we have explored the new conditions under which the "steering of society" is taking place and how the Old Public Administration, the New Public Management, and the New Public Service have responded to the challenges these circumstances present for public managers engaged in the policy process. In contrast to a reliance on bureaucratic expertise or managerial entrepreneurship, the New Public Service argues for a vastly enhanced capacity for citizen involvement in all aspects of the process. We have examined a variety of approaches to engaging citizens in the governance process, as well as some of the important theoretical considerations that must go into any design choice. While we should point out once again that there are differences, even dramatic differences, among these viewpoints, they all share the same concern for democratic governance and civic engagement that is central to the New Public Service, yet missing in the Old Public Administration and the New Public Management. In all cases, these theorists are concerned with improving dialogue, deliberation, or discourse to better meet the tenets of democratic governance.

The first section of this chapter is adapted from a previously published paper: Robert Denhardt and Janet Denhardt, 2001, "The New Public Service, Putting Democracy First," *National Civic Review* 90(4): 391–400. The paper was originally prepared for the Arizona Town Hall.

Chapter 6

Think Strategically, Act Democratically

Think strategically, act democratically. Policies and programs meeting public needs can be most effectively and responsibly achieved through collective efforts and collaborative processes.

In Chapter 4, we argued that the public interest is based upon widespread public dialogue and deliberation about shared values and interests. In the New Public Service, the idea is not merely to establish the vision and then leave the implementation to those in government; rather, it is to join together all parties in the process of both designing and carrying out programs that will move in the desired direction. Through involvement in programs of civic education and by helping to develop a broad range of civic leaders, government can stimulate a renewed sense of civic pride and civic responsibility. We would expect that such a sense of pride and responsibility would evolve into a greater willingness to be involved at many levels, as all parties work together to create opportunities for participation, collaboration, and community. Again, this participation should not be limited to framing the issues, it should also extend to policy implementation.

How might this be done? To begin with there is an obvious and important role for political leadership—to articulate and encourage a strengthening of citizen responsibility and, in turn, to support groups and individuals involved in building the bonds of community. Government can't create community; but government, and, more specifically, political leadership can lay the groundwork for effective and responsible citizen action. People must come to recognize that government is open and accessible—and that won't happen unless government *is* open and accessible, both in the process of policy formulation and in program implementation. People must come to recognize that government is responsive—and that won't happen unless government *is* responsive in both framing programs and delivering services. People must come to recognize that government exists to meet their needs—and that won't happen unless it does. The best way to do so is to create opportunities for participation and collaboration in achieving public purposes. The aim then is to make sure that government is open and accessible, that it is responsive, and that it operates to serve citizens and create opportunities for citizenship in all phases of the policy process.

Accordingly, assumptions regarding the role of public administrators and citizens in the implementation of public policy are key to understanding the nature of citizenship and relationship of public administration to the larger system of democratic governance. Early writers suggested that the role of public administration consisted of the efficient implementation of politically determined goals with little or no direct citizen involvement. Later works portrayed the implementation process as much more complex and multifaceted, but still largely ignored the role of citizens.

In order to understand the underlying principles of implementation in the context of the New Public Service values, this chapter will first briefly consider the evolution of implementation theory from an historical perspective. We then examine contemporary models of implementation and relate them to the assumptions and values of the New Public Management. We follow that with an explanation of the theoretical foundations that support a more democratic and participative approach to implementation will follow.

Implementation in Historical Perspective

Interestingly, the study of "implementation" did not exist per se in the early stages of the development of public administration. This is not because public agencies were not involved in implementation. Rather, in a sense, implementation was invisible as a separate concept or function because it constituted the whole of the field of public administration. Virtually the sole purpose of public agencies was to implement politically determined policies and programs. Because the goal of public administration was to maintain neutrality and to use administrative expertise to achieve efficiency, there was no need to have a concept of implementation because the assumption was that the policy would remain largely unchanged as public agencies acted upon it. After all, as Wilson, Goodnow, and other founding scholars in the field asserted, the political sphere made the decisions, and the administrative apparatus simply and mechanically put them into action. In short, the process of policy implementation didn't call for

study or theory because it wasn't considered important relative to the decisions already made by the politicians.

Accordingly, theory and practice focused on achieving politically determined ends. This lead to a concentration on the structures and functions of
organizations that long characterized the field. Even in the 1940s and 1950s,
with growing recognition that politics and administration were not entirely
separate, the focus remained on the management of organizations to achieve
efficiency and cost effectiveness.

It was not until the emergence of policy studies in the 1970s that the idea
of the activities of public organizations as the implementers of policy (as
opposed to the managers of organizations) took hold. The first significant
work dealing with implementation as a distinct issue was Jeffrey Pressman
and Aaron Wildavsky's 1973 book, *Implementation: How Great Expectations in Washington Are Dashed in Oakland.* These authors chronicled a
series of failures and implementation problems in the implementation of
Federal Economic Development Administration project in Oakland, California, finding that while the program began with good intentions and a
strong commitment, the actual implementation this large-scale federal project
was very difficult and largely unsuccessful. Their conclusion was that policy
is not automatically translated into action, and that the dynamics of the implementation process must be understood as a major determinant of policy outcomes. Pressman and Wildavsky's work was the launching point for numerous
subsequent works that sought to understand and explain the implementation
process. In fact, six years later Wildavsky, in the preface to the second edition of their book, commented that implementation had become a growth
industry (1979).

Although considerable attention has been paid to policy implementation
over the past three decades, mapping the boundaries of implementation theory
remains difficult. This confusion is in part due to the fact that implementation research has continued to overlap with and draw heavily from work in
organizational theory, decision making, organizational change, and intergovernmental relations. Admitting its rather fuzzy boundaries, implementation research has become an important and relatively prominent area of
inquiry. In *Implementation Theory and Practice: Toward a Third Generation*
(1990), Goggin and colleagues divide the development of implementation
into first-, second- and third-generation research. They discuss first-generation research as the work immediately following Pressman and Wildavsky's
book, work that succeeded in shifting the focus from how a bill becomes a
law to how a law becomes a program, and demonstrated the complexity,
difficulty, and frequent failures that occur in the implementation process.
Second-generation research is described as focusing on predictors of imple-

mentation success or failure, such as policy form, organizational variables, and the behavior of individual actors. Third-generation research, which the authors claim has not been achieved, will be more scientific in that it will clarify key concepts, specify causal paths and frequency distributions of behavior variations, and modeling of the process. This typology of three generations of research provides a useful basis for reviewing the historical evolution of implementation theory.

First Generation

First-generation research on implementation, including the work of Wildavsky and Pressman, assumed a top-down linear policy process that was driven by the language of the statute and the intent of elected officials. Top-down models began with the decisions of policymakers, typically expressed in statutory language, and worked "down" the policy process. This model assumed that implementation *ought* to be a linear process wherein policy directives are translated into program activities with as little deviation as possible. It suggests that policymakers are the only important actors and that organization-level actors serve only to thwart the "correct" implementation process. First-generation research was largely based on single-site case studies, and it concentrated on two sources of implementation failure: the content of the policy and the inability of people and organizations to implement it precisely. While early first-generation research on implementation laid out the basics of the study, it was considered methodologically weak as it was generally atheoretical and case specific.

Within this framework, interest in implementation studies began to build in the early 1980s. For example, two articles published in *Public Administration Review* reported the results of specific implementation cases. First, Weimer, in his 1980 analysis of the implementation of an automated case management system, found that three kinds of problems were encountered in such projects: design and cognition problems, organizational cooperation problems, and poor data quality. He concluded that technical assistance might help overcome design and cognition problems.

Second, Menzel studied the implementation of the Federal Surface Mining Control and Reclamation Act concentrated on the role of administrative rulemaking and found that statutory deadlines, complex intergovernmental relationships, and lack of supportive clientele exacerbate implementation problems (1981). In both of these instances, the research was completely program-specific; as a result, few general propositions could be produced.

The issue of implementation was also being discussed in the literature on program evaluation during this time period. Three articles appeared in *Evalu-*

ation and Program Planning in 1982 that underscored the importance of considering what are termed "type III" errors in evaluation. Type III errors are those errors that occur because of the failure to expose the experimental group to the independent variable, in other words, when outcomes are mistakenly attributed to program activities that were never actually implemented. Rezmovic, for example, examined the results obtained on an experiment conducted in criminal justice and found that the original, positive results could not be replicated when experimental and control groups were subdivided between those that actually received treatment and those that did not (1982). Similarly, Cook and Dobson concluded that program implementation data should be included in the analysis of program outcomes (1982). Tornatzky and Johnson explored the specific issue of how evaluation can be used to guide implementation efforts and found that evaluation should specify crucial program elements related to implementation, and could be used as a means to ensure that planned activities actually take place (1982).

In all these cases, the explicit focus was on the idea that implementation often goes awry and confounds the intentions of the policymakers. However, implicit in these findings is an assumption that implementation ought to be a top-down, linear process wherein policy directives are translated into program activities with as little deviation as possible.

Second Generation

In second-generation implementation research, the top-down assumption was turned on its head. In other words, dissatisfaction with the top-down perspective lead theorists to develop of a number of models that viewed implementation from the bottom up. Linder and Peters (1986), for example, suggested that for successful implementation, program design must consider the needs and values of the implementers. Bottom-up models assume the existence of a network of actors whose goals, strategies, and actions must be considered in understanding implementation. In this model, implementing agencies play a positive, necessary, and appropriate role in redefining and refocusing legislation in light of organizational-level realities. The question then becomes, of course, how do you determine success? In top-down models, success occurs when implementers do not deviate from politically determined policy. In bottom-up models, the presumption is that implementers are supposed to exercise discretion and redefine programs and policies as appropriate.

Next, implementation researchers then sought to meld or integrate these top-down and bottom-up models. In the integrated model, implementation is seen as occurring in an interactive, circular policy process. For example,

Nakamura argued that instead of a linear process, implementation activities were a part of a seamless, interacting whole (1987). Adaptation and discretion in the implementation process, therefore, was seen as necessary and desirable. However, legislative leadership was also seen as critical. Likewise, Burke argued that, depending on institutional factors and the degree of internal or external control that could be exercised in the process, public policies should be designed to intentionally allow a range of bureaucratic discretion within legislatively established parameters (1987). This model explicitly acknowledges that both policymakers and administrators are actively involved in the implementation process.

In short, various perspectives on policy implementation emerged. The top-down model assumes implementation to be a linear process controlled by policymakers. The bottom-up perspective views control and the exercise of discretion at the bottom of the bureaucracy to be an appropriate part of implementation. An integrated view incorporates both the top-down and bottom-up perspectives by acknowledging the importance of both leadership from the top and discretion at the bottom.

In addition to debates about the best vantage point from which to view the implementation process, a significant amount of work focused on establishing the predictors of implementation success. For example, Van Meter and Van Horn (1975) argued that in addition to the characteristics of the implementing organization and the political, social, and economic environment, the success of policy implementation is influenced by resource availability, interorganizational communication, as well as the attitude of implementers. O'Toole and Montjoy (1984) found that, in cases in which the cooperation of two or more agencies was required for implementation, the type of interdependence between those agencies is a factor in predicting the likelihood of implementation.

Third Generation

In the third generation of research, questions increasingly focused on policy design and policy networks and their implications for how implementation "success" is most appropriately evaluated. In other words, there was an increasing recognition that the manner in which programs and policies are designed determines how, and how successfully, they will be implemented within a particular policy network.

Unfortunately, implementation is not often considered in policy design. Scholars increasingly argue that implementation is not a failure if the policy is poorly designed or not feasible in the first place; in other words, success must be considered in light of design considerations (Linder and Peters

1987). Dennis Palumbo (1987) claims the problem is that existing research does not differentiate between implementation failure and problems that result from poor policy design. He also criticizes the top-down bias that assumes that the goals and objectives of the policymakers are superior to those of the street-level implementers as well as the failure to see adaptation in implementation as necessary and desirable. Moreover, according to Palumbo, the field of implementation research has an ideological bias that leads investigators to assume that government can't do anything right. As a result, he says, implementation research remains a highly fractured, disjointed body of knowledge.

On the positive side, however, Palumbo argues that inquiry has given us a number of important insights that should change how implementation is understood. Among the most important of these insights is that the tools of implementation rather than management techniques are critical. This becomes particularly important in complex policy networks. Cline (2000) suggests that the implementation process has been defined in two ways: as a problem of organizational management based on administrative process, or as a problem of how to elicit cooperation from participants in the implementation process. He concludes, "Problems of generating cooperation in situations of conflict of interest are likely to stymie implementation before issues of organizational management become an obstacle" (2000, 552). In a similar vein, O'Toole urges scholars to look at the multiple institutional actors in implementation process "whose cooperation and perhaps coordination are needed for implementation success" (2000, 266). In fact, Hall and O'Toole showed that "the great majority of legislation requires multifactor structures spanning governments, sectors, and/or agencies" (2000, 667).

One way to view implementation networks is from an intergovernmental communication perspective. Goggin and colleagues, for example, look at implementation from an intergovernmental policymaking framework based on "messages, messengers, channels, and targets operating within a broader communications system" (Goggin et al, 1990, 33). This communication system provides political messages with regard to inducements, constraints, expectations and exhortations within the intergovernmental framework.

Lynn, Heinrich, and Hill also look at implementation in networked settings: "public, nonprofit, and proprietary sectors through webs of states, regions, special districts, service delivery areas, local offices, independent organizations, collaborative associations, partnerships, or other administrative entities" (2000, 551). Unlike Goggin, these researchers examine implementation from a political economy perspective, emphasizing the "logic of governance." The logic of governance based on the concepts of political economy deals with rational choice and consequences of the mechanisms used by alternative institutional forms to constrain and control behavior. They argue that the logic of political economy has great utility for understanding how agencies, programs, and activities can best be organized to achieve successful outcomes, efficiency and effectiveness. Again, the focus is on "better system performance" (551).

Because top-down models have continued to be prevalent, criticisms of that model of implementation have also continued. Fox (1987) points out that top-down analysis assumes policymakers' directives must be literally and completely followed without deviation, that all program expectations will be met, and that only intended benefits are valid. As a result, implementation research tends to arrive at negative findings and conclude that government can't do anything right. Similarly, Nakamura (1987) also attacks what he calls the textbook policy process, which views policy as a linear series of functionally discrete steps (such as policy formation, implementation, and evaluation) with a feedback loop at the end. He argues that this is unrealistic and that these activities are a part of a seamless, interacting whole. He concludes by urging researchers to develop an alternative, more realistic model of the process. Love and Sederberg (1987) offer one such possibility. They suggest that policy can be seen as a theory and implementation as the attempt to translate theory into action. A number of factors influence how well this translation works: the theory's internal consistency, consistency with conventional wisdom, administrative capacity, and resources and the political support or momentum available.

While much of the most recent literature analyzes implementation from a policy design perspective, Linder and Peters (1986) caution that a design perspective taken to its logical extreme would lead to the view that good policy is that which is most feasible or that which can be most easily implemented. That is, they say, a misdirection of the policy sciences. What would be more fruitful, in their view, is to focus on policy imperatives first, and then consider alternative instruments for their accomplishment. Like Burke, they urge attention to the normative issues which underlie implementation and that researchers concentrate on the design of effective and desirable policy.

In short, moving through various generations of research on implementation, two trends seem evident. First, there has been a shift away from the view of policy implementation as a unidirectional, linear process in which the intent of the elected officials is either followed (successful implementation) or not (failed implementation). Instead, implementation is increasingly seen as an interactive, circular process. Second, numerous variables have been shown to influence the implementation process including individual actors, human behavioral considerations, organizational factors, and institutional and interinstitutional factors, and policy design. As such, implementation studies no longer focus exclusively on a single agency as the unit of analysis. Rather, they look at implementation in the context of policy networks. Nonetheless, most implementation research has ignored or neglected the role of direct citizen involvement in implementation. Using the concepts and questions raised in this review of implementation research, we will now explore the dominant views of implementation evidenced in the Old Public Administration and the New Public Management. We will then discuss how the New Public Service differs from these perspectives, particularly in its recognition of and emphasis on the importance of citizen involvement in program implementation.

The Old Public Administration and Implementation

As noted at the beginning of this chapter, in public administration orthodoxy, there was little differentiation between the administrative process and the implementation process. Implementation was what public administration was responsible for. Consequently, while what later came to be termed "implementation" models did not exist per se, there were a number of implicit assumptions about the nature of implementation (which was largely equivalent to efficient and neutral administration) and the best way to achieve it.

The first assumption was, of course, that the process of policy implementation was top-down, hierarchical, and unidirectional. It was assumed that policy arrived fully formed at the doorstep of administrative agencies. These agencies would then put that policy or program in place with little need to exercise judgment or discretion. In fact, discretion was not acknowledged as a necessary part of a public administrator's job. Instead, agencies and their managers were to apply administrative expertise to control the process so that policies would be put into place precisely as policymakers had intended. The job of administrative agencies was to neutrally execute laws passed by legislative authorities.

Second, because of the influence of scientific management and the emphasis on formal organizations, the focus was on controlling behavior to conform to these scientifically derived principles. The task was, then, to discover the most predictable, regularized, and "correct" procedures and rules to implement a program, and then to use management techniques and controls to ensure that people within the organization did what they were supposed to do. The sole focus was on the management of the organization and the people who were responsible for providing services and functions in support of enacted policy. The preeminent value was efficiency: deliver services at the lowest cost consistent with the law.

The third assumption was that implementation was not part of the policy process. Administrative processes and policymaking (as prescribed by the politics/administration dichotomy) were entirely separate. Accordingly, there was no question about whether a policy was good or bad, "implementable" or not, it simply was the guiding force behind what administrators were obligated to do in the most efficient manner possible. Because of these assumptions, thinking strategically—much less implementing programs democratically—would have seemed both inappropriate and unnecessary.

The New Public Management and Implementation

It is somewhat difficult to tease out the assumptions regarding the implementation process that is embedded in the New Public Management. This is due in part to the fact that the New Public Management doesn't deal with "implementation" directly. Rather, public choice theory and the New Public Management suggests that, in essence, government "get out of the way" as much as possible to allow market forces and incentives to accomplish public purposes. As we will explore more fully in this section, advocates of the New Public Management talk about some of the same mechanisms and approaches to implementation and citizen involvement found in the literature on the New Public Service, however, these approaches are based on different fundamental assumptions and are justified for different reasons. As a result, although the approaches sound the same in some respects, and even use the same terminology, implementation in the New Public Management is different from both the Old Public Administration and the New Public Service.

Two of the primary approaches to implementation applauded by the New Public Management theorists are privatization and coproduction—in other words, get implementation out of the hands of bureaucrats and into a marketlike arena. As noted previously, privatization is a hallmark of the New Public Management movement. Although Osborne and Gaebler did not advocate the wholesale privatization of government, they did state that "It makes sense to put the delivery of many public services in private hands . . . if by doing so a government can get more effectiveness, efficiency, equity or accountability" (1992, 47). In a sense then, the view of implementation advocated by the New Public Management theorists is to remove the implementation function from bureaucracies as much as possible, and instead introduce businesslike incentives to ensure that programs are implemented correctly and efficiently.

While the Old Public Administration sought efficient implementation from the top down, the New Public Management seeks efficient implementation literally from the side—from the private sector into the public domain, and from the bottom—from its customers. Coproduction is the involvement of citizens in producing and delivering public services. Public choice theorists Vincent and Elinor Ostrom were among the first to use the term "coproduction" in their discussion of public goods in relation to institutional arrangements for service delivery (Ostrom and Ostrom, 1971). Ironically, some of the other early proponents of coproduction (discussed in the section that follows) advocated the use of citizen involvement to empower communities, but this idea was quickly overshadowed by the idea of using coproduction to reduce costs.

This emphasis on cost reduction and deemphasis on empowerment was expressed by John Alford, who suggested that problems with coproduction arise when it is too dependent on volunteerism and altruism. "In a climate where market incentives are the dominant currency, [it] seems far too unreliable a motivation on which to based important public functions." The answer is not to rely on the voluntary efforts of citizens, but to base coproduction on clients who are analogous to buyers. "While some of the early theoretical literature mentioned clients or 'consumer producers' . . . it usually collapsed them into 'citizens' or slid into the notion of volunteers" (2000, 129). He goes on to say that, "although no one is seriously suggested a return to an emphasis on direct government production," a more "hard-headed" approach to coproduction by clients is needed (129).

Alford's more hard-headed approach is based on the ideals and norms of the market. He suggests that organizations can provide incentives to clients to behave in ways that can lower organizational costs. For example, if customers write postcards in a particular way, it can make mail sorting easier and reduce costs. If customers can be induced to carry their garbage to the street, it reduces the costs of garbage collection. One way do accomplish this is to simply to require certain actions by the consumer as a condition of receiving the service.

> Derived as it is from the customer in the private sector market, that model assumes an exchange, in which the organization provides goods or services and customer provides money to the amount of the purchase price. Aside from the fact that many public sector clients are beneficiaries who do not pay for the services they receive, client co-production means that the provision of the service is not simply done by the organization in a one-way transfer, but rather is partly done by the client. (Alford 2000, 132)

Brudney and England (1983), on the other hand, argue that coproduction works best to reduce costs and improve performance if it is based on voluntary cooperation on the part of citizens, and on active rather than passive behaviors. But the focus remains on coproduction as a cost-saving measure in response to fiscal constraints: "By supplementing—or perhaps supplanting—the labors of paid public officials with the service-directed activities of urban dwellers, coproduction has the potential to raise both the quality and the efficiency of municipal services" (1983, 959). In other words, in the New Public Management, citizen involvement concerns "*productive* behaviors that can enhance the level and quality of services provided" (Percy 1984, 432, emphasis added).

The New Public Service and Implementation

In the New Public Service, a primary focus of implementation is citizen engagement and community building. Citizens are not treated as potentially interfering with "correct" implementation, nor are they used primarily as vehicles for cost reduction. Instead, citizen engagement is seen as an appropriate and necessary part of policy implementation in a democracy. Because discretion is and must be exercised in policy implementation, that discretion should be informed by citizen participation. Peter deLeon (1999) argues convincingly, for example, that by placing greater emphasis on a democratic, participative forms of implementation, combined with a more postpositivist methodology, we will gain a much better understanding of how implementation can be successful.

In a similar vein, Terry Cooper makes the point that:

> The public administrator should be held ethically responsible for encouraging participation of the citizenry in the process of planning and *providing* public goods and services. Participation may or may not be useful or satisfying to the administrator, but it is essential to the creation and maintenance of a self-governing political community. (Cooper 1991, 143, emphasis added)

In the New Public Service, citizen involvement not limited to setting priorities. In fact, we should manage public organizations so as to enhance and encourage the engagement of citizens in all facets and phases of the policy making and implementation process. Through this process, citizens "come to see themselves as citizens, . . . rather than as consumers, clients, and beneficiaries of the administrative state" (Stivers 1990, 96). Citizens become involved in governance instead of only making demands on government to satisfy their short-term needs. At the same time, the organization becomes "a public space in which human beings [citizens and administrators] with different perspectives . . . act together for the public good" (96). It is this interaction and engagement with citizens that gives purpose and meaning to public service. As Frederickson (1997) puts it, it "ennobles" our work.

From the perspective of the New Public Service, mechanisms like coproduction are derived from the concept of community, not from the concept of the market. Communities are characterized by social interaction, a sense of shared place, and common bonds. As explained by Richard Sundeen (1985), there are three attributes of community—social interaction, shared territory, and common bonds. "These characteristics contribute to the cohesiveness and solidarity of the community with social relations among its members marked by mutual aid, cooperation, and holistic ties—in contrast to segmented, impersonal ties" (388). In this kind of community, citizens and public servants have mutual responsibility for identifying problems and implementing solutions. The absence of these community attributes contribute to self interested and impersonal relationships between people. In this environment, the only way to implement a policy is to offer incentives or disincentives to modify the choices of self-interested individuals.

Worse, we suggest that this view is self-perpetuating. As people are treated as self-interested, utility maximizers, they come to see themselves as consumers of government services not as members of a community. In the New Public Management, citizens generate demands and government is then responsible for producing services to satisfy these demands. The goal is to meet the demands of citizens so that they will favorably judge the performance of government. This model leads to an emphasis on performance measures and productivity indicators to show the citizens that government is doing its job. The consuming public makes demands on government and government sets out to show that it responded. Accordingly, the role of the citizen/customer is limited to demanding, consuming, and evaluating services (Sharpe 1980).

Advocates of the New Public Service argue that too little attention is paid to citizens participating in government decision making and the actual delivery of services. We suggest that coproduction in a community rests on mutual trust, cooperation, and shared responsibility. In the New Public Service, citizens and administrators share responsibility and work together to implement programs. In the process, citizens learn more about government and government learns more about citizens. Charles Levine (1984), for example, speaks directly to this issue, arguing that debates about involving citizens in the delivery of public services too often focus on narrow economic and political criteria. Rather than asking how much money will be saved or how a particular approach will help deal with a contentious political environment, he suggests that we evaluate alternatives according to their potential contribution to enhancing citizenship, including: "(1) citizen trust in government; (2) citizen efficacy; and (3) a shared conception of the 'common good'" (1984, 284).

With regard to privatization, Levine argues that efficiencies will often result because of the advantages of choosing between competitive bidders. However, in the privatization model, the ideal becomes one of government existing to provide a competitive environment where firms provide services to consumers with or without a government contract. Such arrangements do nothing to build citizenship or citizen trust. Rather citizens are viewed and treated as mere consumers of privatized services behaving just as they would buying a service from a business. As a result, "the high citizenship of Pericles, Aristotle, and Rousseau that requires citizens to be active members of a self-governing community is excused by the advocates of privatization as irrelevant in an age of rational, self-centered private interests. . . . Public-spirited action has no place in this scheme" (1984, 285). In short, privatization cannot lead to better citizens, only the possibility of smarter consumers. In contrast, coproduction, as Levine understands it, "lays the foundation for a positive relationship between government and citizens by making citizens an integral part of the service delivery process" (288).

Conclusion

We may conclude by noting that the difference between the New Public Management approach to coproduction and that of the New Public Service is not just a matter of semantics. For example, one of the most widely used applications of coproduction techniques is in area of policing. Think for a minute what a policing program might look like if it were focused only on cost savings and efficiency—the hallmarks of the New Public Management. If a police department sought to enhance efficiency and reduce costs, citizens might, for example, be recruited through a series of incentives or disincentives to report more crime and/or create neighborhood watch activities to prevent criminal activities. These alternatives and others would be evaluated based on the degree to which they reduced the cost of policing services by involving a set of consumers and engaging their assistance to meet police objectives. It might be concluded in some cases and for some functions that privatization is the preferable alternative because of the potential cost savings that can accrue from private firms' hiring less-well-trained and lower-paid security officers. This would also have the advantage of creating competition among security firms to find new and better ways to deliver police services at a lower cost. The role of the police department becomes one of creating a competitive environment. The role of the police officer in relation to coproduction activities would be to ensure that citizens and neighborhood groups understand their objectives clearly and absorb as many policing functions as are practical and cost efficient to reduce and prevent crime. There would be little need for an ongoing relationship between officers and citizens. In fact, such efforts would most likely be costly, as they would divert police personnel from their traditional duties of responding to individual crime calls.

On the other hand, coproduction as derived from the ideals of community and citizenship as in the New Public Service would look very different. Community policing, as it is commonly known, generally involves working with members of community to develop creative solutions to neighborhood problems. Community policing is based on "the concept that police officers and private citizens working together in creative ways can help solve contemporary community problems" (Trajanowicz et al. 1998, 3). This requires a change in the relationship between police officers and citizens, empowering them to set police priorities and involving them in efforts to improve the quality of life in their neighborhoods. While some of the mechanisms employed in these efforts might appear similar to those used in cost-cutting and market-driven strategies, in practice they are different. Neighborhood watches, for example, would be approached as a vehicle for building community ties and the relationship between public employees and citizens to address neighborhood problems. The goal would not be, for example, to reduce the marginal cost of a police officer responding to a call. Rather, the goal would be to build a stronger community, with citizens who are involved and empowered to prevent and reduce crime, and who share with public servants the responsibility for making their communities better. The role of the public servant becomes one of facilitating and encouraging such involvement and helping to build the capacity of citizens.

Chapter 7

Recognize that
Accountability Isn't Simple

Recognize that accountability isn't simple. Public servants should be
attentive to more than the market; they should also attend to statutory and
constitutional law, community values, political norms, professional standards, and citizen interests.

The matter of accountability and responsibility in the public service is extremely complex. Public administrators are and should be held accountable
to a constellation of institutions and standards, including the public interest;
statutory and constitutional law; other agencies; other levels of government;
the media; professional standards; community values and standards; situational factors; democratic norms; and of course, citizens. Indeed, they are
called upon to be responsive to all the competing norms, values, and preferences of our complex governance system. These variables represent overlapping, sometimes contradictory, and ever-evolving points of accountability.
As a result, there are significant challenges involved in "establishing expectations, verifying performance, maintaining responsiveness of agents, assessing blame, sorting out responsibilities, determining who the masters are,
and managing under conditions of multiple accountability systems" (Romzek
and Ingraham 2000, 241–42).

The New Public Service recognizes both the centrality of accountability
in democratic governance and the reality of administrative responsibilities.
We reject the idea that simple measures of efficiency or market-based standards can adequately measure or encourage responsible behavior. Instead,

we argue that accountability in the public sector should be based on the idea that public administrators can and should serve citizens in the public interest, even in situations involving complicated value judgments and overlapping norms. To do so, public administrators must not make these judgments by themselves. Rather, these issues must be resolved based not only on dialogue within organizations, but also on citizen empowerment and broad-based civic engagement. While public servants remain responsible for assuring that solutions to public problems are consistent with laws, democratic norms, and other constraints, it is not a matter of their simply judging the appropriateness of community-generated ideas and proposals after the fact. Rather, it is the role of public administrators to make these conflicts and parameters known to citizens so that these realities become a part of the process of discourse. Doing so not only makes for realistic solutions, it also builds citizenship and accountability.

While accountability in the public service is unavoidably complex, both the Old Public Administration and the New Public Management tend to oversimplify the issue. As will be explored more fully in this chapter, in the classic version of the Old Public Administration, public administrators were simply and directly responsible to political officials. At the other end of the spectrum, in the vernacular of the New Public Management, the focus is on giving administrators great latitude to act as entrepreneurs. In their entrepreneurial role, public managers are called to account primarily in terms of efficiency, cost effectiveness, and responsiveness to market forces.

This chapter considers how our ideas about accountability and responsibility in public administration have evolved and changed over time. First, to define some of the key parameters of the issue, we summarize the classic debate between Carl Friedrich (1940), who argued that professionalism was the best way to ensure accountability, and Herman Finer (1941), who said accountability must be based on external controls. Then we look at the notion of responsibility and the evolution of thought regarding answers to the three big questions of responsibility and accountability: (1) *What* are public administrators are responsible for? (2) To *whom* are they accountable? (3) By what *means* should accountability and responsibility be achieved? Finally, we compare and highlight the implicit and explicit views on accountability and the approaches they suggest, in the Old Public Administration, the New Public Management, and the New Public Service.

The Classic Debate

In a sense, the field of public administration was founded on a claim made by Wilson and others that the question of administrative accountability could be answered by defining the work of public administrators as objective and businesslike—and completely separate from politics. The trouble with accountability, at least intellectually speaking, began anew when the credibility of the politics/administrative dichotomy began to crumble under the pressures of increasingly complex governmental functions. If we cannot explain administrative functions as being largely mechanical and entirely separate from politics, and administrators aren't elected, how then do we hold them responsible? If administrative functions involve discretion, how do we make sure that discretion is exercised in a responsible manner consistent with democratic ideals? What, for that matter, is "responsible" administrative behavior? Finding answers to these questions is as difficult as it is important. As Frederick Mosher said, "Responsibility may well be the most important word in all the vocabulary of administration, public and private" (1968, 7).

Questions about how best to secure accountable and responsible administration encompass some of the most important issues in democratic governance. In fact, one of the defining principles of democracy is the notion of controlled, accountable government. As Dwivedi states, "Accountability is the foundation of any governing process. The effectiveness of that process depends upon how those in authority account for the manner in which they have fulfilled their responsibilities, both constitutional and legal. . . . Consequently, at the very root of democracy lies the requirement for public responsibility and accountability" (1985, 63–64).

The fundamental parameters of the debate about responsibility and accountability in the field of public administration were set forth in a well-known exchange between Carl Friedrich and Herbert Finer. In 1940, as America prepared for war, Friedrich wrote in the journal *Public Policy* that the key to bureaucratic responsibility was professionalism. Friedrich said that administrative responsibility involved much more than simply executing preestablished policy. Policy formulation and execution were, in fact, becoming largely inseparable. Further, administrators were professionals and possessed specialized knowledge and technical expertise that the general citizenry did not have. Because their responsibilities are based on professional knowledge and norms of conduct, administrators should be accountable to their fellow professionals to meet commonly agreed to standards.

It was not, Friedrich said, that being responsive to public sentiment isn't important. Rather, the changing nature of administrative responsibility requires that among technical experts, professionalism, or "craftsmanship" be a central component of accountability (1940, 191). In making this argument, he suggested that there are two aspects of this responsibility: personal and functional. Personal responsibility refers to the administrator's being able to justify his or her actions according to orders, recommendations, and so forth. Functional responsibility involves the administrator's looking to his or her function and professional standards for guidance. There was the potential, he warned, for personal and functional responsibility to conflict. In these cases, both technical knowledge and hierarchy have to be considered.

Friedrich suggested that there are a number of ways to measure and enforce accountability, and "only a combination of all of them offers the prospect of securing the desired results" (1940, 201). But, he said, "officials working in all the more esoteric fields of government service, the ever more numerous scientific activities, both national and international, are more sensitive to and more concerned with the criticism made of their activities by their professional peers than by any superiors in the organizational they serve" (201). Ultimately, as government problems had grown increasingly complex and the need for discretion had expanded, professionalism had become the cornerstone of administrative responsibility.

Herman Finer (1941), from the University of London, disagreed. Writing in response to Freidrich, he said that external controls were the best and only means of ensuring administrative accountability in a democracy. He argued that administrators should be subordinate to elected officials because elected officials are directly responsible to the people. These officials, based on their interpretation of the public's wants, should tell the administrator what to do. Then, the administrator was responsible for carrying out those duties according to those directions. In making this argument, Finer defined responsibility in two ways. The first definition is that "X is accountable for Y to Z." The second (and according to Finer, the wrong-headed) definition involves "a personal sense of moral obligation." He stated, "The second definition puts emphasis on the conscience of the agent, and it follows from the definition that if he commits an error it is an error only when recognized by his own conscience, and that punishment of the agent will be merely the twinges thereof. The one implies public execution; the other hara-kiri" (1941, 336).

Finer argued instead that technical feasibility and knowledge must always be secondary to democratic controls, controls based on three doctrines or ideas. First, he refered to the "mastership of the public," suggesting that public servants don't work for the good of the public based on their sense of what the public *needs*, but rather what the public *says it wants* (1941, 337). The second idea is that institutions must be in place, most particularly an elected body, to express and exert the public authority. Most important, however, is the third idea: that these elected institutions not only to express and channel public wants, but also have the authority to decide and enforce how these wants are to be satisfied.

In this process, if external controls are lacking, abuses of power are inevitable. Finer dismissed Friedrich's argument that administrator's responsibility was more of a moral than a political issue, and that adherence to the standards of their profession was the answer. He further stated that Friedrich "gives the impression of stepping over the dead body of political responsibility to grasp the promissory incandescence of the moral variety" of responsibility (1941, 339). Finer concluded that:

> Moral responsibility is likely to operate in direct proportion to the strictness and efficiency of political responsibility, and to fall away into all sorts of perversions when the latter is weakly enforced. While professional standards, duty to the public, and pursuit of technological efficiency are factors in sound administrative operations, they are but ingredients, and not continuously motivating factors, of sound policy, and they require public and political control and direction. (Finer 1941, 350)

Over the years, Friedrich reaffirmed his position, calling Finer a "pious myth-maker" whose views were unrealistic and outdated (1960). He argued that Finer's views on accountability would not work unless there was clear agreement as to what needed to be done and little or no need for administrative discretion. "When one considers the complexity of modern governmental activities, it is at once evident that such agreement can only be partial and incomplete, no matter who is involved" (3–4). He pointed out that administrative responsibility is more than trying to "keep the government from doing wrong" (4). Rather, the main concern ought to be to ensure effective administrative action. To do this, he said, the interdependencies between the realms of policy making and policy execution had to be considered. "In so far as particular individuals or groups are gaining or losing power or control in a given area, there is politics; in so far as officials act or propose action in the name of public interest, there is administration" (6).

Friedrich once again criticized Finer's contention that external controls must be the basis for ensuring accountability. While political controls are important, "there is arising a type of responsibility on the part of the permanent administrator, the man who is called upon to seek and find the creative solutions for our crying technical needs, which cannot be effectively enforced except by fellow-technicians who are capable of judging his policy in terms of the scientific knowledge bearing upon it" (1960, 14). Besides, external mechanisms of control and measures of accountability "represent approximations, and not very near approximations at that"(14). In other words, unless there is a set of standards based on professional and technical knowledge, that administrators internalize and hold each other accountable to, responsibility cannot be achieved. Friedrich concluded that:

> Responsible conduct of administrative functions is not so much enforced as it is elicited. But it has been the contention all along that responsible conduct is never strictly enforceable, that even under the most tyrannical despot administrative officials will escape effective control-in short, that the problem of how to bring about responsible conduct of the administrative staff of a large organization is, particularly in a democratic society, very largely a question of sound work rules and effective morale. (Friedrich 1960, 19)

In simplest form, Friedrich claims that administrators have to use their technical and professional knowledge in order to be responsible. Therefore, for a public administrator, being accountable means not only following the law and doing what you are told to do by elected officials, but also using the expertise of your profession.

The debate between Friedrich and Finer raised several key questions that remain at the center of contemporary issues regarding democratic accountability. As Dunn and Legee state, "The concepts and methods that define accountability and responsibility constitute fundamental issues in democratic theory because they determine how public policy and administration remain responsive to public preferences" (2000, 74). It is apparent that Friedrich and Finer held very different views of the way in which the policy process ought to work. Friedrich accepted the need for administrative discretion. Finer, on the other hand, wanted to limit it as much as possible. Perhaps most fundamentally, their positions are staked on the rather unsteady foundation of the politics/administration dichotomy: In what manner are the forces of democracy to be balanced with the structure of bureaucracy and professional expertise? What institution or institutions are best suited to articulate public needs and wants? Can the work of administrators be made predictable and objective, and therefore controllable by means of preset measures? Or is it inherently subjective and too complex to reduce to a set of preconceived standards? Is it both? These are questions that have continued to plague efforts to encourage and enforce accountability in the public service, and are not likely to be definitely resolved anytime soon.

Administrative Responsibility: To Whom for What?

The exchange between Friedrich and Finer crystallized some of the key issues with regard to administrative accountability in the democratic process. Not too surprisingly, since that time, most administrators and writers in the field have located themselves somewhere in the middle of the controversy, saying that administrative accountability requires both external controls and professionalism. As Marshall Dimock and Gladys Dimock expressed it, accountability is a legal and moral issue that is enforced both internally and externally:

> To be accountable means to act responsibly, that is, in accordance with predetermined standards of propriety. For the public administrator, however, accountability is more than a matter of manners and custom; it is a matter of law. To be accountable also describes a person on whom one can count. For the administrator, this means knowing his duty and doing it— being honest and acting with probity. Thus the combined modern meaning of accountability is duty, both legal and moral. (Dimock and Dimock 1969, 123)

Accountability in public administration is achieved by both internal and external means. Internal controls are those that are established and enforced within an agency when "the administrator himself or someone alongside or above him in the hierarchy sees that he does his duty" (Dimock and Dimock 1969, 123). External controls may involve legislative supervision, budget and audit activities; the use of an office such as an ombudsman, criticism from the press, and oversight by consumer groups, interest groups, and other concerned individuals.

Unfortunately, despite the appeal of this more balanced view, it does not "solve" the issue of accountability, nor does it tell us exactly what to do about it. As a result, questions about accountability have continued to revolve around a set of tensions in the field of public administration that can be expressed in three deceptively simple questions: (1) *What* are we responsible for? (2) To *whom* are we responsible? and (3) *How* is that responsibility best ensured? Depending on how these questions are answered, and in what order of importance, different perspectives on the most appropriate systems of administrative accountability are suggested. Most problematic is usually the last question: We can set forth propositions about what we are responsible for and to whom, but figuring out how to ensure accountability is not an easy proposition.

For example, Maass and Radaway (1959) clearly state their positions (which they called "working biases") on the first two questions. In fact, they largely dismiss the first question (responsible for what?) in one sentence, stating that administrative agencies should be responsible for formulating as well as executing policy. With regard to the second question (to whom are administrators responsible?), their answers are somewhat more qualified. They begin by saying that administrators should not be held directly responsible to the public at large or to political parties. But administrative agencies should be responsible to pressure groups in order to allow them sufficient access and information to safeguard their interests. The primary responsibility of administrators is "to the legislature, but only through the chief executive, and primarily for broad issues of public policy and general administrative performance"(1959, 169), leading back to the question of for what they are responsible. Maass and Radaway suggest that administrators are responsible for conforming to the general program of the chief executive and coordinating activities with other executive branch agencies to carry out that program. Further, they should be "responsible for maintaining, developing, and applying such professional standards as may be relevant to its activities" (176).

With these answers in hand, Maass and Radaway turn to the question of how accountability is to be achieved under these circumstances. Because the basic principles of administrative responsibility are often equivocal and mutually incompatible, the question of how to ensure accountability cannot be answered generically. They suggest, therefore, that it is necessary to use the more practical and modest language of "criteria" of responsibility. Some of these criteria may conflict with others, "but all of which must be weighted and applied together in any attempt to gauge the responsibility of a specific administrative agency"(1959, 163). There is no one-size-fits-all solution. As we said at the beginning of this chapter, accountability is complex. In the words of Maass and Radaway:

> [A]dministrative responsibility . . . has been termed the sum total of the constitutional, statutory, administrative, judicial, and professional practices by which public officers are restrained and controlled in their official actions. But it is not possible to identify the *criteria* for gauging administrative responsibility by relying on such general language. It becomes necessary, therefore, to relate the general concept of responsibility to the specific functions of power (i.e., responsibility to whom?) and purpose (i.e., responsibility for what?). (Maass and Radaway 1959, 164)

One answer, then, would be to make sure that accountability and responsibility (or authority) were always in balance in a given circumstance. In other words, an administrator would only be held responsible for those things for which he or she had authority and responsibility. But there are potential problems with this as well. Herbert Spiro, in *Responsibility in Government* (1969), points out that such a proposition is not very practical and raises questions that inevitably lead to confusion. Even the word "responsibility" itself has multiple definitions and uses, and it is used more often than it is defined. This lack of definitional clarity, he says, contributes to the controversy and confusion.

His argument is that there are three different connotations used when addressing responsibility: accountability, cause, and obligation. Like several other authors, but using different terms, Spiro argues that accountability can be either explicit or implicit. Explicit accountability refers to having to answer and account for how an administrator carries out his or her official tasks. But, he says, "All of us are implicitly accountable to the extent that we may be unexpectedly affected by the consequences of decisions made by other human beings" (1969, 15). In other words, people can be held implicitly responsible for outcomes that they did not directly cause. Explicit causal responsibility, on the other hand, "consists of four elements, present in varying degrees under different circumstances: resources, knowledge, choice, and purpose" (16). Implicit causal responsibility occurs when one or more of these elements is lacking.

Discussions about responsibility that confuse accountability with causal responsibility, or that assume that responsibility and accountability are in balance are bound to be unrealistic. "As a matter of *fact*, this is simply not so. As a matter of *value*, however, advocacy of a fair balance between causal responsibility and accountability is quite possible (Spiro 1969, 17). But a reasonable imbalance is not necessary a bad thing, according to Spiro. If the function of responsibility is to preserve social conscience, then it might be appropriate that someone is held accountable for an event that he or she did not directly, or solely cause. On the other hand, Spiro writes:

> From the viewpoint of constitutional democracy, however, we would have to advocate a fair balance between these two faces of responsibility, between accountability and causal responsibility. We would not want to hold a person accountable for an event to which he made no causal contribution. . . . We would want him to be in a sound *situation of responsibility*, in which causal responsibility stands in fair balance with accountability. (Spiro 1969, 18)

Under these circumstances, figuring out how to ensure responsibility is difficult. The issue is not whether we want public administrators to be responsible—we do. The more important issue is *how* to ensure accountability, an issue that goes directly back to the Friedrich-Finer debate. If accountability mechanisms focus on the constitutional and legal framework alone, and do not take into account other sources of knowledge and resources, the purpose becomes one of negatively restraining bureaucrats. If we take a broader approach, accountability can have the more positive purpose of enhancing responsibility across the public sphere. Spiro states:

> We must give up excessive preoccupation with the bureaucrat's situation in favor of the individual citizen's. This is true especially because bureau-

crat and citizen are no longer opposites who face each other in attitudes of constant hostility. Moreover, the bureaucrat is also a citizen. By virtue of assuming his delegated, specific, additional responsibility and accountability *qua* bureaucrat, he does not surrender his original, general responsibility *qua* citizen. His situation as a citizen, and that of his fellow citizens, must be the main center of our attention." (Spiro 1969, 101)

From this perspective, then, the focus should be on the character and ethics of the individual administrator. Some have suggested, in fact, that at its core, accountability is a question of ethics, and that the role of administrator should be reconceived as an ethical actor. As Dwivedi states, "Unethical administration is the antithesis of accountable administration" (1985, 65). The work of Terry Cooper exemplifies the thinking of those who would focus on ethics as the basis for accountable and responsible administrative action. In *The Responsible Administrator* (1998), Cooper examines the ethical decision-making process and proposes a model for addressing ethical problems. Like several other writers, Cooper discusses the objective (external) and subjective (internal) natures of responsibility. He argues that the problems that arise when there is conflict between these two forms of responsibility are fundamentally ethical in nature. Ethical conduct, Cooper suggests, is enhanced by both internal and external controls. This is so, he says, because there are four components of responsible conduct: individual attributes, organizational culture, organizational structure, and societal expectations. Individual ethical behavior, he argues, requires individual ethical autonomy and self-awareness as well as limits to the reach and power of organizations.

What can we conclude from all this? We can suggest that several generations of scholars have determined that administrative accountability is difficult to define and even more difficult to enforce. This is in part a function of the complexity of the administrative process as a component of the larger system of governance. The result is the complex web of accountability mechanisms and systems that characterize the current American governmental system. Romzek and Ingraham (2000) provide a useful framework for understanding these multiple perspectives on accountability. They suggest that there are four primary types of accountability based on whether they are internal or external, and whether they assume high or low levels of individual autonomy. The first type is hierarchical accountability, which is "based on close supervision of individuals who have low work autonomy." Second, legal accountability involves "detailed external oversight of performance for compliance with established mandates . . . such as legislative and constitutional structures." This would include fiscal audits and oversight hearings, for example. Third, professional accountability is based on "arrangements that afford high degrees of autonomy to individuals who based their decision making on internalized norms of appropriate practice." Finally, political accountability requires responsiveness to "key external stakeholders, such as elected officials, clientele groups, the general public, and so on" (2000, 242)

Romzek and Ingraham point out that while all of these types of accountability relationships are present, some forms may become more dominant while others may become largely dormant in a given circumstance. In times of reform, they say, "there is often a shift in emphasis and priority among the different types of accountability" (2000, 242). In the sections that follow, we will discuss the assumptions about and forms of accountability that can be seen as dominant in the Old Public Administration, the New Public Management, and the New Public Service.

The Old Public Administration and Accountability

A formal, hierarchical and legal view of accountability characterizes the Old Public Administration and remains, in some ways, the most familiar model for viewing administrative responsibility and accountability today. This view of accountability relies on the assumption that administrators do not and should not exercise significant amounts of discretion. Rather, they simply implement the laws, rules and standards set forth for them by hierarchical superiors, elected officials and the courts. Accountability, according to adherents of the Old Public Administration, focuses on ensuring that administrators adhere to standards and conform to rules and procedures established for them in carrying out their functions. It is not a matter of using discretion appropriately and responsibly, it is a matter of avoiding the use of discretion by closely adhering to the law, regulation, organizational procedures, and directives of the supervisor.

In this view, direct responsiveness or accountability to the public was, implicitly at least, seen as unnecessary and inappropriate. Elected officials were seen as solely responsible and accountable for translating the public will into policy. As Goodnow presented it, "Politics has to do with the guiding or influencing of governmental policy, while administration has to do with the execution of that policy" (1987, 28). The public had little or no direct role in the administrative or policy execution process. Wilson, in fact, seemed to want to buffer the governing process from popular interests, thus preventing the people from becoming "meddlesome" by direct involvement. In the Old Public Administration, responsible administrators were those who possessed and relied on their expertise and "neutral competence." Accordingly, responsible administrative action was based on scientific, value-neutral principles.

It is not difficult to see the continued influence of this perspective in present-day, institutionalized accountability systems. A quick review of the topics included in Rosen's (1998) edition of *Holding Government Bureaucracies Accountable*, for example, presents a broad array of processes, institutions, and mechanisms for ensuring formal accountability. Within the executive branch, hierarchical supervision, the budget and audit process, performance evaluations systems, and oversight by staff agencies such as personnel and purchasing departments are used to hold the actions of administrators in check and to ensure compliance with laws, procedures, and regulations. The legislative branch also uses a range of accountability mechanisms, including the appropriations process, committee oversight, hearings and investigations, reporting requirements, and legislative audit. The courts also employ a number of administrative controls, through judicial review and case law, as well as their oversight and interpretation of the Administrative Procedure Act of 1946 (which governs the procedures and process which executive agencies must use in establishing and applying governmental regulations). Most of these approaches rely, to a greater or lesser degree, on formal, external notions of accountability—that is, that administrators are responsible for adhering to objective external controls and answering for their actions in relation to established standards and the preferences of key stakeholders.

The New Public Management and Accountability

In a sense, the views of accountability advocated by the adherents of the New Public Management echo those of the Old Public Administration in that there is a continued reliance on objective measurement and external controls. There are important differences, however. First, in the New Public Management, the assumption is that traditional bureaucracy is ineffective because it measures and controls inputs rather than results. As Osborne and Gaebler state, "Because they don't measure results, bureaucratic governments rarely achieve them" (1992, 139). Controlling inputs, such as money and personnel, rather than results, such as the cleanliness of streets or the knowledge gained by children, leads to government failure. Osborne and Gaebler argue that the answer is to look to the business model: "Private organizations focus on results because they will go out of business if the key numbers go negative" (139).

Again, as with the New Public Management generally, the assumption is that business and the market model are superior and ought to be emulated in the public sector. Since government agencies cannot go out of business when they do not produce results, performance measurement must be used as a surrogate measure for what in business is the bottom line—profit. The focus of accountability is, then, on meeting performance standards to produce results.

Second, the public is reconceptualized as a market made up of individual customers who each act in a manner to serve their self-interest. In this way, public agencies are not primarily accountable, either directly or indirectly, to citizens or to the public or common good. Rather, they are accountable to their "customers." The responsibility of government then is to offer choices to their customers and to respond to their expressed individual preferences in terms of the services and functions provided. Accountability is a matter of satisfying the preferences of the direct customers of governmental services.

The third difference in the dominant view on administrative accountability suggested in the New Public Management perspective is the reliance on privatization. There is a strong emphasis in the New Public Management on privatizing previously public functions whenever possible. Again, this shifts accountability from a public to a private perspective, focusing again on the bottom line. As such, accountability systems in privatized government emphasize the provision of services and functions that produce desired results in the most cost-effective manner possible while satisfying their customers.

The New Public Service and Accountability

Perspectives on accountability in the New Public Service stand in contrast to both the Old Public Administration and the New Public Management. Measures of efficiency and results are important, but they cannot address or encompass the other expectations we hold for public administrators to act responsibly, ethically, and in accordance with democratic principles and the public interest. In the New Public Service, the ideals of citizenship and the public interest are at center stage.

Accountability in the New Public Service is multifaceted and demanding in recognition of the complex roles played by public administrators in contemporary governance. The New Public Management artificially oversimplifies the issue of accountability in several ways. Kettl expresses it even more strongly: that the pursuit of businesslike practices and market-driven reforms constitutes an "aggressive attack on the tradition of democratic accountability" (1998, v). First, privatization and attempts to mimic the private sector narrow the scope of accountability and place the focus on meeting standards and satisfying customers. Such approaches do not reflect the multiple, overlapping channels of accountability in the public sector because the standards in the private sector are simply less stringent (Mulgan 2000). A private company being responsible to its shareholders is not analogous to a

government agency being responsive to its citizens. While private companies are invariably and primarily accountable for producing a profit, the
public sector must pay more attention to process and policy. In government,
"The emphasis is on the accountability of public power, on how to make
governments, their agencies and officials, more accountable to their ultimate
owners, the citizens" (Mulgan 2000, 87).

Glen Cope (1997) also makes important observations in this regard. She
suggests that there are a number of reasons that responsiveness to citizens is
different than responsiveness to customers. In order to be responsive to customers, private enterprise attempts to provide a product or service that is
desirable and of acceptable quality, as inexpensively as possible. Customers
don't have to like the product or buy it unless they choose to do so. The
serving of customers is driven by the profit motive: Enough customers have
to be satisfied so they will buy the product or service at the designated price.
Response to citizens, on the other hand, is distinctly different. Government
should provide a service or product that the majority of citizens want. Since
buying the product or service is not voluntary in that it is often paid for by
tax revenues, "This creates a special responsibility for government not only
to satisfy its immediate customers and operate in a cost-efficient manner, but
also to deliver services that its citizens have requested" (1997, 464).

Second, the New Public Management does not place an appropriate degree of emphasis on public law and democratic norms. Public accountability
is lessened when governmental services are performed by nonprofit or private organizations that are not bound by public law principles (Leazes 1997).
As Gilmore and Jensen suggest, "Because private actors are not subject to the
same constitutional, statutory, and oversight restrictions as governmental
actors, delegation of public functions outside the bounds of government
profoundly challenges traditional notions of accountability, making it all the
more difficult. . . " (1998, 248).

In the New Public Service, if private administrators are to function as
public ones, they should become subject to public standards of accountability. Based on his examination of a state's child welfare program, Leazes
concludes that, "Efficiency and effectiveness alone are not the only public
administration standards available to measure the success of privatization.
The accountability inherent in public law that relates to the safeguarding of
democratic, constitutional administration should have an equal place at the
privatization policy-implementation table" (1997, 10). Typically, however,
they cannot and do not.

The focus on results or outcomes popularized by advocates of the New
Public Management does not satisfy the need for accountability to democratic norms and values either. As Myers and Lacey state, "The performance

of civil servants should be judged . . . according to the extent to which they uphold such values, just as much, if not more than, on their success at meeting output targets" (1996, 343). That is not to say that attention to results and output measures isn't important. By focusing on results, public organizations can make important improvements to the benefit of the people they serve. But it does suggest that results-oriented performance measures ought to be developed based on an open public process; they should not be developed and imposed by those in government simply to mimic measures of profit.

Third, in the New Public Management, the public administrator is conceived of as an entrepreneur, seeking opportunities to create private partnerships and serve customers. This perspective on the role of the public administrator is narrow, and is poorly suited to achieve democratic principles such as fairness, justice, participation, and the articulation of shared interests. The very qualities that make an administrator a good entrepreneur, may in fact make him or her an ineffective public servant. Cooper states, "The attributes associated with effective administration and management in the business world, such as competitiveness and profit orientation, may be unsuited to, or less appropriate to, the interests of democratic political society" (1998, 149). In fact, he points out, if concern for efficiency is given more than secondary importance, the openness to popular sovereignty may well be compromised.

The New Public Service rejects all three of these assumptions about accountability advanced by the New Public Management. The complexity of public accountability faced by public servants is recognized as a challenge, an opportunity, and a calling. It requires expertise, a commitment to democratic ideals, a knowledge of public law, and judgment informed by experience, community norms, and ethical conduct. Accountability in the New Public Service suggests a reconceptualization of the role of the public servant as leader, steward, and emissary of the public interest, not as an entrepreneur. As Kevin Kearns states, despite "the fact that accountability is an untidy construct . . . debates on accountability should be informed by its poor structure, not deterred by it. To this end, any truly meaningful dialogue should be guided by an analytical framework that embraces the many dimensions of accountability and allows contextual factors and subjective judgments to surface for informed dialogue on assumptions" (1994, 187).

Legal, constitutional, and democratic principles are an incontrovertible centerpiece of responsible administrative action. The New Public Service differs from both the Old Public Administration and the New Public Management in its emphasis on elevating the importance and centrality of citizenship and the public as the basis for accountable and responsible public action. Put simply, the source of public administrators' authority is the citizenry. "Public Administrators are employed to exercise that authority on their behalf. They do so as one of citizenry; they can never divest themselves of their own status as members of the political community with obligations for its well being" (Cooper 1991, 145). Accountability requires that public servants interact with and listen to citizens in a manner that empowers and reinforces their role in democratic governance. As N. Joseph Cayer states, "The purposes of citizen participation is generally to make administration more responsive to the public and to enhance the legitimacy of governmental programs and agencies" (1986, 171). Responsible behavior requires that public administrators interact with their fellow citizens, not as customers but as members of a democratic community.

In *Bureaucratic Responsibility* (1986), John Burke says that in light of the problems with accountability, and of inherent tensions between the values of bureaucracy and democracy, our attention should focus on "how bureaucratic officials conceive of their roles, duties, and obligations and especially what principles might guide them in a more responsible, accountable direction" (1986, 5). He suggests that a "democratically grounded conception of responsibility" is "derived not just from formal rules, regulations, and laws but from a broader understanding of the bureaucrat's place within a more encompassing set of political institutions and processes" (39).

There are two major components of this model of democratic responsibility. The first is a public servant's responsibility to take political authority seriously. The second involves a set of responsibilities that hinge on obligations with respect to the duties of others as well as the role of the responsible public servants in policy formulation and implementation. This democratic model, Burke argues, "attempts to reconcile the potentially conflicting allegiances owed politics and the profession by demarcating a domain within which expertise is granted license and autonomy" (1986, 149).

Importantly, Burke argues that the multiple views of moral obligation, responsibility, and their political relevance cannot be resolved based on an administrator's own sense of what is right. Rather, such judgments must be made as part of a participatory process. Burke states:

> Not only do the specific obligations posited by a democratic conception of responsibility enhance participatory processes and outcomes, but the general sense of responsibility it fosters—especially its democratic source and character—facilitates the goals of participation. It embodies an implicit ethos of taking democracy seriously, whether its structure is formal or informal, centralized or decentralized. (Burke 1986, 214)

This viewpoint is also exemplified by Edward Weber's (1999) discussion of the grass-roots ecosystem management (GREM) model, which looks at administrative accountability "in a world of decentralized governance, shared power, collaborative decision processes, results-oriented management, and broad civic participation" (1999, 451). The GREM model looks at political responsiveness, administrative performance, and a normative dimension when assessing accountability. While Weber is speaking directly to the issue of accountability and responsiveness, his arguments also apply to the question of how we view and evaluate the administrative discretion exercised in policy implementation. He challenges the view that responsiveness is "a one way street" emanating from elected officials, suggesting instead that responsiveness and accountability are "a matter of both top-down policy commands from political and administrative superiors and bottom-up input from community-based stakeholders as well as others" (454–55). Although the model gives weight to bottom-up participation, legal and hierarchical accountability are also important. He is suggesting, in essence, a holistic policy focus that provides for adaptive management and citizen involvement.

In the New Public Service, accountability is broadly defined to encompass a range of professional, legal, political, and democratic responsibilities. But "The ultimate aim of accountability and responsibility mechanisms in democratic policies is to assure responsiveness by government to citizens' preferences and needs" (Dunn and Legge 2000, 75). This accountability and responsibility is best achieved by a public service that acknowledges and responds to the multiple and conflicting norms and factors that can and should influence an administrator's actions. The key to balancing these factors in a responsible and democratically accountable fashion rests with citizen engagement, empowerment, and dialogue. Public administrators are neither neutral experts nor business entrepreneurs. They are called upon to be responsible actors in a complex governance system, in which they may play the roles of facilitators; reformers; interest brokers; public relations experts; crisis managers; brokers; analysts; advocates; and most importantly, moral leaders and stewards of the public interest (Vinzant and Crothers 1998; Terry 1995).

If public functions are privatized, or "reinvented" so as to mirror private sector corporations, democratic values become less important. Instead, the focus is placed on market efficiency and the achievement of the governmental "bottom line." Particularly when privatization involves functions that are vital to the public interest (such as medical care, welfare, or education), the relationship between government and citizen becomes more complex than merely the provision of a service to a customer. Accordingly, more than market-driven measures of efficiency are required to hold the government accountable (Gilmore and Jensen 1998). In the private sector, financial incentives and shareholder preferences guide an administrator's behavior. When public functions are either given over to the private sector or reconfigured to mimic in the private model, public accountability for equity, citizen access, and the constitutional and statutory rights of citizens are almost by definition compromised, if not lost. As Shamsul Haque states, "The hallmark of public bureaucracy is its accountability to the public for its policies and actions. Without the realization of such accountability, public bureaucracy loses its identity of publicness, surrenders its public legitimacy, and may relegate itself to the fetish of self-seeking private interests" (1994, 265).

As Michael Harmon (1995) puts it, responsibility remains a paradox. The paradox is that the nature of responsibility upholds two contrasting ideas: moral accountability versus answerability to an organization. He argues that conceptions of responsibility that rely on the concepts of agency (acting on behalf of), accountability and obligation do not take into account the element of morality. Because of this lack of emphasis on morality, three paradoxes arise: the paradox of obligation, the paradox of blame, and the paradox of accountability. The paradox of obligation suggests that if "public servants are free to choose but at the same time are obliged to act only as others authoritatively choose for them, then they are not, for all practical purposes, free. If on the other hand, public servants do choose freely, their actions may violate authoritative obligations, in which case, their exercise of free choice is irresponsible" (1995, 102). The paradox of agency occurs when taking personal responsibility for acting as a moral agent conflicts with answerability to others. Conversely, "the claim of moral innocence implied in the assertion of ultimate answerability to others can only be achieved by the individual's denial of agency" (128). The paradox of accountability, Harmon says, is that, when

> public servants are accountable solely for the effective achievement of purposes mandated by political authority, then as mere instruments of that authority they bear no personal responsibility as moral agents for the products of their actions. If, on the other hand, public servants actively participate in determining public purposes, their accountability is compromised and political authority is undermined. (Harmon 1995, 164)

Harmon concludes, "the rational reform of government institutions is no substitute for, and in fact may well prevent, strengthening the communal bonds that form the substance of the institutions themselves" (1995, 207). In other words, public servants are rightly called upon to be accountable, answerable, responsible, and moral; to choose any one of these qualities to the exclusion of the others places democratic government at risk. Despite the inherent tensions, and difficulty, if not impossibility, of perfectly and fully satisfying each facets of accountability in every circumstance, that is what we, as a society, demand of our public servants. Fortunately, with courage and professionalism, they are doing so every day in communities across America. It is our responsibility as a field to acknowledge the difficulty of their jobs, prepare them, applaud their successes, and advance the democratic values that surround what they do.

Conclusion

The question of accountability in the public service is a complex one, involving balancing competing norms and responsibilities within a complicated web of external controls; professional standards; citizen preferences; moral issues; public law; and ultimately, the public interest. Or as Robert Behn puts it, "To whom must public managers be accountable? The answer is 'everyone'" (2001, 120). In other words, public administrators are called upon to be responsive to all the competing norms, values, and preferences of our complex governance system. Accountability is not, and cannot be made, simple. The tensions and paradoxes that Harmon and others identify are irreducible and unavoidable in our democratic system of governance. It is a mistake, in our estimation, to oversimplify the nature of democratic accountability by focusing only on a narrow set of performance measures or by attempting to mimic market forces—or, worse, by simply hiding behind notions of neutral expertise. To do so calls into question the nature of democracy, and the role of citizenship and a public service dedicated to serving citizens in the public interest. The New Public Service recognizes that being a public servant is a demanding, challenging, sometimes heroic endeavor involving accountability to others, adherence to the law, morality, judgment, and responsibility.

Chapter 8

Serve Rather than Steer

Serve rather than steer. It is increasingly important for public servants to use shared, value-based leadership in helping citizens articulate and meet their shared interests rather than attempting to control or steer society in new directions.

We noted in Chapter 5 that public policy is increasingly being made through the interaction of many different groups and organizations, overlapping and often competing in their interests and jurisdictions and engaged in efforts to meet both individual and collective goals through an open-ended, fluid, and often chaotic process. We also noted some of the ways in which citizens' views can be brought to bear on that process of building public policy in a democratic fashion. Here we will focus more on the way in which various groups and interests can be brought together in a collaborative manner to achieve mutually satisfactory ends. More particularly, we will ask how leadership can be brought to bear where "no one is in charge." Under those circumstances, in which there is little evidence of formal or traditional leadership, there may seem to be a vacuum of leadership—at least if we think of leadership primarily as the exercise of power over others. Leadership is still needed; in fact, leadership is needed more than ever. What is needed, however, is leadership of a new kind.

Changing Perspectives on Leadership

Certainly there is agreement that the traditional top-down models of leadership we associate with such groups as the military are outdated and unworkable in modern society. This is an idea, in fact, that is even accepted in the military. As we have seen, today's society can be described as (1) highly turbulent, subject to sudden and dramatic shifts; (2) highly interdependent, requiring cooperation across many sectors; and (3) greatly in need of creative and imaginative solutions to the problems facing us. Under these conditions, public (and private) organizations need to be considerably more adaptable and flexible than in the past. Yet the traditional command and control form of leadership doesn't encourage risk and innovation. Quite to the contrary, it encourages uniformity and convention. For this reason, many people now argue that a new approach to leadership is desirable.

Leadership is changing in many ways, and we should be attentive to those changes. First, in today's world and certainly in tomorrow's, more and more people are going to want to participate in the decisions that affect them. In the traditional top-down model of organizational leadership, the leader was the one who established the vision of the group, designed ways of achieving that vision, and inspired or coerced others into helping to realize that vision. But increasingly those in organizations want to be involved; they want a piece of the action. Moreover, clients or citizens also want to participate, as they should. As Warren Bennis correctly predicted a few years ago, "leadership . . . will become an increasingly intricate process of multilateral brokerage. . . . More and more decisions will be public decisions, that is, the people they affect will insist on being heard" (1992, 311).

Second, leadership is increasingly being thought of not as a position in a hierarchy, but as a process that occurs throughout organizations (and beyond). In the past, a leader was considered the person who held a formal position of power in an organization or a society. Increasingly, however, we are coming to think of leadership as a process occurring throughout organizations and societies. Leadership is not just something reserved for the presidents, governors, mayors, or department heads; rather, it is something that everyone throughout our organizations and our society will become involved in from time to time. Indeed, there are many who argue that such a shift in the distribution of leadership will be necessary for our survival. John Gardner, the former cabinet secretary and founder of the public interest group Common Cause, states, "In this country leadership is dispersed among all elements of society and down through all levels, and the system simply won't work as it should unless large numbers of people throughout society are prepared to take leader-like action to make things work at their level" (1987, 1).

It's safe to predict that, over the coming years, we will see more and more instances of what we will term "shared leadership" in public organizations, both within public organizations and as administrators relate to their many external constituencies. In our view, the notion of shared leadership is especially important in the public sector as administrators work with citizens and citizen groups of all kinds. As was suggested in Chapter 5, public administrators will need to develop and employ new leadership skills that include important elements of empathy, consideration, facilitation, negotiation, and brokering.

Third, we should understand that leadership is not just about doing things right, it's about doing the right things. In other words, leadership is inevitably associated with important human values, including the most fundamental public values, values such as freedom, equality, and justice. Through the process of leadership people work together to make choices about the directions that they want to take; they make fundamental decisions about their futures. Such choices cannot be made simply on the basis of a rational calculation of costs and benefits. They require a careful balancing of human values, especially as citizens and governmental officials work together in the development of public policies. Leadership, as we will see, can play a "transformational" role in this process, helping people to confront important values and to grow and develop individually and collectively. Accordingly, a number of recent writers on leadership have urged that we examine the "servant" role of leadership and that we be attentive to "leading with soul."

We will suggest in this chapter that the public administrator of today and especially tomorrow will have to develop quite a different understanding of leadership than that associated with the Old Public Administration or the New Public Management. Leadership will need to be dramatically reconceptualized. At a minimum, the role of public leaders will be (1) to help the community and its citizens to understand their needs and their potential, (2) to integrate and articulate the community's vision and that of the various organizations active in any particular area, and (3) to act as a trigger or stimulus for action. This reconceptualization of public leadership is variously described as shared leadership, values-based leadership, and street-level leadership. Before we examine these alternatives, which we associate most clearly with the New Public Service, we should briefly review the approaches to leadership taken by the Old Public Administration and the New Public Management.

The Old Public Administration and Executive Management

As we saw earlier, the prevailing view of leadership in the Old Public Administration was based on a model of executive management. Recall that Woodrow Wilson first argued for creating single centers of power and responsibility, an admonition upon which a number of early writers elaborated. W.F. Willoughby, for example, argued that administrative authority should first be vested in a chief executive, who should have the power and authority necessary to create a "single, integrated piece of administrative machinery" (1927, 37). The next step is to group similar activities together in units reflecting a division of labor. In turn, a management hierarchy can be created through which the executive can essentially control the behavior of those lower in the organization. The key principles underlying this interpretation of executive leadership were exactly those found in business organizations of the time—unity of command, hierarchical/top-down authority, and the division of labor.

This preoccupation with organizational design, that is designing organizations through which control might be effectively exercised, was certainly a topic of great interest to business leaders of the time. For example, two former General Motors executives, James Mooney and Alan C. Reiley (1939) identified four "principles" around which organizations might be built. The first was coordination through unity of command, the idea that strong executive leadership should be exercised through a hierarchical chain of authority. In such a structure, each person would have only one boss and each boss would supervise a limited number of subordinates, leaving no question about whose orders were to be obeyed. Second, Mooney and Reiley described the "scalar" principle, the vertical division of labor among various levels of the organization. For example, in the military, the difference between a general and a private would be a "scalar" difference. A third principle, the "functional" principle described the horizontal division of labor, as in the distinction between infantry and artillery. Fourth, there was the distinction between line and staff, with line offices reflecting directly the chain of command through which authority flows, and staff offices providing advice to line officers. Not surprisingly, these concerns for administrative structure were frequently illustrated by examples from the military, seen as the epitome of rationalized authority.

The top-down nature of internal organizational management in the Old Public Administration was, for the most part, paralleled by a similar approach to relations between government agencies and the citizenry or their "clients." As we noted earlier, administrators came to play a more and more influential role in the process of policy development, though always with an eye toward maintaining the primacy of the elected official. In this process the role of the citizenry was seen as limited—largely one of periodically electing officials, then standing on the "sidelines" to watch them perform. At least until the mid-1960s, citizen involvement in agency operations was extremely limited. True enough, some writers questioned that omission. Leonard White, for example, argued against excessive centralization of power in part because citizens need to gain experience in assuming their civic responsibility. "If administration is to be the work of a highly centralized bureaucracy, it is impossible to expect a sense of personal responsibility (on the part of citizens) for good government" (1926, 96, parenthesis added). Luther Gulick, on the other hand, pursued a much more active and independent role for the administrator, one in which citizen involvement was at best a device for securing compliance, at worst an unnecessary inconvenience. According to Gulick, "the success of the operation of democracy must not be made to depend upon extended or continuous political activity by citizens nor upon unusual knowledge of intelligence to deal with complicated questions" (1933, 558). Policy determination, in other words, should be left to the "experts."

For the most part, agencies and their leaders were either concerned with the regulation of behavior or with direct service delivery. In either case, detailed policies and procedures were devised, mostly to protect the rights and responsibilities of both agency personnel and their clients. Despite their noble purposes, these policies and procedures often became so cumbersome that they restricted the capacity of the agency to meet clients' needs. Thus, government agencies and their managers came to be viewed as inefficient and rule-bound, hopelessly wrapped in "red tape."

The New Public Management and Entrepreneurship

In the New Public Management, the need for leadership is at least partially eclipsed by decision rules and incentives. In such cases, leadership does not reside in a person; rather the aggregation of individual choices replaces the need for some leadership functions. For example, Don Kettl says that a key issue in market-based reform is "How can government use market-style incentives to root out the pathologies of bureaucracy?" (2000a, 1). In some cases, governments have completely set adrift certain public functions, such as those performed by telephone companies, airlines, and power companies, so that they might simply compete in the market. In many other cases, governments have contracted out the delivery of services ranging from trash collection to prisons. Still others have tried to create mechanisms for consumer choice, through alternative systems of service delivery or through such efforts as providing "vouchers" for needed services. In any case, the New Public Management aims to replace traditional, rule-based service delivery with market-based, competition-driven tactics. Citizens are "led" by their preferences to one choice or another.

Osborne and Gaebler (1992) explicitly describe a reduced service delivery role for government as a better way of "leading" society. They recommend that government should move increasingly away from a service delivery role (which they call "rowing") and instead attend to policy development (which they call "steering"). Steering organizations set policy, provide funding to operational agencies (whether governmental or nongovernmental), and evaluate performance. They establish a structure of "incentives" for

which agencies can compete or for which citizens can choose. But they are
not actually involved in delivering services. What are the benefits of such an
approach? Osborne and Gaebler write:

> Freeing policy managers to shop around for the most effective and effi-
> cient service providers helps them squeeze more bang out of every buck. It
> allows them to use *competition* between service providers. It preserves
> maximum *flexibility* to respond to changing circumstances. And it helps
> them insist on *accountability* for quality performance, contractors know
> they can be let go if their quality sags; civil servants know they cannot.
> (Osborne and Gaebler 1992, 35, italics in original)

Another element of New Public Management's approach to public leadership is its insistence on injecting competition into areas that previously were
governmental "monopolies." By establishing competitive bidding processes
for such services as trash collection, many cities have substantially reduced
their costs; but even more dramatic departures from tradition have been urged.
For example, many jurisdictions are experimenting with school choice as a
device for creating competition within the educational system. The idea is
simply that schools should be given enough autonomy to manage their own
resources and then the market would determine which school is most effective
as students "vote with their feet." The incentive mechanism works in several
directions. Schools have an incentive—high enrollments—to demonstrate high
quality. Students have an incentive to seek out the best school system.

What is important for our discussion here is that market incentives are
employed by the New Public Management *as a substitute for public leadership.* Osborne and Gaebler, for example, enthusiastically endorse a statement
from John Chubb, coauthor of an important book on school choice.

> You can get effective schools through other means—such as the force of
> powerful leadership. But if we have to rely on the development of truly
> unusual leaders in order to save our schools, our prospects simply aren't
> going to be very good. The current system is simply not set up to encour-
> age that kind of leadership. A system of competition and choice, on the
> other hand, automatically provides the incentives for schools to do what is
> right. (quoted in Osborne and Gaebler 1992, 95)

The New Public Service and Leadership

The New Public Service sees leadership in terms of neither the manipulation
of individuals nor the manipulation of incentives. Instead, leadership is seen

as a natural part of the human experience, subject to both rational and intuitive forces, and concerned with focusing human energy on projects that benefit humanity. Leadership is no longer seen as a prerogative of those in high public offices, but as a function that extends throughout groups, organizations, and societies. What is needed, in this view, is the principled leadership by people throughout public organizations and throughout society. Here we will examine several prominent and representative interpretations of this new approach to leadership.

Values Based Leadership

Perhaps the most powerful formulation of leadership, whether applied to politics, business, or management, is the idea of "transformational leadership." Transformational leadership is the key concept in a classic, indeed, a Pulitzer Prize–winning study, written by Harvard political scientist James MacGregor Burns and titled simply *Leadership* (1978). In this monumental work, Burns goes far beyond trying to understand the dynamics of leadership in terms of rational efficiency, getting things done, or meeting organizational objectives. Rather he seeks to develop a theory of leadership that would extend across cultures and time and apply to groups, organizations, and societies. Specifically, Burns seeks to understand leadership not as something leaders do to followers but as a relationship between leaders and followers, a mutual interaction that ultimately changes both:

> [T]he process of leadership must be seen as part of the dynamics of conflict and power; . . . leadership is nothing if not linked to collective purpose; . . . the effectiveness of leaders must be judged not by their press clippings but by actual social change; . . . political leadership depends on a long chain of biological and social processes, of interaction with structures of political opportunity and closures, of interplay between the calls of moral principles and the recognized necessities of power; . . . in placing these concepts of political leadership centrally into a theory . . . we will reaffirm the possibilities of human volition and of common standards of justice in the conduct of peoples' affairs. (Burns 1978, 4)

Burns starts by noting that, while historically we have been preoccupied with the relationship between power and leadership, there is an important difference between the two. Typically, power is thought of as carrying out one's own will, despite resistance. Such a conception of power neglects the important fact that power involves a relationship between leaders and followers and that a central value in that relationship is *purpose*—what is being sought and what is intended, both by the one who is exercising power and the one who is on the receiving end. In most, though perhaps not all, situations the recipient has some flexibility in his or her response to an attempted exercise of power, so the power one can exercise is dependent on the way both parties view the situation. Power wielders draw on their own resources and their own motives, but these must be relevant to the resources and motivations of the recipient of power.

Leadership, according to Burns, is an aspect of power, but it is also a separate process. Power is exercised when potential power wielders, acting to achieve goals of their own, gather resources that enable them to influence others. Power is exercised to realize the purposes of the power wielders, whether or not those purposes are also the purposes of the respondents (1978, 18). Leadership, on the other hand, is exercised "when persons with certain motives and purposes mobilize, in competition or conflict with others, institutional, political, psychological, and other resources so as to arouse, engage, and satisfy the motives of the followers (18). The difference between power and leadership is that power serves the interests of the power wielder, while leadership serves both the leader's interests *and* those of the followers. The values, motivations, wants, needs, interests, and expectations of both leaders and followers must be represented in order for leadership to occur.

There are actually two kinds of leadership, Burns argues. The first is "transactional" leadership, which involves an exchange of valued things (whether economic, political, or psychological) between initiator and respondent. For example, a political leader might agree to support a particular policy in exchange for votes in the next election. Or a student might write a superb paper in exchange for an "A" grade. In the case of transactional leadership, the two parties come together in a relationship that advances the interests of both, but there is no deep or enduring link between them. "Transformational" leadership, on the other hand, occurs when leaders and followers engage with one another in such a way that they raise one another to higher levels of morality and motivation. While the leaders and the led may initially come together either out of pursuit of their own interests or because the leader recognized some special potential in the followers, as the relationship evolves, their interests become fused into mutual support for common purposes. The relationship between leaders and followers becomes one in which the purposes of both are elevated through the relationship; both parties become mobilized, inspired, uplifted. In some cases, transformational leadership even evolves into *moral* leadership as leadership raises the level of moral aspiration and moral conduct of both leaders and followers. Moral leadership results in actions that are consistent with the needs, interests, and aspirations of the followers, but these are also actions that fundamentally change moral understandings and social conditions. In the end, leadership, especially transformational or moral leadership, has the capacity to move groups, organizations, even societies toward the pursuit of higher purposes.

A similar, though somewhat more contemporary, interpretation of leadership is provided by Ronald Heifetz in his book, *Leadership without Easy Answers* (1994). Heifetz argues, as we did at the beginning of this chapter, that leadership is no longer just about establishing a vision and then getting people to move in that direction. More bluntly, leadership is no longer about "telling people what to do." Instead, leadership, whether it comes from someone in a position of formal authority or someone with little or no formal authority, is concerned with aiding a group, an organization, or a community in recognizing its own vision and then learning how to move in a new direction. As an illustration of the difference between these two views of leadership, think about the following two definitions of leadership, "leadership means influencing the community to follow the leader's vision" versus "leadership means influencing the community to face its problems" (Heifetz 1994, 14). Heifetz argues that the latter view is better suited to contemporary life, where the tasks of leadership are not merely getting a job done, but rather "adapting" to new and unusual circumstances. The work of leadership, then, is "adaptive work"—work that may either involve reconciling conflicting values that people hold or finding ways to reduce the discrepancy between the values people hold and the realities they face. Leadership is all about values and learning, specifically helping people learn to identify and actualize their values. In this way, leadership is basically an educative function.

From this theoretical standpoint, Heifetz identifies several practical lessons for leaders—again even leaders with no formal authority:

1. *Identify the Adaptive Challenge*: Diagnose the situation in light of the values at stake, and unbundle the issues that come with it.
2. *Keep the Level of Distress Within a Tolerable Range for Doing Adaptive Work*: To use the pressure cooker analogy, keep the heat up without blowing up the vessel.
3. *Focus Attention on Ripening Issues and Not on Stress-Reducing Distractions*: Identify which issues can currently engage attention; and while directing attention to them, counteract work avoidance mechanisms like denial, scapegoating, externalizing the enemy, pretending the problem is technical, or attacking individuals rather than issues.
4. *Give the Work Back to People, But at a Rate They Can Stand*: Place and develop responsibility by putting the pressure on the people with the problem.

5. *Protect Voices of Leadership Without Authority*: Give cover to those
    who raise hard questions and generate distress—people who point to
    the internal contradictions of the society. These individuals often will
    have latitude to provoke rethinking that authorities do not have (Heifetz
    1994, 128).

Shared Leadership

John Bryson and Barbara Crosby (1992) set the stage for their discussion of
shared leadership by contrasting the traditional model of bureaucratic leadership with more contemporary leadership—where no one is in charge. On
the one hand, there is the traditional, hierarchical bureaucracy, which has the
capacity to "get its hands around problems" and to engage in rational and
expert problem-solving and planning processes to arrive at solutions that it
can then implement "on its own." On the other hand, as we saw in our
discussion of the new processes of governance, today's problems increasingly require the involvement of networks of many different organizations
with different styles, agendas, and concerns. Those groups that are concerned may have serious differences—in direction, motivation, timing, as-
sets, and so on—and these differences may be severe. In these more fluid
and chaotic circumstances, the rational model of formal leadership no longer
works. Instead, someone, often someone who is not in a formal position of
authority, must assume leadership, bringing together all those concerned
with the problem and helping to resolve or mediate their differences, while
never controlling, but rather leading by example, persuasion, encouragement, and empowerment.

This alternative model of leadership, which Bryson and Einsweiler describe as "shared transformative capacity" (1991, 3), is sometimes slow and
often tedious, but for good reason. Leaders in a world of shared power and
shared capabilities have needs which require special time and attention, "the
need to be sure the move is politically acceptable, technically workable, and
legally and ethically defensible; the need to have the move endorsed by a
coalition large enough to support and protect it; and the desire to keep as
many options as possible open as long as possible" (Bryson and Crosby
1992, 9). While shared leadership takes time, because more people and groups
are involved, ironically, it is often far more successful for exactly the same
reason—because more people and more groups are involved!

But success requires an understanding of the various places in which policy
decisions take place and the various steps that individuals and groups must
work through to be successful. Bryson and Crosby (1992) suggest three
settings that are becoming more frequently employed in bringing people

together and negotiating or brokering their different points of view. *Forums* are spaces in which people can engage in discussion, debate, and deliberation. They may include discussion groups, formal debates, public hearings, task forces, conferences, newspapers, radio, television, and the Internet. *Arenas*, on the other hand, are more formal and have a more delimited domain. Examples might be executive committees, city councils, faculty senates, boards of directors, and legislatures. Finally, *courts* are settings that focus on dispute resolution according to established societal norms. Here examples might be the Supreme Court, traffic courts, professional licensing bodies, and ethics enforcement bodies.

Bryson and Crosby then lay out several key steps in effectively solving public problems:

1. *Forging an Initial Agreement to Act*: An initial group of leaders, key decision makers, and ordinary citizens come together and agree on the need to respond to a particular problem. As more people become involved and as each phase informs the next, this step is likely to recur in a continuous loop (as are the next two). Leaders must secure the involvement and participation of all affected groups (and perhaps some that are not).

2. *Developing an Effective Problem Definition to Guide Action*: The way in which problems are framed will dramatically affect the way different parties respond to and engage in the process and the way in which eventual solutions are structured. People must rethink problems before moving to their solution. Here public leadership is perhaps most intense, because leaders can "help people see new problems or see old problems in new ways."

3. *Searching for Solutions in Forums*: In this phase, a search for solutions to the problems previously identified takes place. Especially in this phase, leaders facilitate the construction of alternative scenarios for moving from a problem-filled past to a problem-free future. A key here is to be sure that proposed solutions meet the problem as defined before and don't just capture the interests of particular groups. Leadership is required to transcend the private interests that may come forward during this phase.

4. *Developing a Proposal that Can Win in Arenas*: Here the focus shifts to the development of policies that can be put on the agendas of formal decision-making bodies. The key is that action in forums and less formal groups must produce proposals that will likely be adopted, proposals that are both technically sound and politically acceptable.

5. *Adopting Public Policy Solutions*: In this phase, those advocating change

seek the adoption of their proposals by those with formal decision-making authority and the resources and support necessary for successful implementation.

6. *Implementing New Policies and Plans*: Policies don't implement themselves, so extending the newly adopted policy throughout the system involves a multitude of details and arrangements associated with the implementation process. Until these concerns are attended to, the change cannot be considered complete.

7. *Reassessing Policies and Programs*: Even following implementation, there is a need to reevaluate the situation. Things change, people change, resource commitments change—and any of these can lead to a new round of policy change. (Adapted from Bryson and Crosby 1992, 119–338)

A similar argument is developed by Jeffrey Luke in *Catalytic Leadership* (1998). Consistently with our earlier discussion of network-based governance, Luke points out that public organizations are increasingly limited in what they can do on their own. Many other groups and organizations must be involved in addressing issues such as teenage pregnancy, traffic congestion, and environmental pollution. In addition, traditional leadership, the type Luke associates with business corporations and bureaucractic government agencies, is largely based on hierarchical authority and cannot be easily transferred to situations that are dispersed, chaotic, and complex. In contrast, in these circumstances, which increasingly characterize the public policy process, leadership must "focus attention and mobilize sustained action by multiple and diverse stakeholders" (1998, 5).

The problem, on one hand, is that government is no longer "in charge" of the policy process. "Governance in the United States is characterized by a dynamic interplay among government agencies, nonprofit service providers, business enterprises, multinational corporations, neighborhood groups, special-interest and advocacy groups, labor unions, academia, the media, and many other formal and informal associations that attempt to influence the public agenda" (Luke 1998, 4). Moreover, the most substantial problems we face today cross organizational, jurisdictional, and sector boundaries. What happens in one place or what one organization does is likely to affect the problem only in a marginal way; all the other groups and organizations interested in the same issue are also affecting the issue. In other words, there is an underlying web of interdependence and interconnectedness that ties many different groups together. Without the involvement of all these interconnected groups and organizations, little can be done to effectively address complex public problems. Moreover, given the passionate commitment and highly focused interest of most of these parties, it's often difficult to exclude anyone.

According to Luke, effective public leadership in an interconnected world, what he calls "catalytic" leadership, involves four specific tasks:

1. Focus attention by elevating the issue to the public and policy agendas. Moving a particular problem onto the public agenda involves identifying the problem, creating a sense of urgency about its solution, and triggering broad public interest.
2. Engage people in the effort by convening the diverse set of people, agencies, and interests needed to address the issue. Engaging people involves identifying all the stakeholders and those with understanding of the problems, enlisting core group members, and convening the initial meetings.
3. Stimulate multiple strategies and options for action. This step requires building and nurturing an effective working group, with a unifying purpose and a credible process for discussion and group learning. Strategic development involves identifying desired outcomes, exploring multiple options, and promoting commitment to the strategies that are developed.
4. Sustain action and maintain momentum by managing the interconnections through appropriate institutionalization and rapid information sharing and feedback. In this stage, it is necessary to build support among "champions," power holders, advocacy groups, and those holding important resources. The leader must then turn to institutionalizing cooperative behavior and becoming a network facilitator. (Adapted from Luke 1998, 37–148)

As we have noted before, the New Public Service requires developing skills quite different from those associated with controlling public agencies or those involved in strict economic analysis—though particular skills may be appropriate from time to time. Instead, those interested in a New Public Service will need to develop skills in other areas. Luke specifically addresses this concern by describing three specific skill sets required for catalytic leadership (1998, 149–240). The first is thinking and acting strategically—framing and reframing issues, identifying desired outcomes and connecting those with specific actions or strategies that might be undertaken, identifying stakeholders and others whose involvement is essential to success, and drawing out the interconnections so essential to effective leadership in the complex public policy universe. The second is facilitating productive work groups—engaging in skillful interventions that move a group forward, helping the group cope with conflict, and forging multiple agreements, hopefully through consensus building. The third is leading from personal passion and inner values:

Catalytic leaders lead from strength of character, not strength of personality. Successful catalysts exhibit a strength of character that establishes their credibility to convene diverse groups. They have the personal confidence to facilitate and mediate sometimes difficult agreements, and they possess a long-term perspective that helps focus and refocus groups members' attention in the face of small defeats. (Luke 1998, 219)

Once again, as in our discussion of the dignity and worth of public service, we argue that passion, commitment, and perseverance in the face of difficult problems are often required to "make a difference."

Servants, Not Owners

In the New Public Service, there is an explicit recognition that public administrators are not the business owners of their agencies and programs. Accordingly, the mindset of public administrators is that public programs and resources do not belong not to them. Rather, public administrators have accepted a responsibility to serve citizens by being stewards of public resources (Kass 1990), conservators of public organizations (Terry 1995), facilitators of citizenship and democratic dialog (Box 1998; Chapin and Denhardt 1995; King and Stivers 1998), and catalysts for community engagement (Denhardt and Gray 1999; Lappe and duBois 1994). This is a very different perspective from that of a business owner focused on profit and efficiency. Accordingly, the New Public Service suggests that public administrators not only must share power, work through people, and broker solutions but also must reconceptualize their role in the governance process as responsible participant, not entrepreneur.

Accordingly, when public administrators take risks, they are not entrepreneurs of their own businesses who can make such decisions knowing that the consequences of failure will fall largely on their own shoulders. Risk in the public sector is different (Denhardt and Denhardt 1999). In the New Public Service, risks and opportunities reside within the larger framework of democratic citizenship and shared responsibility. Because the consequences of either success or failure are not limited to a private business concern, public administrators do not single-handedly decide what is best for a community. This need not mean that all short-term opportunities are lost. If dialog and citizen engagement are ongoing, opportunities and potential risks can be explored in a timely manner. The important factor to consider is whether the benefits of a public administrator's taking immediate and risky action in response to an opportunity outweigh the costs to trust, collaboration, and the sense of shared responsibility.

Finally, in the New Public Service, shared and value-based leadership is seen as a function and responsibility at all levels of the organization, from the executive suite to the street level. Vinzant and Crothers (1998), for example, describe how public servants on the front lines are called upon to exercise discretion, involve others, and make decisions that respect and reflect a variety of factors and values. They must be responsive to agency rules, their supervisor, the community they serve, their supervisors, and their coworkers, as well as to situational and ethical variables. Vinzant and Crothers argue that in many of these cases, front line public servants are called upon to behave as value-based leaders: "They make choices and take action to elevate the goals, attitudes, and values of the participants in a given situation in ways that may be counter to their immediate interests and desires, but that can legitimated through reference to the broader complex of ideals and values involved in the case" (1998, 112).

Conclusion

In the New Public Service, leadership is based on values and is shared throughout the organization and with the community. This change in the conceptualization of the public administrator's role has profound implications for the types of leadership challenges and responsibilities faced by public servants. First, public administrators must know and manage more than just the requirements and resources of their programs. The narrow view is not very helpful to a citizen whose world is not conveniently divided up by programmatic departments and offices. The problems citizens face are often, if not usually, multifaceted, fluid, and dynamic—and they do not easily fall within the confines of a particular office or the narrow job description of an individual. To serve citizens, then, public administrators must not only know and manage their own resources; they must also be aware of and connected to other sources of support and assistance, engaging citizens and the community in the process. They do not seek to control, nor do they assume that self-interested choice serves as a surrogate for dialog and shared values. In short, they must share power and lead with passion, commitment, and integrity in a manner that respects and empowers citizenship.

The material in the section entitled "The Old Public Administration and Executive Management" and the discussion of James Burns's *Leadership* (1978) are adapted from a book by Robert B. Denhardt, Janet V. Denhardt, and Maria P. Aristigueta, *Managing Human Behavior in Public and Nonprofit Organizations* (Thousand Oaks, CA: Sage, 2002).

Chapter 9

Value People, Not Just Productivity

Value people, not just productivity. Public organizations and the networks in which they participate are more likely to be successful in the long run if they are operated through processes of collaboration and shared leadership based on respect for all people.

In its approach to management and organization, the New Public Service emphasizes the importance of managing through people. Systems of productivity improvement, process reengineering, and performance measurement are seen as important tools in designing management systems. But the New Public Service suggests that such rational attempts to control human behavior are likely to fail in the long term if, at the same time, insufficient attention is paid to the values and interests of individual members of an organization. Moreover, while these approaches may get results, they do not build responsible, engaged, and civic-minded employees or citizens.

The evolution of thought with regard to how to best manage people involves a number of related topics and ideas including motivation, "supervision" and leadership, organizational culture, organizational structure, and organizational power. It involves questions about the nature of authority, definitions of performance and responsibility, and the establishment of trust. Most fundamentally, however, it is grounded in our most basic assumptions about the nature of people and behavior. In this chapter we will explore the very different assumptions and conceptual foundations for the views about managing people exemplified in the Old Public Administration, the New Public Management, and the New Public Service. We will begin by looking at the major concepts and ideas related to motivation and management in historical perspective. We then compare the assumptions and models that underlie the management of people from the perspective of the Old Public Administration, the New Public Management, and the New Public Service.

Human Behavior in Organizations: Key Concepts

Our beliefs about what motivates human behavior in large measure determine how we interpret, respond to, and try to influence the behavior of others. When theorists initially began to study human behavior in organizations the assumptions they made about the nature of people was relatively simplistic and generally negative. One of the first and most central ideas in the study of organizational management was that in order for organizations to function, workers had to be induced or forced to produce certain behaviors and perform particular tasks. These tasks were to be accomplished by people within an organization that was understood principally as a "structure" for regularizing interactions and processes. The goal of this structure was to obtain efficient and consistent performance of tasks.

While we now talk of the structure of the organization as being one factor among several in influencing worker behavior, initially, it was *the* focus of management. Ott states, "The structure—an organization's shape, size procedures, production technology, position descriptions, reporting arrangements, and coordinating relationships—affects the feelings and emotions, and therefore the behavior of the people and groups inside them" (1996, 304). These feelings and emotions were largely ignored in the study of organizations and management for many decades. Rather, it was assumed that if the work was designed well and authority relationships were appropriately structured and regularized, optimum efficiency could be realized.

Hierarchy and Scientific Management

The German sociologist Max Weber is perhaps most closely associated with the structural approach to managing and controlling human behavior in organizations. Weber described bureaucratic organizational structure as characterized by a hierarchy of authority, regularized rules and procedures, and formalized positions with fixed duties, and said that such a structure would lead to predictable and efficient performance. "Precision, speed, unambiguity, knowledge of the files, continuity, discretion, unity, strict subordination, reduction of friction and of material and personal costs—these are raised to the optimum point in the strictly bureaucratic administration" (Weber, quoted in Gerth and Mills 1946, 214). In part because bureaucracy was the best way to attain efficiency, Weber said, bureaucracy is the "most rational known means of carrying out imperative control over human beings" (337). This is accomplished, in part, by making the administrative processes as objective, rational and depersonalized as possible. "The objective discharge of business primarily means a discharge of business according to calculable rules and 'without regard to persons'" (215). Weber went on to say that this dehumanization of work, "is the specific nature of bureaucracy and it is appraised as its special virtue" (216).

Yet, Weber himself was concerned about the consequences of bureaucracy for both democratic values and the individual human spirit. He said "'democracy' as such is opposed to the 'rule' of bureaucracy" (Weber, quoted in Gerth and Mills 1946, 231). Even so, Weber thought that ultimately, bureaucratic power would exceed that of the political sphere: "Under normal conditions, the power position of a fully developed bureaucracy is always overpowering" (232).

Not only was Weber concerned about the implications of bureaucracy for democratic governance, he was worried about its consequences for people. "The individual bureaucrat cannot squirm out of the apparatus in which he is harnessed (Weber, quoted in Gerth and Mills 1946, 228). He referred to bureaucratization as creating an "iron cage" in which "all forms of value-oriented social conduct would be suffocated by the almighty bureaucratic structures and by the tightly-knit networks of formal-rational laws and regulations, against which the individual would no longer stand any chance at all" (Mommsen 1974, 57).

Despite these concerns, the values of bureaucracy and efficiency found particularly fertile ground with early management theorists who sought to find the best means to control workers and achieve efficiency. These early management theorists viewed workers primarily as extensions of their tools and machines. It was thought that the fear of physical or economic punishment was needed to get people to work. Only those "motivated" by money or fear would complete their assigned tasks.

For example, as we saw earlier, Frederick Taylor argued that workers would do what they were told if they were given specific instructions and then paid a piece rate to follow them. He urged managers to study the tasks to be performed, establish the best way to perform them, and then scientifically select and train workers to do the job. The workers could then be induced to perform by paying a set amount of money for each task performed or product produced. Although Taylor saw this as a mutually beneficial approach for workers and managers, it was clear that he assumed workers to be naturally lazy and stupid. For example, in his comments about inducing men to haul big iron, he said it is "possible to train an intelligent gorilla" to do their job (1911, 40). He also expected employees to obey their superiors without question.

The Human Factor

These ideas about obedience to authority and hierarchy were the dominant management doctrine in the early 1900s and still exert considerable influence today. Although there were a few early humanistic writings on management and workers (e.g., Follett 1926; Munsterberg 1913); it was not until the publication of the Hawthorne studies in the 1930s, that there was any significant recognition of the importance of social (as opposed to economic or technical) factors in work motivation. Even the Hawthorne experiments themselves began as a study of "the relation between conditions of work and the incidence of fatigue and monotony among employees" (Roethlisberger and Dickson 1939, 3). But the study did not go as planned, and the researchers ultimately found that human relationships (including the worker's relationship with the researchers) influenced worker behavior. Consequently, new models were needed to explain worker behavior. The researchers found that behavior and motivation are complex, influenced by attitudes, feelings, and the meanings that people assign to their work and their relationships at work. As Roethlisberger and Dickson stated, "It is [our] simple thesis that a human problem requires a human solution" (1939, 35).

Research that immediately followed the Hawthorne studies resulted in the beginnings of a more sophisticated understanding of the relationship between people, work and organizations. Ideas such as the importance of human cooperation (Barnard 1948) and the influence of groups (Knickerbocker and McGregor 1942) were studied by researchers to determine how these factors might influence work performance. By the 1950s, there was growing agreement among management theorists that motivation was a psychological concept rather than a purely economic one.

This recognition was exemplified in McGregor's (1957) work in which he distinguished between what he called Theory X and Theory Y assumptions about workers. He argued that traditional command and control approaches (Theory X), based on the assumption that people are lazy, uninvolved, and motivated solely by money, actually cause people to behave in a manner consistent with that expectation. Theory Y, on the other hand, is based on a much more optimistic and humanistic view of people, and emphasizes the inherent dignity and worth of individuals in organizations. Holding these assumptions, and acting on them, would allow these more positive qualities of workers to manifest themselves in organizations.

Other theorists looked at different aspects of worker motivation and conducted research on the behavior of individuals under differing circumstances. In simple terms, contemporary motivation theory seeks to explain voluntary, goal directed behavior. There are a variety of models that emphasize different aspects of motivation: human needs (e.g., Herzberg 1968; McClelland 1985; Maslow 1943); an individual's expectations, skills, and desires (Vroom 1964); goal setting (Locke 1978); perceptions of equity and fairness (Adams 1963); opportunities for participation (Lawler 1990); and, more recently, motivation based on public service values and norms (Perry and Wise 1990).

As assumptions about workers and their motivations changed, so did the dominant framework for an understanding of the role of management and leadership. Management's role was originally conceived of as documenting tasks and procedures, and then supervising and controlling workers accordingly. With the recognition of the psychological components of human motivation came the need to broaden the definition of management to include "human relations" in order to keep workers satisfied and productive. Importantly, however, while the parameters of management changed, the goals typically remained the same—to improve and maintain productivity. In many cases, the idea was to treat people better and more humanely in order to get better performance from them. It wasn't until the last several decades that the argument that treating people with respect and dignity is important in its own right, not simply as a means to improve production, gained currency in the management literature.

Groups, Culture, and Democratic Administration

A number of other perspectives on managing the workers' behavior have also emerged and gained recognition. It has been argued, for example, that group norms and behaviors influence individual behavior (e.g., Asch 1951; Homans 1954; Lewin 1951; Sherif 1936; Whyte 1943). These theorists suggest that human beings are social, and readily form groups both inside and outside of organizations. These groups create norms, roles, and expectations for members that both meet individuals' needs for affiliation and belongingness, but also require a level of conformity in order to maintain membership. Accordingly, work groups, both formal and informal, create a normative context for our behavior in organizations. Mary Parker Follett, for example, argued that group dynamics and the motivations of the individual should form the basis of administration. Rather than simply responding to orders, managers and workers should define administrative problems jointly, and respond accordingly—taking their "orders" from the circumstances. She wrote in 1926, "One *person* should not give orders to another *person*, but both should agree to take their orders from the situation" (quoted in Shafritz and Hyde 1997, 56). Still other theorists looked at how individual characteristics influence organizational behavior such as those who emphasize the life stage of workers (Schott 1986) or personality characteristics (e.g., Myers Briggs or similar inventories). Power and politics, once the province of political scientists and philosophers, have also been used as a lens for understanding human behavior in organizations (French and Raven 1959; Kotter 1977; Pfeffer 1981).

Critiques of bureaucracy and hierarchy have also been launched from the standpoint of the inconsistency between bureaucracy and democratic governance. Waldo in his book *The Administrative State* (1948), for example, argued not only that administrative questions were inherently value-laden, but that administration itself must be made more consistent with democratic principles. "*The Administrative State* contains a strong message: that an uncritical acceptance of an administrative outlook constitutes a rejection of democratic theory and that this is a societal problem, not simply a problem of administrative management" (Denhardt 2000, 66–67). In other words, Waldo's argument is that the extension of the hierarchical and "neutral" bureaucracy would ultimately undermine democracy.

Only by making the administrative machinery adhere to democratic norms and principles could this threat be addressed. This requires not only expanding the role of citizens in policy administration, but it also requires reforming the administrative process itself. As suggested by Levitan "a democratic state must not only be based on democratic principles but also democratically administered, the democratic philosophy permeating its administrative machinery" (1943, 359). Waldo was even more direct in his criticism of hierarchy and bureaucratic control and his hope for reform, saying that what was needed was:

> Substantial abandonment of the authority—submission, superordinate—subordinate thought patterns which tend to dominate our administrative theory. . . . In rare moments of optimism, one permits himself the luxury of a dream of society of the future in which education and general culture are consonant with a working world in which all participate both as "leaders" and "followers" according to "rules of the game" known to all. Such a society would be postbureaucratic. (Waldo 1948, 103)

This critique of bureaucracy and the call to make administration more democratic dovetailed neatly with the developments that were occurring in motivation theory. For instance, making administration more democratic and less hierarchical would allow for individuals to express their natural tendencies to work and be responsible as suggested by McGregor, to meet social/esteem/self-actualization needs as suggested by Maslow, and to take orders from the situation as advocated by Follett.

Another important idea with regard to managing the behavior of people in organizations is the concept of organizational culture. Rather than seeing an organization as a static "structure," the organizational culture perspective draws from the field of anthropology to understand how norms, beliefs, and values are shared by members of an organization and, in turn, define its boundaries. These shared norms and values are manifest in organizational members' language and behaviors, rituals, and symbols, and in the artifacts they produce. Culture expresses the ideas and overall values that define an organization and has a significant and long-lasting influence on its members. Schein (1987) suggested that there are three levels of organizational culture: (1) the observable social and physical environment, such as physical layout, technological preferences, language patterns, or the day-to-day operating routines that guide people's behavior; (2) the values and ideas about the way the organization "should" be; and (3) the often hidden and largely unquestioned assumptions and beliefs held by members of the organization that guide their behavior. Schein suggests that the last category constitutes the core definition of culture: "a pattern of basic assumptions . . . that has worked well enough to be considered valid and, therefore, to be taught to new members as the correct way to perceive, think, and feel in relation to those problems" (1987, 9). Or as Ott states, "It functions as an organizational control mechanism, informally approving or prohibiting behaviors" (1989, 50).

Despite this evolution of thought, there remains a lack of consensus about what motivates people and how best to influence behavior in organizations. As will be explored in the sections that follow, public choice theorists argue strenuously for a model of human behavior and motivation based on solely on self-interested, individual decision making, to the exclusion of other explanations of human behavior. For others, there has been a growing recognition that in addition to self-interest, human motivation involves both social and psychological factors. This leads to a much more complex view of the relationship between organizations and human behavior in which both the structure of the organization and interactions and relationships between individuals and groups influence behavior. In this more complex view, it is also assumed that individuals with different experiences and personalities will respond to organizational life in different ways. Organizational politics are also believed to influence behavior as people seek to obtain and maintain power. Finally, in this view, organizational culture is understood as creating the normative context for our behavior in organizations. In short, for these theorists, people are seen as bringing their social and emotional needs to work. In the sections that follow, we will explore how these issues are dealt with from the perspectives of the Old Public Administration, the New Public Management, and the New Public Service.

The Old Public Administration: Using Control to Achieve Efficiency

The Old Public Administration is based on the ideas that efficiency is the preeminent value and that people won't be productive and work hard unless you make them. In this view, workers will be productive only when they are provided with monetary incentives, and when they believe that management can and will punish them for poor performance. Employee motivation is not considered in a direct way. In the early twentieth century, when Old Public Administration was the dominant model, people were expected to simply follow orders, and for the most part, they did. Public employment was considered to be a simple quid pro quo arrangement analogous to employment in the private sector: In exchange for a steady salary, workers would carefully and methodically carry out assigned tasks. The treatment of workers as human beings with emotions and needs, with contributions and insights, with value in their own right, was not part of the equation.

Efficiency, defined as the ratio of costs to outputs, demanded that cost control and productivity were the primary, if not the sole, objectives of management. The challenge was to organize and structure the work so as to minimize costs and maximize production. Employees were considered to be costs. Accordingly, the goal was to minimize the cost of labor by obtaining the maximum output from each employee while providing the least salary and other monetary incentives possible. The emphasis was on the potential gain in efficiency, not on the long-term well-being of the people who worked in the organization, much less the citizens or the community. It was assumed that the issues of community, citizenship, and democracy fell squarely within the political sphere and completely outside the realm of administration. To the extent that "humanistic" approaches can be accommodated in the Old Public Administration, they were seen merely as vehicles to secure more productivity. For example, in the Hawthorne experiments it was recommended that managers institute a "suggestion box" for employees, to make them feel more involved and therefore potentially more productive. But there was no consideration of the idea that the suggestions might actually be useful or important in their own right.

The idea was that the organization itself should be the primary concern of management. If it could be structured according to the ideals of bureaucracy, if it could advance the values of neutral competence and expertise, and if management systems could be put into place to control and account for the expenditure of funds, then public organizations would fulfill their intended function.

The New Public Management: Using Incentives to Achieve Productivity

As we saw earlier, public choice theory is based on a number of important assumptions about the behavior of people and how to best manage that behavior to achieve public policy objectives. Principal agent theory applies these assumptions to explain the relationship between executives and the workers in an organization using the metaphor of a contract. This contract is necessary because, although the employee (the agent) acts on behalf of the executive (the principal), their goals and objectives are different. As a result, the principal has to obtain enough information to monitor the agent, determine results, and provide sufficient incentives to consistently obtain them. Because the goal is efficiency, the question then becomes a matter of what is the least-cost approach that the organization can use to keep employees from seeking their own, rather than organizational, goals and to verify that they are doing so.

The New Public Management, with its reliance on public choice and principal agent theory, has made some important contributions to our understanding of human behavior. It is important to note, however, that it relies on economic rationality as the explanation of human behavior *to the exclusion of other ways of understanding motivation and the human experience.* If that is so, the only way to successfully influence their behavior is by altering the decision-making rules or incentives so as to alter their self-interest to be more in line with organizational priorities.

The New Public Service: Respecting Public Service Ideals

The assumptions about the motivations and treatment of people in the New Public Service differ starkly from both the Old Public Administration and the New Public Management. The Old Public Administration assumed people to be as McGregor's Theory X described them: lazy, stupid, lacking in drive, and unwilling to accept responsibility. Accordingly, they had to be controlled and threatened with punishment to secure their performance. The New Public Management has a different, but no more trusting, view of people. It assumes that they are self-interested and will seek to meet their own objectives unless they are monitored and provided with enough incentives to do otherwise. As such, the New Public Management, like Taylor's scientific management, excludes consideration of group norms and values, organizational culture, emotional/social considerations, and psychological and other "irrational" needs. It negates the idea that people act in response to shared values, loyalty, citizenship, and the public interest.

We are not suggesting that people are never lazy or self-interested. Rather, relying on self-interest as the sole explanation of human behavior represents a very narrow, and largely negative, view of people that is neither borne out by experience nor can be justified from a normative standpoint. In other words, people don't typically act that way. More importantly, they shouldn't.

The elements of human behavior that are at the core of the New Public Service, such as human dignity, trust, belongingness, concern for others, service, and citizenship based on shared ideals and the public interests, are deemphasized in the Old Public Administration and the New Public Management. In the New Public Service, ideals such as fairness, equity, responsiveness, respect, empowerment, and commitment do not negate but often outweigh the value of efficiency as the sole criterion for the operation of government. As Frederickson states, "Persons who practice public administration must be increasingly familiar with issues of both representational and direct democracy, with citizen participation, with principles of justice and individual freedom" (1982, 503). Frederickson was talking about the relationship between public servants and citizens, but the same principal applies in how public managers ought to treat other public servants.

If you assume that people are capable of other-mindedness, of service, of acting on shared values as citizens, then it is only logically consistent that you assume public employees are capable of the same motivations and behaviors. We cannot expect public servants to treat their fellow citizens with respect and dignity if they themselves are not treated with respect and dignity. We cannot expect them to trust and empower others, to listen to their ideas, and to work cooperatively unless we are willing to do the same for them. In the New Public Service, the enormous challenges and complexities of the work of public administrators are recognized. Service and democratic ideals are applauded. Public servants are viewed not just as employees who crave the security and structure of a bureaucratic job (the Old Public Administration), nor as participants in a market (the New Public Management); rather, public servants are people whose motivations and rewards are more than simply a matter of pay or security. They want to make a difference in the lives of others (Denhardt 1993; Perry and Wise 1990; Vinzant 1998).

Elmer Staats, former comptroller of the United States and a distinguished public servant, once wrote that public service is far more than an occupational category. It is better defined, he said, as "an attitude, a sense of duty—yes even a sense of public morality" (1988, 602). This is consistent with the notion that public service motives are very important and powerful in motivating the behavior of the public servants. Public service motivation is based on an individual's predisposition to respond to motives grounded primarily or uniquely in public institutions and organizations (Perry and Wise, 1990).

In other words, there are particular motives that are associated with the nature of public service work that revolve around service to others and the public interest. These motives are related to values such as loyalty, duty, citizenship, equity, opportunity, and fairness. Research has shown that these norm-based, and affective motives are unique to public service and critical to understanding behavior in public organizations (Balfour and Weschler 1990; Denhardt, Denhardt, and Aristigueta 2002; Frederickson and Hart 1985; Perry and Wise 1990; Vinzant 1998).

As we saw earlier, Frederickson and Hart (1985) argue that too frequently we fail to make a distinction between what they call the "moral entailments" of service in the public sector and employment in the private sector. When we do so, we denigrate the ideals of both democratic citizenship and public service. They call for a return to what they call "the patriotism of benevolence" based first on the love of and patriotism to democratic values, and second, on benevolence defined as "extensive and non-instrumental love of others" (1985, 547). This means that we should serve and care for others, and work to protect their rights, not because it advances our own interests, but because it is the right thing to do for its own sake. This patriotism of benevolence, they argue, ought to be "the primary motivation of public servants in the United States" (547).

Similarly, Hart points out that that the primary obligations of public servants are "to encourage civic autonomy; to govern by persuasion, to transcend the corruptions of power; and to become civic exemplars" (1997, 967). Accordingly, he says, "public servants are obligated to embody those values intentionally in all their actions, *whether with superiors, colleagues, subordinates, or the general public*" (1997, 968, emphasis added). Put simply, in public organizations, we need to treat each other and our fellow citizens in a manner consistent with democratic ideals, trust, and respect. We do so because we believe that people respond to and are motivated by such values, and because we believe that public service plays a special role in advancing and encouraging those aspects of human character.

Practically speaking, then, the values of the New Public Service dictate that we encourage, model, and enact our commitment to democratic ideals and our trust of others. As managers, we can encourage public service motives and values by making them a central part of organizational identity and culture. Because we know and trust that the people we work with want to serve others, we need to treat them as partners in the pursuit of the public interest. This suggests, even demands, a highly inclusive, participative approach to management—not just as an instrumental means to enhance productivity, but as a means to advance the values at the core of public service. Roy Adams puts it succinctly: "Efficiency is not enough" (1972, 18). Participative approaches are needed in order to for people in organizations to have "a decent and dignified existence" (18). Moreover, although participation often improves performance, its value should not be dependent upon its contribution to something else. Participation is an important value in and of itself.

Robert Golembiewski (1977), as we saw earlier, has argued that organizational democracy is based on participation by all organization members in decision making, frequent feedback of the results of organizational performance, sharing of management-level information throughout the organization, guarantees for individual rights, the availability of appeal or recourse in cases on intractable disputes, and a set of supporting attitudes or values. He suggested that the closer an organization is to these criteria, the more democratic the organization will be. Edward Lawler (1990) advocates what he calls "high-involvement" management, based on information sharing, training, decision making, and rewards as the four key components of a successful employee participation program. He argues that participation enhances motivation because it helps people understand what is expected and see the relationships between performance and outcomes.

According to Kearny and Hays (1994), public managers are beginning to realize how vitally important it is to use participatory management approaches. These authors argue that participatory approaches should begin with the premise that workers are an organization's most important asset, and should be treated accordingly. All employees must be empowered by management to participate in decision making, and must be allowed to do so without fear. Based on their review of the research of a participative approach to organizational decision making, they conclude that this approach is an effective way to increase employee satisfaction and productivity.

In the New Public Service, the facts that these approaches "work better" to enhance satisfaction, boost productivity, and enhance an organization's capacity for change are important. In fact, it has been shown that although both quality management and participation in decision making have positive effects on employee performance, participation in decision making has a much greater effect (Stashevsky and Elizur 2000). What is most important from the standpoint of the New Public Service is that participative and inclusive approaches are the only ones that build citizenship, responsibility, and trust, and advance the values of service in the public interest. They are the only approaches that make sense if you begin with the assumption that public servants are, and ought to be, motivated by democratic ideals and service to others. To treat them otherwise discourages this important source of pride and the motivation to be selfless in the pursuit of the public interest. It is this normative core of public service that the nation found so compelling on watching the police and firefighters, the health care and emergency workers, as well as the citizen volunteers, in the aftermath of the September 11, 2001, attacks on New York and Washington, D.C. This devotion to public service represents what is best, and most important to the achievement of public values and democractic ideals.

As discussed in Chapter 8, the notion of shared leadership is critical in providing opportunities for employees and citizens to affirm and act upon their public service motives and values. In the New Public Service, shared leadership, collaboration, and empowerment become the norm both inside and outside the organization. Shared leadership focuses on the goals, values, and ideals that the organization and community want to advance. As Burns (1978) would say, leadership exercised by working through and with people transforms the participants and shifts their focus to higher-level values. Through shared (or transformational) leadership, the purposes and ends of organizations, groups, and communities are transformed to another, higher set of goals and values. This process must be characterized by mutual respect, accommodation, and support. The public service motives of citizens and employees alike can be recognized, supported, and rewarded in the process.

Conclusion

Writing about management in the private sector, Plas (1996) states that organizational culture must evolve and find a "place for the heart again" in the workplace. Workers should be permitted, she says, to participate with their labor, with their minds, and with their hearts. Managers should be, and should encourage their employees to be, "authentic." Managers and workers should share their feelings, values, and ethics within the corporate environment. Plas says this requires a new social contract between employees and employers. The old contract assumed that the employee would work hard and the organization would look after the employee. Modern society has shown that these contracts do not work, if, in fact, they ever did. The new contract is based on the assumption that both the individual and the organization have responsibilities to each other and accordingly, to creating and maintaining a successful relationship.

Public sector managers have a special responsibility and a unique opportunity to capitalize on the "heart" of public service. People are attracted to the public service because they are motivated by public service values. These values—to serve others, to make the world better and safer, and to make democracy work—represent the best of what it means to be a citizen in the service of a community. We need to nourish and encourage these higher-level motivations and values, not extinguish them by treating people as if they were cogs in a machine or as if they were only capable of self-serving behavior. How many of us have seen what happens when an idealistic public servant comes to a public organization and is treated as if his or her idealism is naiveté—and is told that what is expected and rewarded is to do what they are told and keep quiet? If we treat people as bureaucrats, as self-serving and self-interested individuals, we encourage them to become just that. Believing in the public service, and our role in serving the public interest, is what allows us to sacrifice, to give our best, to go, as the firefighters and police officers did in the World Trade Center disaster, where others would not go.

If we can help others to see that the work they are doing is larger and more important than the individual, if we can help people to understand that public service is honorable and valuable, they will act accordingly. Treating our fellow public servants with the dignity and respect that they deserve in public organizations, and empowering them to help find ways to serve their communities, allows us to attract and empower those who are willing and able to serve in the public interest. It is the duty, obligation, and privilege of every public manager to do so. As MacKenzie put it a century ago,

> We must try to see once more, as the wisest of Greeks saw, that there is nothing nobler in human life than politics, in the most comprehensive sense of that term. Few of us can do much to serve humanity in the widest sense: the best thing probably on the whole that most of us can do is serve our country. (MacKenzie 1901, 22)

Chapter 10

Conclusion

In the preceding chapters, we have presented a theoretical framework that gives full priority to democracy, citizenship, and service in the public interest. We have called this framework the New Public Service. We have argued that the New Public Service offers an important and viable alternative to both the traditional and the now-dominant managerialist model of public management. It is an alternative that has been built on the basis of theoretical explorations and practical innovations in public agencies. The result is a normative model, comparable to other such models.

We began with a description of what we called the Old Public Administration or the orthodoxy of the field. We suggested that, under the Old Public Administration, the purpose of government was simply to deliver services efficiently, and that problems were to be addressed primarily by changing the organization's structure and control systems. While some in the field called for greater attention to democratic values, the voices calling for hierarchy and control, little citizen involvement, and neutral expertise largely prevailed.

More recently, the New Public Management has come to dominate thought and action in the field of public administration. The New Public Management, as we have seen, is grounded in the idea that the best way to understand human behavior is to assume that governmental and other actors make choices and undertake action based on their own self-interest. In this view, the role of government is to unleash market forces so as to facilitate individual choice and to achieve efficiency. Citizens are seen as customers and problems are addressed by manipulating incentives. Public servants are expected to be entrepreneurial risk takers who get the "best deals" and reduce costs.

In contrast, we have made an argument for what we call the New Public Service. We have suggested that public administrators should begin with the recognition that an engaged and enlightened citizenship is critical to democratic governance. We assert that this "high" citizenship is both important and achievable because human behavior not only is a matter of self-interest, but also involves values, beliefs, and a concern for others. Citizens are seen as the owners of government and as capable of acting together in pursuit of the greater good. Accordingly, we have argued that the public interest transcends the aggregation of individual self-interests. The New Public Service seeks shared values and common interests through widespread dialogue and citizen engagement. Public service itself is seen as an extension of citizenship, motivated by desire to serve others and to achieve public objectives.

From this perspective, the role of public administrator is to bring people "to the table" and to serve citizens in a manner that recognizes the multiple and complex layers of responsibility, ethics, and accountability in a democratic system. The responsible administrator should work to engage citizens not only in planning, but also implementing programs to achieve public objectives. This is done not only because it makes government work better, but because it is consistent with our values. The job of the public administrator is not primarily control or the manipulation of incentives; it is service. In this model, democratic ideals and respect for others not only permeate our interactions with citizens, but also are modeled within public organizations.

In short, we have argued for a model of New Public Service based on citizenship, democracy, and service in the public interest as an alternative to the now dominant models based on economic theory and self-interest. While debates among theorists will continue and while administrative practitioners will test and explore new possibilities, it is important to acknowledge that this is not just an abstract debate. The actions that public administrators take will differ markedly depending on the types of assumptions and principles upon which those actions are based. If we assume that the responsibility of government is to facilitate individual self-interest, we will take one set of actions. If, on the other hand, we assume that the responsibility of government is to promote citizenship, public discourse, and the public interest, we will take an entirely different set of actions. As stated in *Street-Level Leadership:*

> [O]ne of the most potent and effective ways to influence practice is to change the theory and language used to understand that practice. . . . From this perspective, it is not an overstatement to suggest that the capacity of the governance system and efficacy of public administration as a compo-

nent of that system are products of the acceptance of a particular set of theories which undergird them. (Vinzant and Crothers 1998, 143–44)

Put simply, the theories we ascribe to *matter.* Theories, values, and beliefs are what facilitate or constrain, encourage or discourage particular kinds of action. Consider, for example, the implications for action of the following two statements: (1) "The customers are waiting to see us," and (2) "The owners are waiting to see us." In the first instance, we may respond to the preferences of each individual, in the order that they appear, in the most efficient manner possible. We respond as politely and as quickly as possible to their demands. When we have completed the transaction, the relationship is over until the next demand is made. The customer is satisfied and goes away. In the second case, the people we serve are the owners. In responding to owners, we recognize that each owner has a stake in what we do and that the guidance and involvement of all owners are both needed and appropriate. They are allowed to keep their dignity and are treated with respect in the context of a long term relationship. They and we recognize that instead of responding only to the self-interest of each, we must engage in an extended conversation about the larger public interest. In short, there are clear practical and behavioral implications in the ways we see, understand, and talk about the people we serve. As we change how we think and how we talk, we will change what we do.

It is also important to note that, while changing a single word can have important implications for how we think and behave, realizing the values of the New Public Service will require simultaneous attention to all the factors and principles discussed in this book. The New Public Service is a call for not only a redefinition of how we see the citizens we serve, but also a change in how we see ourselves and our responsibilities—how we treat each other, how we define our purpose and goals, how we evaluate ourselves and others, how we make decisions, how we view success and failure, and how we think about the legitimacy of our actions. It refocuses our attention on the ideals of democracy and the public interest, of citizenship and human dignity, of service and commitment as the foundation of *everything* we do.

So the lessons and principles of New Public Service are not sequential steps or a linear process; all rely on and are expressions of the same core principles. They form the interdependent threads of the whole fabric of public service. Without each other, they are simply frayed pieces of the newest management fashion. They become "looks" or styles of management without the substance—briefly tried and then abandoned when the desired results cannot be consistently and continually shown.

In the concluding chapter of *The Pursuit of Significance* (1993), Denhardt argued that the central and most basic concept in traditional views of management was the idea of self-interest. He pointed out that standard approaches to management flow from the assumption of self-interest, whether pay and performance, motivation and control, communication and conflict. He then asked:

> What if we turned the whole thing upside down and suggested that what is central to the operation . . . of public organizations is not a concern for self-interest but the pursuit of significance? This would change the way we think about public organizations in some very interesting ways. Using this new assumption, for example, wouldn't we want to state more clearly what is significant about the work of the organization so that people could focus their energy and excitement? Wouldn't we want to place the needs of clients and citizens at the forefront of all our activities? Wouldn't we want to give persons throughout our organizations the strength and power and responsibility to be significant? And wouldn't we want everything we do to be touched, indeed propelled by a commitment to public service? In others words, wouldn't we be doing all of those things that the best public managers already seem to be doing? (Denhardt 1993, 276)

The New Public Service is not just the latest management fad or technique. It is, instead, a definition of who we are and why we serve others. It is a fundamental reordering of values. We don't embrace these values because they increase satisfaction, motivation, retention, effectiveness, and service and improve decision making (although we would argue that they do). Rather, we simply act on them because we believe they are, and always have been, integral components of American democracy.

Decades ago, Herbert Kaufman (1956) suggested that, while administrative institutions are organized and operated in pursuit of different values at different times, during the period in which one idea is dominant, others are never totally neglected. Building on this idea, it makes sense to think of one normative model as prevailing at any point in time, with the other (or others) playing a somewhat lesser role *within* the context of the prevailing view. Currently, the New Public Management and its surrogates have been established as the dominant paradigm in the field of governance and public administration. In this process, a concern for democratic citizenship and the public interest have not been fully lost, but rather have been subordinated.

We would argue, however, that in a democratic society, a concern for democratic values should be paramount in the way we think about systems of governance. Values such as efficiency and productivity should not be lost, but should be placed in the larger context of democracy, community, and the public interest. In terms of the normative models we have examined here, the New Public Service clearly seems most consistent with the basic foundations of democracy in this country and, therefore, provides a framework *within which* other valuable techniques and values, including the best elements of the Old Public Administration and the New Public Management, might be played out. The New Public Service provides a rallying point around which we might envision a public service based on and fully integrated with civic discourse and the public interest.

How do we realize these ideals? As individual public servants, each of us has the opportunity and responsibility to serve others in the public interest, though, at present, many of us wouldn't, or couldn't, express it this way. Rather, we might say that we have the responsibility to process claims, investigate cases, process paperwork, teach classes, supervise workers, or answer the phone. But if we think about how we can contribute to service in the public interest and to building active citizenship, it not only changes how we feel about our work, but also how we approach our daily tasks. As Louis Gawthrop suggests, "To labor in the service of democracy is to recognize that all of us are called, in varying degrees of responsibility, to be watchmen, sentinels, or prophets for others—any others—as well as for one another, in attempting to attain the common good" (1998, 100).

Perhaps we should each start with ourselves. Think about what brought *you* to the public service? What gives your work meaning? Do you remember feeling when you started your public service career that you were about to become part of something important? How can you do your job in a way that affirms these larger purposes? What can you do to reawaken in yourself that feeling of purpose, of calling, or of service? Through this process of self-reflection, we can begin to rediscover our desire to serve our fellow citizens and to think about our public service work in a way that celebrates its "soul" and meaning.

We are often struck by how our students, many of whom are midcareer public servants, react to classroom discussions about the values and meaning of the public service and their role in enacting those values. Their attention is captured; they listen more carefully to each other and the conversation is more charged with emotion. Reticent students become engaged and involved. Many seem excited and almost grateful to have the chance to talk about what public service means to them. Some confess that they had never thought about the larger meaning and societal value of their work. Perhaps most telling is the frequency of such comments as, "I wish my supervisor/employees felt this way (and talked this way) about the public service."

Most of us probably do value the significance, the meaning, the "soul" of public service. We just don't think or talk about it very much. Or worst of all, we think it applies to someone other than ourselves. In our efforts to improve productivity and efficiency, we seem to have lost the ability to speak with passion about each other and about what we do. Perhaps our speech and our professional self-identity have instead become overrun with words and concepts like efficiency, deadlines, productivity, measures, objectives, analysis, performance, alignment, structure, customers, and procedures. Consider how you talk about your work to other people. If we fail to talk about the public service in a way that reflects its inherent value and societal meaning, we contribute to the loss of the soul of the field—a loss that robs us of our own excitement and satisfaction, and robs citizens of our caring and commitment. If we fail to infuse our own professional identity, as well as our conversations with others, with words and phrases like public service, citizenship, public interest, meaning, values, ethics, community, and democracy, to name just a few, we miss opportunities to enhance and advance the heart of public service.

Self-reflection is both important and difficult. It is only through self-reflection that we can develop our capacity to serve others and recapture the pride we are missing as public servants. Through the process, we can strive to be proud without being arrogant; to be strong without being morally insensitive; to be respectful without being timid; to be vigilant without being oppressive; to be cautious without letting fear control us; and to be caring without being patronizing. Finding this balance through honest self-reflection is hard work, but it can make each of us a better person, a better citizen, and a better public servant.

We are convinced that, at the core, public servants want to do something that matters and has value. If that is true, it is critical that we find a voice in ourselves that applauds, recognizes, and advances these ideas. We need to find and use the words. The next time you talk to an employee, a student, a colleague, or even a friend, ask yourself how your speech reflects the soul of public administration. Think about the specific words and phrases you use. Do they motivate and inspire? As public servants we would be well served if each of us consciously, deliberately, and frequently reminded ourselves and others that what we do profoundly matters.

As we said earlier, if we change how we think and talk, we also change how we behave. What do we think about the people we serve? Are they simply cases to be dispensed with as quickly as possible? Are they, fundamentally, unlike us? Do we treat the people we serve in a way that reflects both our self-respect and our respect for them? Do we look them in the eye and honestly try to help, serve, respond, and/or engage them? Are they treated as the citizen-owners of our organization? Do they feel valued as people? Do they leave our interactions feeling better or worse about their government? Do our interactions create a good foundation for continued involvement and participation, or will the people we serve dread their next interaction with government? We can begin by treating citizens as citizens, remembering that in a democracy these people are not just our clients or customers, they are our "bosses," and as such they deserve no less than sincere respect and full and complete involvement in the work of government.

What can we do as citizens and members of communities to contribute to the creation of a civil society and the ideals of democracy? The short answer is that we can do what comes naturally—we can act on our desire to belong and to join with others. Again, this begins with how we think about our role in democratic governance. In a sense, our rightful role in government has been taken from us, not because of evil intent or elitist plot, but as a natural outgrowth of approaches to governance and management that begin and end with the assumption that we are incapable of anything other than self-interest. But for us as citizens, it is important to recognize that making our country and our communities better requires at the very least our cooperation, and ideally, our active involvement. By definition, our government belongs to us and is our responsibility. We can and should have high expectations for government; but for government to work well, it needs active citizenship. We can expect that our fellow citizens, who work for government, will treat us with respect and invite our active participation in their work. It is our right, duty, and privilege to do so. In return, we can honor and respect their contribution, not just during times of national disaster, but in everyday service to others.

Finally, we can ask ourselves whether we would perhaps find more meaning, higher purpose, and greater significance in our lives if we were to make public service our life's work. There are great opportunities and tremendous satisfactions to be gained in working toward making the world and our communities better, serving others, and pursuing something larger and more important than ourselves. As individuals, as public servants, and as a nation, we must have the integrity, the strength, and the commitment to be honest with ourselves and to work continually to be true to our shared values. Whether we express our citizenship by becoming more involved in our community dialogue, participating directly in democratic processes and institutions, or renewing our commitment or by becoming public servants ourselves—whatever form it takes—an expansion of democratic citizenship will not only benefit citizens in their work together but also help build the spirit of public service throughout society to the benefit of all. Recall Portia's characterization of mercy in the Shakespearean play *The Merchant of Venice:*

> The quality of mercy is not strained. It droppeth as the gentle rain from heaven upon the place beneath. It is twice blest: It blesseth him that gives and him that receives.

The same is true of public service. We invite you to join in building the New Public Service.

References

Adams, J. Stacey. 1963. "Toward an Understanding of Inequity." *Journal of Abnormal Social Psychology* 67(1): 422–36.

Adams, Roy J. 1992. "Efficiency Is Not Enough." *Labor Studies Journal* 17(1): 18–29.

Albretch, Karl, and Ron Zemke. 1985. *Service America.* Homewood, IL: Dow Jones–Irwin.

Alford, John. 2000. "A Public Management Road Less Traveled: Clients as Co-Producers of Public Service." *Australian Journal of Public Administration* 57(4): 128–37.

American Heritage Dictionary. 2000. Boston: Houghton Mifflin.

American Society for Public Administration (ASPA). 2001. *Code of Ethics.* http://aspanet.org/ethics/coe.html.

Appleby, Paul. 1945. *Big Democracy.* New York: Knopf.

———. 1949. *Policy and Administration.* Tuscaloosa: University of Alabama Press.

———. 1950. *Morality and Administration in Democratic Government.* Baton Rouge: Louisana State University Press.

Argyris, Chris. 1957. *Personality and Organization.* New York: Harper and Row.

———. 1962. *Interpersonal Competence and Organizational Effectiveness.* Homewood, IL: Dorsey Press.

———. 1973. "Some Limits of Rational Man Organization Theory." *Public Administration Review* 33(3): 253–67.

Asch, Solomon. 1951. "Effects of Group Pressure upon the Modification and Distortion of Judgments." In *Groups, Leadership, and Men,* ed. Harold Guetzkow. Pittsburgh: Carnegie Press.

Bailey, Stephen K. 1966. "Ethics and the Public Service." In *Public Administration: Readings in Institutions, Processes, Behavior,* ed. Robert T. Golembiewski, Frank Gibson, and Geoffrey Cornog, 22–31. Chicago: Rand McNally.

Balfour, Danny, and Barton Weschler. 1990. "Organizational Commitment: A Reconceptualization and Empirical Test of Public-Private Differences." *Review of Public Personnel Administration* 10(3): 23–40.

Barber, Benjamin. 1984. *Strong Democracy: Participatory Politics for a New Age.* Berkeley: University of California Press.

———. 1998. *A Passion for Democracy.* Princeton, NJ: Princeton University Press.

Barnard, Chester. 1948. *The Function of the Executive.* Cambridge, MA: Harvard University Press.

Barzelay, Michael. 1992. *Breaking Through Bureaucracy.* Berkeley: University of California Press.

———. 2001. *The New Public Management.* Berkeley: University of California Press.

Behn, Robert. 1999. "The New Public Management Paradigm and the Search of Democratic Accountability." *International Public Management Journal* 1(2): 131–265.

———. 2001. *Rethinking Democratic Accountability.* Washington, DC: Brookings Institution.

Bell, Daniel, and Irving Kristol. 1965. "What Is the Public Interest?" *Public Interest* 1(Autumn): 3–5.

Bellah, Robert; Richard Madsen; William Sullivan; Ann Swidler; and Steve Tipton. 1985. *Habits of the Heart.* Berkeley: University of California Press.

———. 1991. *The Good Society.* New York: Knopf.

Bennett, William, ed. 1993. *The Book of Virtues.* New York: Simon and Schuster.

Benhabib, Seyla. 1996. "Toward a Deliberative Model of Democratic Legitimacy." In *Democracy and Difference*, ed. Seyla Benhabib, 67–94. Princeton, NJ: Princeton University Press.

Bennis, Warren. 1992. "The Artform of Leadership." In *Public Administration in Action*, ed. Robert B. Denhardt, and Barry S. Hammond, 311–15. Pacific Grove, CA: Brooks-Cole.

Berry, Jeffrey M.; Kent Portney; and Ken Thomson. 1993. *The Rebirth of Urban Democracy.* Washington, DC: Brookings Institution.

Boston, Jonathan. 1991. "The Theoretical Underpinnings of Public Sector Restructuring in New Zealand." In *Reshaping the State*, ed. Jonathon Boston et al., 1–24. Oxford: Oxford University Press.

Boston, Jonathan; John Martin; June Pallot; and Pat Walsh. 1996. *Public Management: The New Zealand Model.* New York: Oxford University Press.

Box, Richard. 1992. "The Administrator as Trustee of the Public Interest: Normative Ideals and Daily Practice." *Administration and Society* 24(3): 323–45.

———. 1998. *Citizen Governance.* Thousand Oaks, CA: Sage.

Boyte, Harry C., and Nancy N. Kari. 1996. *Building America.* Philadelphia: Temple University Press.

Brudney, Jeffrey L., and Robert E. England. 1983. "Toward a Definition of the Coproduction Concept." *Public Administration Review* 43(1): 59–65.

Bryson, John, and Barbara Crosby. 1992. *Leadership for the Common Good.* San Francisco: Jossey-Bass.

Bryson, John M., and Robert Einsweiler. 1991. "Introduction." In *Shared Power*, ed. John M. Bryson and Robert Einsweiler, 1–24. Minneapolis, MN: Humphrey Institute of Public Affairs.

Burke, John. 1986. *Bureaucratic Responsibility.* Baltimore, MD: Johns Hopkins Press.

———. 1987. "A Prescriptive View of the Implementation Process: When Should Bureaucrats Exercise Discretion?" *Policy Studies Review* (7): 1, 217–31.

Burns, James MacGregor. 1978. *Leadership.* New York: Harper and Row.

Carlson, Margaret S., and Roger Schwarz. 1995. "What Do Citizens Really Want?" *Popular Government* (Spring): 26–33.

Carnavale, David. 1995. *Trustworthy Government.* San Francisco: Jossey-Bass.

Carroll, James, and Dahlia Bradshaw Lynn. 1996. "The Future of Federal Reinvention: Congressional Perspectives." *Public Administration Review* 56(3): 299–304.

Casinelli, C.W. 1962. "The Public Interest in Political Ethics." In *Nomos V: The Public Interest,* ed. C.J. Friedrich. New York: Atherton Press.

Cayer, N. Joseph. 1986. *Public Personnel in the United States.* 2d ed. New York: St. Martin's Press.

Chapin, Linda W., and Robert B. Denhardt. 1995. "Putting 'Citizens First!' in Orange County, Florida." *National Civic Review* 84(3): 210–15.

Cleveland, Frederick A. 1920. *The Budget and Responsible Government.* New York: Macmillan.

Cleveland, Harlan. 1985. "The Twilight of Hierarchy." *Public Administration Review* 45(2): 185–95.

Cline, Kurt D. 2000. "Defining the Implementation Problem: Organizational Management versus Cooperation." *Journal of Public Administration Research and Theory* 10(3): 551–71.

Cochran, Clarke. 1974. "Political Science and 'The Public Interest.'" *Journal of Politics* 36(2): 327–55.

Cook, Brian J. 1996. *Bureaucracy and Self-Government.* Baltimore, MD: Johns Hopkins University Press.

Cook, Thomas, and L. Douglas Dobson. 1982. "Reaction to Reexamination: More on Type III Error in Program Evaluation." *Evaluation and Program Planning* 5(1): 119–21.

Cooper, Terry L. 1991. *An Ethic of Citizenship for Public Administration.* Englewood Cliffs, NJ: Prentice-Hall.

———. 1998. *The Responsible Administrator.* 4th ed. San Francisco: Jossey-Bass.

Cope, Glen. 1997. "Bureaucratic Reform and Issues of Political Responsiveness." *Journal of Public Administration Research and Theory* 7(3): 461–71.

Dagger, Richard. 1997. *Civic Virtues.* New York: Oxford University Press.

Dahl, Robert A. 1947. "The Science of Public Administration." *Public Administration Review* 7 (Winter): 1–11.

———. 1956. *A Preface to Democratic Theory.* Chicago: University of Chicago Press.

———. 1961. *Who Governs?* Princeton, NJ: Yale University Press.

The Declaration of Independence. [1776]1970. Worcester, MA: A.J. St. Onge.

deLeon, Linda, and Robert B. Denhardt. 2000. "The Political Theory of Reinvention." *Public Administration Review* 60(2): 89–97.

deLeon, Peter. 1997. *Democracy and the Policy Sciences.* Albany: State University of New York Press.

———. 1999. "The Missing Link Revisited: Contemporary Implementation Research." *Policy Studies Review* 16(3/4): 311–38.

Denhardt, Robert B. 1981. *In the Shadow of Organization.* Lawrence: Regents Press of Kansas.

———. 1993. *The Pursuit of Significance*. Pacific Grove, CA: Wadsworth.

———. 1999. *Public Administration: An Action Orientation*. 3d ed. Fort Worth, TX: Harcourt Brace.

Denhardt, Robert B., and Janet Vinzant Denhardt. 1999. *Leadership for Change: Case Studies in American Local Government*. Arlington, VA: Pricewaterhouse-Coopers Endowment for the Business of Government.

———. 2000. "The New Public Service, Serving Rather than Steering." *Public Administration Review* 60(6): 549–59.

———. 2001a. "The Power of Public Service." Available at: http://aspanet.org/publications/COLUMNS/archives/2001/Sep/denhardts0913.html.

———. 2001b. "Citizenship and Public Service." Available at: http://aspanet.org/publications/COLUMNS/archives/2001/Nov/denhardts1109.html.

———. 2001c. "The New Public Service, Putting Democracy First." *National Civic Review* 90(4): 391–400.

Denhardt, Robert B.; Janet Vinzant Denhardt; and Maria Aristigueta. 2002. *Managing Human Behavior in Public and Nonprofit Organizations*. Thousand Oaks, CA: Sage.

Denhardt, Robert B., and Joseph E. Gray. 1998. "Targeting Community Development in Orange County, Florida." *National Civic Review* 87(3): 227–35.

———. 2000. *Theories of Public Organization*. 3d ed. Fort Worth, TX: Harcourt Brace.

———. 2001. "The Big Questions in Public Administration Education." *Public Administration Review* 61(5).

de Tocqueville, Alexis. [1835]1969. *Democracy in America*, trans. George Lawrence, ed. J.P. Mayer. Garden City, NY: Doubleday.

Dimock, Marshall E. 1936. "Criteria and Objectives of Public Administration." In *The Frontiers of Public Administration*, ed. John M. Gaus, Leonard D. White, and Marshall E. Dimock, 116–34. Chicago: University of Chicago Press.

Dimock, Marshall E., and Gladys O. Dimock. 1969. *Public Administration*. 4th ed. Hinsdale, IL: Dryden Press.

Dobel, Patrick. 1990. "Integrity in the Public Service." *Public Administration Review* 50(3): 354–67.

Dryzek, John S. 1990. *Discursive Democracy*. New York: Cambridge University Press.

———. 1999. *Deliberative Democracy and Beyond*. Oxford: Oxford University Press.

Dunleavy, Patrick. 1991. *Democracy, Bureaucracy and Public Choice*. New York: Harvester Wheatsheaf.

Dunn, Delmer D., and Jerome S. Legge, Jr. 2000. "U.S. Local Government Managers and the Complexity of Responsibility and Accountability in Democratic Governance." *Journal of Public Administration Research and Theory* 11(1): 73–88.

Dwivedi, O.P. 1985. "Ethics and Values of Public Responsibility and Accountability." *International Journal of Administrative Sciences* 51(1): 61–66.

Eisenhardt, Kathleen. 1989. "Agency Theory: An Assessment and Review." *Academy of Management Journal* 14(1): 57–74.

Etzioni, Amitai. 1988. *The Moral Dimension*. New York: Free Press.

———. 1995. *The New Communitarian Thinking*. Charlottesville: University of Virginia Press.

Evans, Sara M., and Harry C. Boyte. 1986. *Free Spaces.* New York: Harper and Row.

Farmer, John David. 1995. *The Language of Public Administration.* Tuscaloosa: University of Alabama Press.

Finer, Herman, 1941. "Administrative Responsibility in Democratic Government." *Public Administration Review* 1: 335–50.

———. 1972. "Administrative Responsibility in Democratic Government." In *Bureaucratic Power in National Politics,* ed. Francis Rourke, 326–36. Boston: Little, Brown.

Fishkin, James S. 1991. *Democracy and Deliberation.* New Haven, CT: Yale University Press.

———. 1995. *The Voice of the People.* New Haven, CT: Yale University Press.

Follet, Mary Parker. 1926. "The Giving of Order." In *Scientific Foundations of Business Administration.* Baltimore, MD: Williams and Wilkins.

Fox, Charles. 1987. "Biases in Public Policy Implementation." *Policy Studies Review* 7(1): 128–41.

———. 1996. "Reinventing Government as Postmodern Symbolic Politics." *Public Administration Review* 56(3): 256–61.

Fox, Charles, and Hugh Miller. 1995. *Postmodern Public Administration.* Thousand Oaks, CA: Sage.

———. 1997. "The Depreciating Public Policy Discourse." *American Behavioral Scientist* 41(1): 64–120.

Frederickson, H. George. 1980. *New Public Administration.* Tuscaloosa: University of Alabama Press.

———. 1982. "The Recovery of Civism in Public Administration." *Public Administration Review* 43(6): 501–08.

———. 1991. "Toward a Theory of the Public for Public Administration." *Administration and Society* 22(4): 395–417.

———. 1992. "Painting Bulls-Eyes around Bullet Holes." *Governing* 6(1): 13.

———. 1996. "Comparing the Reinventing Government Movement with the New Public Administration." *Public Administration Review* 56(3): 263–69.

———. 1997. *The Spirit of Public Administration.* San Francisco: Jossey-Bass.

Frederickson, H. George, and Ralph Clark Chandler, eds. 1984. "A Symposium on Citizenship and Public Administration." *Public Administration Review* 44 (Special Issue): 99–206.

Frederickson, H. George, and David K. Hart. 1985. "The Public Service and Patriotism of Benevolence." *Public Administration Review* 45(5): 547–53.

Friedrich, Carl J. 1940. "Public Policy and the Nature of Administrative Responsibility." *Public Policy* 1: 1–20.

———. 1960. "The Dilemma of Administrative Responsibility." In *Responsibility,* ed. Carl J. Friedrich, 189–202. New York: Liberal Arts Press.

———. 1972. "Public Policy and the Nature of Administrative Responsibility." In *Bureaucratic Power in National Politics,* ed. Francis Rourke, 165–75. Boston: Little, Brown, 1972.

French, John R., Jr., and Bertram Raven. 1959. "The Bases of Social Power." In *Studies in Social Power,* ed. Dorwin Cartwright. Ann Arbor, MI: Institute for Social Research.

Gardner, John. 1987. "Remarks to the NASPAA Conference." *Enterprise: The Newsletter of NASPAA* (October 23): 1.

———. 1991. *Building Community.* Washington, DC: Independent Sector.

Gawthrop, Louis C. 1998. *Public Service and Democracy.* New York: Chandler.

Gerth, H.H., and C. Wright Mills. 1946. *From Max Weber: Essays in Sociology.* New York: Oxford University Press.

Gilmore, R.S., and L.S. Jensen. 1998. "Reinventing Government Accountability: Public Functions, Privatization, and the Meaning of State Action." *Public Administration Review* 58(3): 247–58.

Glaser, Mark; Janet Denhardt; and Linda Hamilton. 2002. "Community v. Self-Interest: Citizen Perceptions of Schools as Civic Investments." *Journal of Public Administration Theory and Practice* 12(1): 103–27.

Glaser, Mark; Lee Parker; and Stephanie Payton. 2001. "The Paradox Between Community and Self-Interest: Local Government, Neighborhoods, and the Media." *Journal of Urban Affairs* 23(1): 87–102.

Goggin, Malcolm; Ann Bowman; Laurence O'Toole; and James Lester. 1990. *Implementation Theory and Practice: Toward a Third Generation.* Glenwood, IL: Scott Foresman/Little, Brown.

Golembiewski, Robert T. 1967. *Men, Management, and Morality.* New York: McGraw-Hill.

———. 1977. "A Critique of 'Democratic Administration' and Its Supporting Ideation." *American Political Science Review* 71 (December): 1488–507.

Goodnow, Frank. 1987. "Politics and Administration." In *Classics of Public Administration.* 2d ed., ed. Jay Shafritz and Albert Hyde, 26–29. Chicago: Dorsey Press.

Goodsell, Charles T. 1994. *The Case for Bureaucracy.* Chatham, NJ: Chatham House.

Gore, Al. 1993. *From Red Tape to Results.* Washington, DC: *The Review.*

Gray, Joseph, and Linda Chapin. 1998. "Targeted Community Initiative." In *Government Is Us,* ed. Cheryl S. and Camilla Stivers, 175–94. Thousand Oaks, CA: Sage.

Gulick, Luther. 1933. "Politics, Administration, and the New Deal." *Annals of the Academy of Political and Social Science* 169 (September): 545–66.

———. 1937. "Notes on the Theory of Organization." In *Papers on the Science of Administration,* ed. L. Gulick and L. Urwick, 1–46. New York: Institute of Government.

Gutman, Amy, and Dennis Thompson. 1996. *Democracy and Disagreement.* Cambridge, MA: Harvard University Press.

Habermas, Jurgen. 1996. *Between Facts and Norms.* Boston: MIT Press.

Hall, John Stuart. 2002. "Reconsidering the Connection Between Capacity and Governance." *Public Organization Review* 2(1): 5–22.

Hall, Thad E., and Laurence J. O'Toole, Jr. 2000. "Structures for Policy Implementation." *Administration and Society* 31(6): 667–87.

Hamilton, Alexander; James Madison; and John Jay. [1787]1982. *The Federalist Papers.* New York: Bantam Books.

Haque, M. Shamsul. 1994. "The Emerging Challenges to Bureaucratic Accountability: A Critical Perspective." In *Handbook of Bureaucracy,* ed. Ali Farazmand. New York: Marcel Dekker.

———. 2001. "The Diminishing Publicness of Public Service Under the Current Mode of Governance." *Public Administration Review* 61(6): 65–82.

Harmon, Michael. 1981. *Action Theory for Public Administration.* New York: Longman.

———. 1995. *Responsibility as Paradox*. Thousand Oaks, CA: Sage.

Hart, David K. 1984. "The Virtuous Citizen, the Honorable Bureaucrat, and 'Public' Administration," *Public Administration Review* 44 (Special Issue): 111–20.

———. 1997. "'A Partnership in Virtue Among All Citizens': The Public Service and the Civic Humanist Tradition." *International Journal of Public Administration* 20(4, 5): 967–80.

Heifetz, Ronald A. 1994. *Leadership Without Easy Answers*. Cambridge, MA: Harvard University Press.

Herring, E. Pendleton. 1936. *Public Administration and the Public Interest*. New York: Russell and Russell.

Herzberg, Frederick. 1968. "One More Time: How Do You Motivate Employees?" *Harvard Business Review* 46 (January–February): 53–62.

Homans, George. 1954. *The Human Group*. New York: McGraw-Hill.

Hood, Christopher. 1991. "A Public Administration for All Seasons." *Public Administration* 69(1): 3–19.

———. 1995. "The 'New Public Management' in the Eighties." *Accounting, Organization and Society* 20(2–3): 93–109.

Hood, Christopher, and Michael Jackson. 1991. *Administrative Argument*. Aldershot, UK: Dartmouth Press.

Hummel, Ralph. 1994. *The Bureaucratic Experience*. 4th ed. New York: St. Martin's Press.

Ignatieff, Michael. 1995. "The Myth of Citizenship." In *Theorizing Citizenship*, ed. Ronald Beiner, 53–78. Albany: State University of New York Press.

Ingraham, Patricia W., and Carolyn Ban. 1988. "Politics and Merit: Can They Meet in a Public Service Model?" *Review of Public Personnel Administration* 8(2): 1–19.

Ingraham, Patricia W.; Barbara S. Romzek; and Associates. 1994. *New Paradigms for Government*. San Francisco: Jossey-Bass.

Ingraham, Patricia W., and David H. Rosenbloom. 1989. "The New Public Personnel and the New Public Service." *Public Administration Review* 49(2): 116–25.

Jefferson, Thomas. 1903. *The Writings of Thomas Jefferson*. Memorial Edition. Washington, DC: Thomas Jefferson Memorial Association.

Kaboolian, Linda. 1998. "The New Public Management." *Public Administration Review* 58(3): 189–93.

Kantor, Rosabeth Moss. 1972. *Commitment and Community*. Cambridge, MA: Harvard University Press.

Kass, Henry. 1990. "Stewardship as Fundamental Element in Images of Public Administration." In *Images and Identities in Public Administration*, ed. H. Kass and B. Catron, 112–30. Newbury Park, CA: Sage.

Kaufman, Herbert. 1956. "Emerging Conflicts in the Doctrines of Public Administration." *American Political Science Review* 50(4): 1057–73.

Kearney, Richard C., and Steven Hays. 1994. "Labor Management Relations and Participative Decision Making: Toward a New Paradigm." *Public Administration Review* 54(1): 44–51.

Kearns, Kevin P. 1994. "The Strategic Management of Accountability in Nonprofit Organizations: An Analytical Framework." *Public Administration Review* 54(2): 185–92.

Kettl, Donald F. 1993. *Sharing Power.* Washington, DC: Brookings Institution.
———. 1998. *Reinventing Government: A Fifth-Year Report Card.* Washington, DC: Brookings Institute.
———. 2000a. *The Global Public Management Revolution.* Washington, DC: Brookings Institution.
———. 2000b. "The Transformation of Governance." *Public Administration Review* 60(6): 488–97.
Kettl, Donald F., and Jon J. DiIulio, eds. 1995. *Inside the Reinvention Machine.* Washington, DC: Brookings Institution.
Kettl, Donald F., and H. Brinton Milward, eds. 1996. *The State of Public Management.* Baltimore, MD: Johns Hopkins University Press.
King, Cheryl Simrell; Kathryn M. Feltey; and Bridget O'Neill. 1998. "The Question of Participation: Toward Authentic Public Participation in Public Administration." *Public Administration Review* 58(4): 317–26.
King, Cheryl Simrell, and Camilla Stivers. 1998. *Government Is Us: Public Administration in an Anti-Government Era.* Thousand Oaks, CA: Sage.
Kirlin, John J. 1996. "What Government Must Do Well: Creating Value for Society." *Journal of Public Administration Research and Theory* 6 (January): 161–86.
Knickerbocker, I., and D. McGregor. 1942. "Union Management Cooperation: A Psychological Analysis." *Personnel* 19(3): 520–39.
Kotter, John P. 1977. "Power, Dependence, and Effective Management." *Harvard Business Review* 55 (July–August): 125–36.
Landy, Marc. 1993. "Public Policy and Citizenship." In *Public Policy for Democracy*, ed. Helen Ingram and Steven Rathgeb Smith, 19–44. Washington, DC: Brookings Institution.
Lappé, Frances Moore, and Paul Martin Du Bois. 1994. *The Quickening of America: Rebuilding Our Nation, Remaking Our Lives.* San Francisco: Jossey–Bass.
Lawler, Edward. 1990. *High Involvement Management.* San Francisco: Jossey Bass.
Leazes, Francis J., Jr. 1997. "Public Accountability: Is It a Private Responsibility?" *Administration & Society* 29(4): 395–412.
Lester, James; Ann Bowman; Malcolm Goggin; and Laurence O'Toole. 1987. "Public Policy Implementation: Evolution of the Field and Agenda for Future Research." *Policy Studies Review* 7(1): 200–16.
Levine, Charles. 1984. "Citizenship and Service Delivery: The Promise of Coproduction." *Public Administration Review* 44 (Special Issue): 178–87.
Levitan, David. 1943. "Political Ends and Administrative Means." *Public Administration Review* 4(4): 353–59.
Lewin, Kurt. 1951. *Field Theory in Social Science.* New York: Harper and Row.
Lewis, Eugene. 1980. *Public Entrepreneurship.* Bloomington: Indiana University Press.
Light, Paul. 1997. *The Tides of Reform.* New Haven, CT: Yale University Press.
Linder, Stephen, and B. Guy Peters. 1986. "A Design Perspective on Policy Implementation: The Fallacies of Misplaced Prescriptions." *Policy Studies Review* 6(3): 459–75.
———. 1987. "Relativism, Contingency, and the Definition of Success in Implementation Research." *Policy Studies Review* 7(1): 102–27.

Lippman, Walter. 1955. *Essays in the Public Philosophy.* Boston: Little, Brown.

Locke, Edwin. 1978. "The Ubiquity of the Technique of Goal Setting in Theories of and Approaches to Employee Motivation." *Academy of Management Review* (July): 594–601.

Love, Janice, and Peter Sederberg. 1987. "Euphony and Cacophony in Policy Implementation: SCF and the Somali Refugee Problem." *Policy Studies Review* 7(1): 155–73.

Luke, Jeffrey. 1998. *Catalytic Leadership.* San Francisco: Jossey-Bass.

Lukes, Steven. 1974. *Power: A Radical View.* London: Macmillan.

Lynn, Laurence E. 1996. *Public Management as Art, Science, and Profession.* Chatham, NJ: Chatham House.

Lynn, Laurence E.; Carolyn Heinrich; and Carolyn Hill. 2000. "Studying Governance and Public Management: Challenges and Prospects." *Journal of Public Administration Research and Theory* 10(2): 233–62.

Maass, Arthur A., and Lawrence I. Radaway. 1959. "Gauging Administrative Responsibility." In *Democracy, Bureaucracy, and the Study of Administration,* ed. Camilla Stivers. 163–81. Boulder, CO: Westview Press.

Macedo, Stephen, ed. 1999. *Deliberative Politics.* New York: Oxford University Press.

MacKenzie, J.S. 1901. "The Use of Moral Ideas in Politics." *International Journal of Politics* 12(1): 1–23.

Madison, James; Alexander Hamilton; and John Jay. [1787]1987. *The Federalist Papers,* ed. Isaac Kramnick. Harmondsworth, UK: Penguin.

Mansbridge, Jane, ed. 1990. *Beyond Self-Interest.* Chicago: University of Chicago Press.

———. 1994. "Public Spirit in Political Systems." In *Values and Public Policy,* ed. Henry J. Aaron, Thomas Mann, and Timothy Taylor, 146–72. Washington, DC: Brookings Institution.

Marini, Frank. 1971. *Toward a New Public Administration.* San Francisco: Chandler.

Maslow, Abraham. 1943. "A Theory of Human Motivation." *Psychological Review* 50: 370–96.

Mathews, David. 1994. *Politics for People.* Urbana: University of Illinois Press.

McCabe, Barbara, and Janet Vinzant. 1999. "Governance Lessons: The Case of Charter Schools." *Administration and Society* 31(3): 361–77.

McClelland, David. 1985. *Human Motivation.* Glenview, IL: Scott, Foresman.

McGregor, Douglas. 1957. "The Human Side of the Enterprise." *Management Review* (November): 22–28, 88–92.

McSwite, O.C. 1997. *Legitimacy in Public Administration.* Thousand Oaks, CA: Sage.

———. 2000. "On the Discourse Movement: A Self-Interview." *Administrative Theory and Praxis* 22(1): 49–65.

Menzel, Donald. 1981. "Implementation of the Federal Surface Mining Control and Reclamation Act of 1977." *Public Administration Review* 51(2): 212–19.

Merton, Robert. 1985. *Social Theory and Social Structure.* Glencoe, IL: Free Press.

Mill, John Stuart. 1862. *Considerations on Representative Government.* New York: Harper, II, 2.

Miller, Hugh, and Charles Fox. 1997. *Postmodern "Reality" and Public Administration.* Burke, VA: Chatelaine Press.

Miller, Trudi. 1989. "The Operation of Democratic Institutions." *Public Administration Review* 49(6): 511–21.

Milward, H. Brinton. 1991. "Current Institutional Arrangements that Create or Require Shared Power." In *Shared Power*, ed. John M. Bryson and Robert C. Einsweiler, 51–77. Minneapolis, MN: Humphrey Institute of Public Affairs.

Mintzberg, Henry. 1996. "Managing Government, Governing Management." *Harvard Business Review* 74 (May–June): 75–83.

Mommsen, Wolfgang. 1974. *The Age of Bureaucracy.* New York: Harper and Row.

Monypenny, Philip. 1953. "A Code of Ethics for Public Administration." *George Washington Law Review* 25(3): 247–62. Also available at http://aspanet.org/ethics/coe.html.

Mooney, James, and Alan C. Reiley. 1939. *The Principles of Organization.* New York: Harper and Row.

Mosher, Frederick. 1968. *Democracy and the Public Service.* New York: Oxford University Press.

Mulgan, Richard. 2000. "Comparing Accountability in the Public and Private Sectors." *Australian Journal of Public Administration* 59(1): 87–98.

Munsterberg, Hugo. 1913. *Psychology and Industrial Efficiency.* Boston: Houghton Mifflin.

Myers, R., and R. Lacey. 1996. "Consumer Satisfaction, Performance and Accountability in the Public Sector." *International Review of Administrative Sciences* 62(2): 331–50.

Nakamura, Robert. 1987. "The Textbook Policy Process and Implementation Research." *Policy Studies Review* 7(1): 142–54.

Nalbandian, John. 1999. "Facilitating Community, Enabling Democracy: New Roles of Local Government Managers." *Public Administration Review* 59(3): 187–98.

Nelissen, Nico. 2002. "The Administrative Capacity of New Types of Governance." *Public Organization Review* 2(1): 23–43.

Nelissen, Nico; Marie Louise Bemelmans Videc; Arnold Godfroij; and Peter de Goede. 1999. *Renewing Government.* Utrecht: International Books.

Organization for Economic Cooperation and Development (OECD). 2001. *Citizens as Partners: Information, Consultation, and Public Participation in Policy Making.* Paris: OECD.

Osborne, David, and Ted Gaebler. 1992. *Reinventing Government: How the Entrepreneurial Spirit Is Transforming the Public Sector.* Reading, MA: Addison-Wesley.

Osborne, David, with Peter Plastrik. 1997. *Banishing Bureaucracy.* Reading, MA: Addison-Wesley.

Ostrom, Vincent. 1974. *The Intellectual Crisis in American Public Administration.* Tuscaloosa: University of Alabama Press.

Ostrom, Vincent, and Elinor Ostrom. 1971. "Public Choice: A Different Approach to the Study of Public Administration." *Public Administration Review* 31 (March–April): 203–16.

O'Toole, Laurence. 2000. "Research on Policy Implementation: Assessment and Prospects." *Journal of Public Administration Research and Theory* 10(2): 263–88.

O'Toole, Laurence, and Robert Montjoy. 1984. "Intergovernmental Policy Implementation: A Theoretical Perspective." *Public Administration Review* 54(6): 491–503.

Ott, J. Steven, ed. 1989. *Classic Readings in Organizational Behavior.* Belmont, CA: Brooks/Cole Publishing.

———. 1996. *Classic Readings in Organizational Behavior.* 2d ed. Fort Worth: Harcourt Brace.

Palumbo, Dennis. 1987. "What Have We Learned and Still Need to Know?" *Policy Studies Review* 7(1): 91–102.

Pateman, Carole. 1970. *Participation and Democratic Theory.* Cambridge, UK: Cambridge University Press.

Percy, Stephen. 1984. "Citizen Participation in the Coproduction of Urban Services." *Urban Affairs Quarterly* 19(4): 431–46.

Perry, James L., ed. 1996. *Handbook of Public Administration.* 2d ed. San Francisco: Jossey-Bass.

Perry, James L., and Lois Wise. 1990. "The Motivational Bases of Public Service." *Public Administration Review* 50(3): 367–73.

Peters, B. Guy, and Donald Savoie. 1996. "Managing Incoherence: The Coordination and Empowerment Conundrum." *Public Administration Review* 56(3): 281–89.

Peters, Tom, and Robert Waterman. 1982. *In Search of Excellence.* New York: HarperCollins.

Pfeffer, Jeffrey. 1981. *Power in Organizations.* Cambridge, MA: Ballinger Publishing.

Plas, Jeanne M. 1996. *Person-Centered Leadership: An American Approach to Participatory Management.* London: Sage.

Pocock, J.G.A. 1995. "The Ideal of Citizenship Since Classical Times." In *Theorizing Citizenship*, ed. Ronald Beiner, 29–52. Albany: State University of New York Press.

Pollitt, Christopher. 1988. "Bring Consumers into Performance Measurement." *Policy and Politics* 16(2): 77–88.

———. 1993. *Managerialism and the Public Service.* 2d ed. Cambridge, UK: Basil Blackwell.

Pollitt, Christopher, and Geert Bouckaert. 2000. *Public Management Reform.* Oxford, UK: Oxford University Press.

Potter, Jenny. 1988. "Consumerism and the Public Sector." *Public Administration* 66 (Summer): 149–64.

Pranger, Robert J. 1968. *The Eclipse of Citizenship.* New York: Holt, Rinehart and Winston.

Pressman, Jeffrey, and Aaron Wildavsky. 1973. *Implementation.* Berkeley: University of California Press.

———. 1979. *Implementation.* 2d ed. Berkeley: University of California Press.

Pusey, Michael. 1991. *Economic Rationalism in Canberra.* New York: Cambridge University Press.

Putnam, Robert. 2000. *Bowling Alone.* New York: Simon and Schuster.

Rabin, Jack, W. Bartley Hildreth, and Gerald J. Miller, eds. 1998. *Handbook of Public Administration.* 2d ed. New York: Marcel Dekker.

Redford, Emmett. 1954. "The Protection of the Public Interest with Special Reference to Administrative Regulation." *American Political Science Review* (48): 1103–08.

———. 1969. *Democracy in the Administrative State*. New York: Oxford University Press.

Reich, Robert B. 1988. "Policy Making in a Democracy." In *The Power of Public Ideas*, ed. Robert B. Reich. Cambridge, MA: Ballinger.

Rezmovic, Eva. 1982. "Program Implementation and Evaluation Results." *Evaluation and Program Planning* 5(1): 111–18.

Roethlisberger, F.J., and William Dickson. 1939. *Management and the Worker.* Cambridge, MA: Harvard University Press.

Rohr, John A. 1986. *To Run a Constitution: The Legitimacy of the Administrative State*. Lawrence: University Press of Kansas, Studies in Government and Public Policy.

———. 1998. *Public Service, Ethics and Constitutional Practice*. Lawrence: University Press of Kansas.

Romzek, Barbara S., and Melvin Dubnick. 1987. " Accountability in the Public Sector: Lessons from the Challenger Tragedy." *Public Administration Review* 47(3): 227–38.

Romzek, Barbara S., and Patricia Ingraham. 2000. "Cross Pressures of Accountability: Initiative, Command, and Failure in the Ron Brown Plane Crash." *Public Administration Review* 60(3): 240–53.

Rosen, Bernard. 1989. *Holding Government Bureaucracies Accountable*. 2d ed. New York: Praeger.

Ruscio, Kenneth. 1996. "Trust, Democracy, and Public Management: A Theoretical Argument." *Journal of Public Administration Research and Theory* 6(3): 461–77.

Sandel, Michael. 1996. *Democracy's Discontent*. Cambridge: Belknap Press of Harvard University Press.

Schachter, Hindy Lauer. 1997. *Reinventing Government or Reinventing Ourselves*. Albany: State University of New York Press.

Schattschneider, E.E. 1952. "Political Parties and the Public Interest." *Annals of the American Academy of Political and Social Science* 280:13–31.

Schein, Edgar. 1987. *Organizational Culture and Leadership*. San Francisco: Jossey-Bass.

Schmidt, Faye, with Teresa Strickland. 1998. *Client Satisfaction Surveying*. Ottawa: Canadian Centre for Management Development, Citizen-Centered Service Network.

Schneider, Anne Larason, and Helen Ingram. 1997. *Policy Design for Democracy*. Lawrence: University Press of Kansas.

Schott, Richard. 1986. "The Psychological Development of Adults: Implications of Public Administration." *Public Administration Review* 46(6): 657–67.

Schubert, Glendon. 1957. "'The Public Interest' in Administrative Decision-Making: Theorem, Theosophy, or Theory." *American Political Science Review* 51(2): 346–68.

———. 1960. *The Public Interest: A Critique of the Theory of a Political Concept*. Glencoe, IL: Free Press.

———. 1962. "Is There a Public Interest Theory?" In *The Public Interest*, ed. Carl Friedrich, 162–76. New York: Atherton Press.

Schwartz, N.L. 1988. *The Blue Guitar: Political Representation and Community*. Chicago: University of Chicago Press.

Selznick, Phillip. 1992. *The Moral Commonwealth*. Berkeley: University of California Press.

Shafritz, Jay, and Albert Hyde. 1997. *Classics of Public Administration*. 2d ed. Fort Worth, TX: Harcourt Brace.

Sharpe, Elaine. 1980. "Toward a New Understanding of Urban Services and Citizen Participation." *Midwest Review of Public Administration* 14(2): 105–18.

Sherif, M. 1936. *The Psychology of Social Norms*. New York: Harper.

Simon, Herbert A. 1957. *Administrative Behavior*. 2d ed. New York: Free Press.

Simon, Herbert A.; Donald W. Smithburg; and Victor A. Thompson. 1950. *Public Administration*. New York: Knopf.

Sirianni, Carmen, and Lewis Friedland. 2001. *Civic Innovation in America*. Berkeley: University of California Press.

Smith, Howard. 1960. *Democracy and the Public Interest*. Athens: University of Georgia Press.

Sorauf, Frank. 1957. "The Public Interest Reconsidered." *Journal of Politics* 19(4): 616–39.

Spiro, Herbert J. 1969. *Responsibility in Government: Theory and Practice*. New York: Van Nostrand Reinhold.

Staats, Elmer.1988. "Public Service and the Public Interest." *Public Administration Review* (March–April): 601–5.

Stashevsky, Shmuel, and Dov Elizur. 2000. "The Effect of Quality Management and Participation in Decision-Making on Individual Performance." *Journal of Quality Management* 5: 53.

Stivers, Camilla. 1990. "The Public Agency as Polis: Active Citizenship in the Administrative State." *Administration & Society* 22(1): 86–105.

———. 1993. *Gender Images in Public Administration*. Newbury Park, CA: Sage.

———. 1994a. "Citizenship Ethics in Public Administration." In *Handbook of Administrative Ethics*, ed. Terry Cooper, 583–602. New York: Marcel Dekker.

———. 1994b. "The Listening Bureaucrat." *Public Administration Review* 54(4): 364–69.

Stone, Deborah. 1988. *Policy Paradox and Political Reason*. New York: HarperCollins.

———. 1997. *Policy Paradox: The Art of Political Decision Making*. New York: W.W. Norton.

Sundeen, Richard. 1985. "Coproduction and Communities." *Administration & Society* 16(4): 387–402.

Taylor, Frederick W. 1923. *Scientific Management*. New York: Harper and Row.

Terry, Larry D. 1993. "Why We Should Abandon the Misconceived Quest to Reconcile Public Entrepreneurship with Democracy." *Public Administration Review* 53(4): 393–95.

———. 1995. *Leadership of Public Bureaucracies*. Thousand Oaks, CA: Sage.

———. 1998. "Administrative Leadership, Neo-Managerialism, and the Public Management Movement." *Public Administration Review* 58(3): 194–200.

Thomas, John Clayton. 1995. *Public Participation in Public Decisions*. San Francisco: Jossey-Bass.

Thompson, Dennis. 1970. *The Democratic Citizen*. Cambridge: Cambridge University Press.

Tornatzky, Louis, and Elmina Johnson. 1982. "Research on Implementation: Implications for Evaluation Practice and Evaluation Policy." *Evaluation and Program Planning* 5(1): 193–98.

Trajanowicz, R.; V. Kappeler; L. Gaines; and B. Bucqueroux. 1998. *Community Policing: A Contemporary Perspective*. Cincinnati, OH: Anderson.

Turner, Bryan S., ed. 1993. *Citizenship and Social Theory.* London: Sage.

Van Meter, D.S., and C.E. Van Horn. 1975. "The Policy Implementation Process: A Conceptual Framework." *Administration & Society* 6(4): 445–88.

Vinzant, Janet. 1998. "Where Values Collide: Motivation and Role Conflict in Child and Adult Protective Services." *American Review of Public Administration* 28(4): 347–66.

Vinzant, Janet, and Lane Crothers. 1998. *Street-Level Leadership: Discretion and Legitimacy in Front-Line Public Service.* Washington, DC: Georgetown University Press.

Vroom, Victor. 1964. *Work and Motivation.* New York: John Wiley.

Waldo, Dwight. 1948. *The Administrative State.* New York: Ronald Press.

———. 1952. "The Development of a Theory of Democratic Administration." *American Political Science Review* 46 (March): 81–103.

Walzer, Michael. 1995. "The Civil Society Argument." In *Theorizing Citizenship,* ed. Ronald Beiner, 153–74. Albany: State University of New York Press.

Wamsley, Gary; Robert Bacher; Charles Goodsell; Philip Kronenberg; John Rohr; Camilla Stivers; Orion White; and James Wolf. 1990. *Refounding Public Administration.* Newbury Park, CA: Sage.

Wamsley, Gary, and James Wolf. 1996. *Refounding Democratic Public Administration.* Thousand Oaks, CA: Sage.

Weber, Edward P. 1999. "The Question of Accountability in Historical Perspective." *Administration & Society* 31(4): 451–95.

Weeks, Edward C. 2000. "The Practice of Deliberative Democracy." *Public Administration Review* 60(4): 360–72.

Weimer, David. 1980. "CMIS Implementation: A Demonstration of Predictive Analysis." *Public Administration Review* 50(3): 231–40.

White, Leonard D. 1926. *Introduction to the Study of Public Administration.* New York: Macmillan.

Whyte, W.F. 1943. *Street Corner Society.* Chicago: University of Chicago Press.

Willoughby, W.F. 1927. *Principles of Public Administration.* Baltimore: Johns Hopkins University Press.

Wilson, Woodrow. [1887]1987. "The Study of Administration." *Political Science Quarterly* 2 (June). Reprinted in 1997 in *Classics of Public Administration,* 2d ed., ed. Jay Shafritz and Albert Hyde, 10–25, Chicago: Dorsey Press.

Wolfe, Alan. 1989. *Whose Keeper? Social Science and Moral Obligation.* Berkeley: University of California Press.

Woolum, Janet. 2000. "Social Capital as a Community Resource: Implications for Public Administration." Unpublished manuscript.

Wolin, Sheldon. 1960. *Politics and Vision.* Boston: Little, Brown.

Yankelovich, Daniel. 1991. *Coming to Public Judgment.* Syracuse, NY: Syracuse University Press.

———. 1999. *The Magic of Dialogue.* New York: Simon and Schuster.

Yeatman, Anna. 1987. "The Concept of Public Management and the Australian State." *Australian Journal of Public Administration* 46(4): 339–53.

Index

About the Authors

Janet V. Denhardt is a professor in the School of Public Affairs at Arizona State University. Her teaching and research interests focus on organizational theory, organization behavior, and leadership. Her books include *Managing Behavior in Public and Nonprofit Organizations* (with Robert Denhardt and Maria Aristigueta) and *Street-Level Leadership: Discretion and Legitimacy in Front-Line Service* (with Lane Crothers). She has also published numerous articles in journals such as *Public Administration Review*, *Administration & Society*, *American Review of Public Administration*, and *Journal of Public Administration Research and Theory*. Prior to joining the faculty at Arizona State University, she taught at Eastern Washington University and served in a variety of administrative positions for the state of Washington and the U.S. Department of Health and Human Services. Her doctorate is from the University of South Carolina.

Robert B. Denhardt is a professor in the School of Public Affairs at Arizona State University and Visiting Scholar at the University of Delaware. He is past president of the American Society for Public Administration (ASPA) and was founder and first chair of ASPA's National Campaign for Public Service, an effort to assert the dignity and worth of public service across the nation. He is also a member of the National Academy of Public Administration. He has published fifteen books, including *Theories of Public Organization*; *Public Administration: An Action Orientation*; *In the Shadow of Organization*; *The Pursuit of Significance*; and most recently, *Managing Behavior in Public and Nonprofit Organizations* (with Janet Denhardt and Maria Aristigueta). He has published more than seventy-five articles in professional journals, primarily in the areas of leadership, management, and organizational change. His doctorate is from the University of Kentucky.